D0771787

NO TIME TO MOURN

Central Europe, with boundaries prior to 1939.

No Time to Mourn

The True Story of a Jewish Partisan Fighter

Leon Kahn

as told to Marjorie Morris

Introduction by Allan Levine

RONSDALE PRESS & VANCOUVER HOLOCAUST EDUCATION SOCIETY

RONSDALE PRESS
3350 West 21st Avenue
Vancouver, B.C., Canada
V6S 1G7

Typesetting: Julie Cochrane, in Adobe Garamond 12 pt on 14.5
Cover Design: Susan Mavor, Metaform, Vancouver, B.C.
Paper: Ancient Forest Friendly Rolland "Enviro" — 100% post-consumer waste, totally chlorine-free and acid-free

Ronsdale Press wishes to thank the Canada Council for the Arts, the Government of Canada through the Book Publishing Industry Development Program (BPIDP), and the Province of British Columbia through the British Columbia Arts Council for their support of its publishing program.

National Library of Canada Cataloguing in Publication

Kahn, Leon, 1925–2003
    No time to mourn: the true story of a Jewish partisan fighter / Leon Kahn; introduction by Allan Levine.

Co-published by: Vancouver Holocaust Education Centre.
Includes index.
ISBN 1-55380-011-7

    1. Kahn, Leon, 1925–2003. 2. Holocaust, Jewish (1939–1945) — Personal narratives.
3. World War, 1939–1945 — Jewish resistance. 4. World War, 1939–1945 — Participation, Jewish. 5. Jews — Persecutions — Lithuania. I. Vancouver Holocaust Education Centre II. Title.

D802.P6K34 2004   940.53'183'092   C2004-901654-7

At Ronsdale Press we are committed to protecting the environment. To this end we are working with Markets Initiative (www.oldgrowthfree.com) and printers to phase out our use of paper produced from ancient forests. This book is one step towards that goal.

Printed in Canada by AGMV Printing, Quebec, Canada

I dedicate this book to all the "lost souls" including my own:

Shael Kaganowicz, FATHER
Miriam Kaganowicz, MOTHER
Benjamin Kaganowicz, BROTHER
Freidke (Frieda) Kaganowicz, SISTER
Liebe Gitl Rudzian, GRANDMOTHER
Alter Kaganowicz, UNCLE
Basha Kaganowicz, AUNT
Mote Kaganowicz, COUSIN
Moshe Kaganowicz, COUSIN
Mashe Kaganowicz, COUSIN
Gniese Kaganowicz, COUSIN
Samuel Bastunski, UNCLE
Rebecah Bastunski, AUNT
Leib Bastunski, FIRST COUSIN
Sarah Bastunski, FIRST COUSIN
Moshe Bastunski, FIRST COUSIN
Elijah Bastunski, UNCLE
Ethel Bastunski, AUNT
Motl Bastunski, UNCLE
Chana Bastunski, AUNT
Meier Bastunski, COUSIN
Jankel Bastunski, COUSIN
Abraham Kaplan, UNCLE
Alta Kaplan, AUNT
Moshe Kaplan, FIRST COUSIN
Rachele Kaplan, FIRST COUSIN
Abraham Mordecai Pacianko, UNCLE
Sarah Pacianko, AUNT
Ita-Malka Pacianko, FIRST COUSIN

Acknowledgements

Special recognition is extended to Morris Wosk, *z"l,* businessman, community leader and philanthropist and to his son Rabbi Yosef Wosk, who, through a major gift to the Vancouver Holocaust Education Centre in 2000, established the Wosk Publishing Program. In recognition of the Wosk family's deep interest in Jewish history, the mandate of the Wosk Publishing Program is to publish original writings that advance our understanding of the events of the Holocaust, its history, implications and effects.

Thanks are also extended to those who have helped to bring *No Time to Mourn* to completion, in particular Dr. Ronald B. Hatch and Fernanda Gonçalves in their editorial capacity, Carol McConnell for her proofreading and indexing skills, Jonathan Friedrichs for research assistance, Sarah Ruediger for producing the maps, Dr. Allan Levine for his splendid introduction, Susan Mavor for her striking cover, Dr. Roberta Kremer for her overall involvement in the project, and Hodie, Saul and Mark Kahn for contributing the Afterword in memory of their father.

"The fear of death is still here. Do you feel it?
Beating its cold black wing and freezing the roots of your
hair. And here and there look! Eyes, mute eyes are
staring. These are the souls of the slain. Outcast, lost souls
that have assembled here and stare at you with
their mute eyes, mutely repeating the ancient plaint that
has never yet reached heaven. Why? Why?
and once again why?"

— CH. N. BIALIK

Lithuania and Poland, 1939, showing the location of Eisiskes.

Contents

Introduction by Allan Levine / 1

Prologue / 5

Vancouver: 1948 / 7

CHAPTER ONE
Eisiskes: 1925–1939 / 9

CHAPTER TWO
Eisiskes: September 1939–September 1941 / 17

CHAPTER THREE
Radun: September 1941–May 1942 / 46

CHAPTER FOUR
Nomads: June–October 1942 / 72

CHAPTER FIVE
Grodno: October–December 1942 / 90

CHAPTER SIX
To the Forest: January–July 1943 / 105

CHAPTER SEVEN
Partisan: July–October 1943 / 123

CHAPTER EIGHT
The Yureli Forest: October 1943 / 137

CHAPTER NINE
Return to the Partisans: April–June 1944 / 152

CHAPTER TEN
Mopping Up: Midsummer 1944 / 165

CHAPTER ELEVEN
Lodz: May–September 1945 / 190

CHAPTER TWELVE
Salzburg: 1945–1948 / 197

Epilogue / 203

Afterword / 209

Index / 213

Introduction

BY ALLAN LEVINE

In 1944 and 1945 as the Second World War ended and the Soviet Union's Red Army liberated the cities and towns of Eastern Europe, approximately 25,000 Jews walked out of the forests of Poland, Belarus, Lithuania, the Ukraine and Russia. For three years or more, these men, women and children had miraculously survived, eluding Nazi hunts as well as Soviet, Polish and Ukrainian partisans, who also resisted the Nazis but cared little about the Jews' plight.

Some of these Jews had also joined Soviet partisan brigades, whose leaders were more favourable to them, and fought against the Nazis, in armed combat and through the sabotage of railway tracks and bridges. Some lived on the run, others built military-style camps. Many more Jews had escaped to the forests — during 1942 and 1943 there were likely 100,000 Jews seeking refuge — from the ghettos where the Nazis had imprisoned them. Most, however, were later killed. Survival in the woods was not impossible, but to do so meant confronting vicious enemies and coping with the ravages of nature.

One among this multitude who defied the overwhelming odds facing any Jew trying to stay alive during the dark days of the Second World War was Leon Kahn, then known as Leibke Kaganowicz. He was only sixteen years old at the end of June 1941, when the Nazis invaded Soviet-occupied territory. Soon after they arrived in Leon's small town of Eisiskes or Ejszyszki, where Jews had resided for centuries alongside Christian Poles and Lithuanians. Until the Soviet occupation of the region in September 1939, the town located near Vilna (or Vilnius, as it is now called), had been part of Poland for nearly two decades.

Within a few months of the Nazi occupation, most of Eisiskes' three thousand Jews were dead, murdered by Nazi death squads with the able assistance of Lithuanian collaborators. From a distance, Leon and his younger brother Benjamin witnessed this gruesome slaughter, a memory, he writes, he "can never forget." Owing to the efforts of historian Yaffa Eliach, a child survivor of the town, hundreds of photographs of the Jews of Eisiskes, including ones of Leon and his parents and siblings, are displayed in a three-storey picture tower at the United States Holocaust Memorial Museum in Washington, D.C.

The Kahn family had initially survived the first wave of killings by relocating to the ghetto in nearby Radun, but death soon engulfed that community as well. By this time, in mid-1942, Leon had heard rumours of Soviet partisans in the forests. Although his father Shael was sceptical, Leon eventually persuaded him that survival in the forest was the family's only option. Leon's mother Miriam refused to leave her own mother in the ghetto and both women eventually died. Leon's recollection of his farewell to his mother, whom he never saw again, is one of many poignant moments in his memoir.

During the next few months, he was able to link up with a Soviet partisan group, to be, as he writes, "one of the hunters instead of one of the hunted," and participated in many sabotage operations against the Nazis. But death was always around every corner. And in October 1943, he watched in horror as his father was shot and sixteen-year-old sister Freidke murdered by a group of Polish soldiers of the Armia Krajowa or Home Army, who regarded most Jewish fugitives as Communist sympathizers and a threat to an independent Poland. Freidke was bayoneted and died instantly, while Shael Kaganowicz lingered with his wounds for several days before he, too, died.

In general, Leon's survival, like that of many partisans, was dependent on a variety of factors. The first was geography, since one had to be close to the forest to reach it safely. The jungle-like forests of eastern Poland, Lithuania and Belarus, so thick in spots that during the day one cannot see the sunlight, provided adequate yet primitive shelter. Second was age, because it was difficult for those individuals who were more than forty years old and younger than fifteen to deal with the hardships and dangers of life as an escaped Jew from a ghetto. Third was access to weapons: the Soviet officers who waged a guerrilla war against the Nazis from behind enemy lines usually demanded that Jewish recruits to their brigades supply their own guns. It was a dangerous and almost impossible challenge to meet. Leon was able to acquire weapons from friendly farmers his father had done business with prior to the war.

Fourth was the attitude of the local rural population. Food and aid were always welcome, but helping a Jew under the Nazi occupation meant an instant death to the peasant and his family. Fear of Nazi retribution was endemic and naturally impacted on Jewish and Christian interactions. At the same time, anti-Semitism, widespread in Europe for generations, did not vanish during the war. Informing on Jewish fugitives for as little as a piece of sugar or salt was not unheard of. Fifth was the leadership and courage shown by such Jewish partisan leaders as Aba Kovner, Tuvia Bielski, Shalom Zorin, Dr. Yeheskel Atlas, Misha Gildenman and dozens more like them. Without their strength, perseverance, and determination in rescuing Jews from the ghettos, providing shelter for them once they reached the forests, negotiating with the Soviets, and protecting and feeding camps of families, thousands more Jews would have perished. Finally, there was sheer luck. As Leon's own saga shows over and over again, fate often intervened and being in the right place at the right time meant the difference between life and death.

The war and its hectic aftermath dictated a different set of morals and standards. Leon, like many partisan survivors, was young and understandably intent on avenging the murders of his family. He makes no apologies for stealing food or taking the law into his own hands. He was not perfect. He made mistakes, and often reacted impetuously and not always, in hindsight, with the best judgment. But this grave time did not usually present moments for reflection. Hesitation meant death.

His relations with his Christian Polish and Russian neighbours and comrades were complex and not always easy to explain or understand. War brings out the best and worst in some people. Leon's tale is filled with episodes of hatred, revenge, greed, and murder, but he also recounts numerous acts of kindness, and writes of hope and optimism.

The history of the partisans is the least-known aspect of the Holocaust, although in recent years there have been several books published on the subject in addition to memoirs like Leon's that relate the experience in the forest from a personal perspective. Many historians dismiss as inconsequential the Jewish partisans' resistance — pointing, for example, to the small numbers of those who survived compared to the millions who perished — yet they fail to appreciate the immensity of the struggle. The question should not be, why did more Jews not resist, but rather, how, under the circumstances, was any resistance possible at all?

The answer can be found in Leon Kahn's memoir. The story he tells is one about ordinary people like himself whose lives were altered forever by a war that stained the history of civilization. His is a chronicle that testifies to the strength and fortitude of the human spirit. It is a tale that deserves to be told and told again.

Allan Levine is a historian and writer based in Winnipeg. He is the author of eight books including *Fugitives of the Forest: The Heroic Story of Jewish Resistance and Survival During the Second World War*, which won the 1999 Canadian Yad Vashem Prize for Holocaust History.

Prologue

There may be those of you who will question why I have written this book. Why I feel so compelled to tell my story to the world. Reliving the details has been a painful and heartbreaking experience for me. Memories that had faded with time once more assume a fresh reality, and I am torn with grief and anguish as I recall the sufferings of my lost family and friends. In spite of this, I am glad I persisted, and for several reasons. One is the hope that in the telling I may help to ensure against the possibility of a repetition of the past. Painful as it may be for all of us who survived, I believe it essential to remember and put down what happened to six million of our people. Innocent souls who died only because they were Jews.

In addition, I wished to show that the German nation alone was not totally responsible for the destruction. The Germans could never have succeeded as well as they did without the wholehearted support of many Poles, Lithuanians, Ukrainians, and thousands of other Jew-hating, pro-Nazi collaborators. Nurtured for two thousand years on the seeds of anti-Semitism fed to them by the Catholic Church and the educational system, they were more than willing to cooperate with the Germans in the liquidation of the towns and ghettos, in the operation of the execution squads, and in the running of the death camps.

Lastly, I believe it is absolutely imperative to mention the responsibility of the Roman Catholic Church and its clergy for their part in the wholesale and unprecedented slaughter of Central Eastern European Jewry. They were well aware of the daily persecutions, the indignities, the murders, and indescribable horrors inflicted on Jews by their devout Catholic parishioners. Yet not once did Rome or any of its deputies throughout Eastern Europe raise a voice in protest. This shocking and complete disregard for the spilling of innocent Jewish blood indicated their tacit approval of what was happening. It will remain forever as a black and shameful chapter in the annals of Catholicism, which time can never erase.

In conclusion, I would like to thank Marjorie Morris for more than two years of hard work on the manuscript, Betty Keller for editing the material, and Cherie Smith for her support and encouragement.

— Leon Kahn

Vancouver: 1948

In the fall of 1948 I arrived in Vancouver, British Columbia, as a refugee. I spoke no English, but this did not worry me because I already spoke Polish, Lithuanian, and Yiddish and could make myself understood in Russian and German. I knew I could learn one more language. I was told that the best place to learn English was the movie theatre, and so night after night I sat listening and watching as the famous lips of Hollywood moved and formed words for me to copy. It is surprising how well this system worked.

One evening, after the last show was over, I came out the back door of the Capitol Theatre onto Seymour Street. The street was quite deserted, except for two drunks coming noisily along the sidewalk toward me. For a moment I watched them approach, then I crossed the sidewalk and stood in the gutter, hoping they would not notice me. But they did.

Still arguing drunkenly, they paused to look at me, obviously surprised at what I had done. Then off they went again down the street, shouting and shoving one another. I didn't know whether to laugh or cry. Neither of them had made a move to strike me. They had not called me names. They had not even understood why I was standing in the gutter. Where I had come from, no drunk ever forgot — even when he forgot his own name — that Jews were there to be beaten, abused, and thrown in the gutter.

CHAPTER ONE
Eisiskes: 1925-1939

When I was a boy, every day began with the sound of Shavel the Cowherd's horn. Early in the morning, he would stand in the centre of the town square blowing his horn to call the cows from their stables and lead them to pasture in the meadows beyond the town. At sunset he would lead them home again, each cow finding her way to her own stable for milking time.

Shavel and his horn were just one small part of the centuries-old pattern of the little town or shtetl of Eisiskes. It had been founded nine centuries earlier by the Lithuanians as a way station between the fortresses of Vilnius, Lida, and Nowogrudek, and it still retained the form common to most medieval towns: a square enclosing a square. The perimeter of the main square in the heart of the town was packed with houses side-by-side facing toward it, nearly two dozen of them to each side of the square. Some were built of brick, but many of them were constructed in the old way of square-hewn logs fitted tightly at the corners. Behind each house was a stable for the family horse and cow and behind the stable was the vegetable garden where each thrifty housewife tended cabbages and pumpkins and gooseberry bushes and apple trees. Beyond this was a final square of houses a few individuals had built in straggling solitude, but since the entire life of the town focused on the activities that took place in the square, few people wished to be far away from it. Life in Eisiskes was always somewhat precarious, for the town lies in that part of middle Europe that has passed back and forth between Poland, Lithuania, and Russia through many centuries and many wars. When I was a boy, the Poles were our masters and we were subject to the special laws and discriminatory practices that they had devised for oppressing the Jewish minority.

Jews had first acquired land in the vicinity of Eisiskes in the middle of the twelfth century, but had been dispossessed of it by anti-Semitic governments in the centuries that followed. A few managed to stay on the land by acquiring ninety-nine year leases, while some others worked as overseers for absentee farm landlords. The remainder reluctantly established themselves as shopkeepers and merchants and professional men in the town itself so that by 1900, almost seventy percent of the town's population was Jewish. But they never lost their connection with the land and, as a result, the life of the countryside flowed through the town square in a constant stream. In Eisiskes, commerce was carried on in our homes, and so closely knit was our community that no one needed a surname. One man was known as Moishe the Baker, another as Shmuel the Milkman, and another as Benjamin the Harness-maker. And their children were known as the son of Moishe the Baker, and the daughter of Shmuel the Milkman. This familiarity and interdependence kept the community united and gave everyone a sense of security despite constant threats from the outside world.

In 1895, Eisiskes had been levelled by fire but soon after had been rebuilt with many improvements. The market square had been cobbled and a row of shops built near its centre. Many of the homes, including our own, were rebuilt of brick to decrease the risk of fire in the future. Unfortunately, the incidence of fires did not decrease, for a few of the town's less upstanding citizens had found that there was time for looting before the fire tore through the entire house. As a result, unexplained fires kept on occurring in Eisiskes. As fast as the homeowners passed their goods into the street to helpful "friends," the goods and the "friends" disappeared. These friends, of course, were part of Eisiskes' underworld, a small group of men who dabbled in highway robbery, looting and arson, and even in a certain amount of blackmail. The people of Eisiskes never reported them for fear of reprisal.

In the mid-1930s, the town at last bought a fire engine. Alas, the machine worked perfectly during parades and demonstrations, but never in emergencies. The firemen, however, became the pride of the town; they formed a brass band, which was so good that it helped us to forget the fire department's inadequacies.

Almost without exception, the Jewish people of Eisiskes attended synagogue regularly, for it was the most powerful influence in their lives. All the events of the week were directed toward the preparation for Sabbath when families would gather to thank God that another Sabbath had come to pass in peace and harmony.

This was the town where I was born in 1925, the second son of Shael and Miriam Kaganowicz. My brother, Benjamin, was three years older than I; my sister Freidke would be born two years later. My father was a dark, slim man, extremely good-looking and about 5'8" in height. He was warm, easygoing and friendly. Everyone regarded him with affection, including the non-Jewish farmers whom he dealt with. Mother was plump, prematurely grey and about 5'5" in stature. She had a strong but loving personality and was the strength and mainstay of our family. I adored her and depended completely on her good judgment in all decisions. She was the most important human being in my life.

Benjamin, my older brother, stood about 5'8". He had reddish hair and a kind, freckled face. He was extremely sensitive, bright and intelligent, and found the events of the war, which engulfed all of us, terribly hard to cope with. Although I was the younger brother, I always felt very protective toward him. Last of all was Freidke, my little sister — a bit spoiled perhaps, being the only girl, but she had courage and stamina. In appearance, she was very pretty with fair hair and a lovely figure.

The house we lived in faced the southeast side of the square. Pressed into the mortar over its door were the numbers 1895, the year of its construction. It was home to our small family and to my two grandmothers as well. My father's mother was very old. My keenest memory is of her sitting in her rocking chair, knitting and smiling serenely. She seldom spoke and never ventured an opinion on family matters. Occasionally, she went to visit relatives on the other side of town, a tiny figure still knitting as she walked across the square. I was ten when she died. My maternal grandmother was a complete contrast to my father's mother because, in addition to being nearly thirty years younger, she was a strong-willed and determined woman. She lived with us because my mother had married a relatively poor man. Since we could not afford to hire help, she came to ease the burden of work on my mother's shoulders. Well-educated and opinionated, she had made sure that her daughters were given all the advantages her husband's wealth could ensure. Her daughters held her in great esteem and always addressed their mother by the respectful pronoun "eer" rather than the usual "du" of close family ties. I remember her shaping the family bread in huge, twenty-five pound loaves and preparing the family soup, but I do not remember feeling for her the love I felt for my other grandmother.

As a small boy I often sat on the steps of our house to watch wagons piled high with produce cross the cobbled square. And since the highway passed right through the middle of it, there was plenty of traffic en route to Grodno in the southwest or Vilnius in the northeast. Sometimes a fancy carriage with spirited horses would careen through the square without breaking pace, causing people and animals to dash off in all directions in an effort to escape. When I grew older, automobiles drove through the square honking their horns to warn us out of the way, or sometimes stopping at the gas pump that had been installed in the centre of the square.

The best time to watch the square was Thursday morning when the farmers arrived for the weekly market. As soon as the permanent shops in the square opened, the farmers would stand by their wagons waiting to bargain with the Jewish housewives shopping for the Sabbath feast. It was exciting to follow my mother as the weekly ritual began: the thoughtful trip from wagon to wagon, looking, touching, pinching, smelling the produce, and bargaining. Oh, the bargaining! — the housewives and the farmers had refined bargaining to an art. At last a decision would be made. She would take "these apples, please," and "these vegetables," and the farmer would put them in a bag. Standing there, as she made her purchases, I could watch all the other mothers pinching and poking the produce, also trailed by their offspring. Finally my mother would choose a wriggling chicken, its feet tied together with string, and take it straight away to the shochet, the ritual slaughterer, across the square.

There was always something especially wonderful about the Sabbath, which only a Jew who has lived in a shtetl can truly understand. I believe that its observance was one of the most important reasons the Jews continued to survive in Central Europe when merely existing was almost impossible at times. Its preparation, and the revitalization of the spirit in communion with God, was something every Jew could look forward to, regardless of his financial status or the weight of his burdens.

I will never forget the exquisite peace that would descend on our little town every Friday when Lipa the Shammes would come into the square. He would be dressed in his finest Sabbath attire, and amid the activity would tap his gold-topped cane on the street, announcing in a loud, authoritative voice, *"In Shul arein!"* (Come to the synagogue!) Then like a magical prophecy, the sounds of commerce would fade away and, after a short while, the families would emerge from their homes. Mothers and fathers, calm and reverent. The children, scrubbed and shiny. All with wide, expectant eyes and smiling lips, making their way to synagogue. Then after services, the Sabbath meal awaited us: the chicken soup, warm and soothing to the spirit, and all the other special treats our mothers had prepared.

As I grew older the carefree days came to an end. I had to begin classes in the parochial school next to the synagogue in Eisiskes. There, with all the other Jewish children of the town, I learned my lessons in Hebrew. Polish, the language of the countryside around Eisiskes, was only taught for a couple of hours each week as if it were a foreign language. Within our tight community we could manage with very little command of Polish, but by paying so little attention to the language of the country, we isolated ourselves even more from its people. My mother, however, had aspirations for me to go beyond our little town. She was one of the most respected women of Eisiskes and wanted her sons to command the same respect. She decided that I should become an engineer and, knowing that I would not be accepted into an engineering university without fluency in Polish, she made up her mind that I would transfer to Polish school for my sixth and seventh years.

My brother, Benjamin, had earlier turned down this opportunity. A gentle and creative person, he wanted only to be apprenticed in the leather industry where he could learn to design and fashion shoes. My nature was entirely different from my brother's and I leapt at the challenge that my mother dangled before me. Satisfied that I would succeed, my mother hired a tutor, and during the summer after my fifth year of school he drummed Polish grammar into my young head. So thorough was he that I had no difficulty being accepted by the school, but the students certainly did not accept me. For the first time in my life, I was subjected to the full brunt of anti-Semitism. Centuries of hatred fed by the local Catholic clergy incited my Polish schoolmates to make daily attacks on me. I was beaten, kicked and teased unmercifully. I could not defend myself against these gang onslaughts and no one, not even my teachers, tried to defend me. Each day my mother would challenge me to return on the following day.

"Of course, you can stay home, Leibke," she would say. "We can apprentice you to the harness-maker or maybe the baker," knowing perfectly well that I would not give up my dream of becoming an engineer.

Her persistence won in the end. Gradually, the attacks decreased and in time I won a degree of respect from my fellow students and even from my teachers. This was the result not only of my stubborn refusal to quit, but also of my good progress in school. My tutor had provided me with a better grounding in Polish grammar than the rest of the class possessed. Eventually, even the anti-Semitic princi-pal congratulated me on my achievement and assigned me a group of six Polish boys to tutor. They would walk home with me each day, and over sweets and cakes we would review grammar. Although we never became good friends, they at least left me in peace after that.

At home in the evenings, I still helped with chores in the dairy that my mother operated. She prepared butter, sour cream, and cottage cheese, selling them along with milk and sweet cream. The milk came from the farm of a wealthy Polish landowner about two miles from town. Often I was allowed to take the horse and wagon to collect the big cans of milk. It was a great treat for me to be in charge. Sometimes I would take a friend or two along to show them the great estate with its magnificent house and acres of rolling land. As we loaded the cans onto the old slat-sided wagon we would pretend we had come to visit royalty. Sometimes I went with my handsome father on his expeditions to buy grain or cattle or horses for resale in Eisiskes or the neighbouring villages. These were marvellous trips, for my father had such a wonderful ability to make friends that we were welcomed in villages and on farms almost as far away as Vilnius. In turn, many of these farmers, both Poles and Lithuanians, would stay overnight with us in Eisiskes on the night before market day. Another of our family businesses was shipping live crabs to retail outlets in Vilnius. This meant that every member of the family had to help pack them in moss for shipment. Ours was a busy family but there was good reason for this.

A few years after my birth, my father had heard of a huge tract of land to be sold by the government because the owner had been unable to pay his taxes. Like so many of the Jews of Eisiskes, my father longed for land of his own, and so he took his savings and borrowed money from all his relatives in order to pay for a ninety-nine year lease on the land. But after he had paid over the money, the original owners refused to leave the land and the government would not respect father's right to the property because they had already collected the tax arrears from him. For five years father tried to insist on his rights while gun battles raged between the original owners and the men my father hired to work the land. At last, in despair, he gave up and began the awful struggle to repay those who had loaned him the money. All through the early 1930s he and my mother worked hard to pay off this debt.

Then one day in 1936, the Polish police walked into our home. Without permission they searched it from room to room and arrested my father. He was imprisoned in Vilnius but neither he nor my mother was told the charge. Mother hired an expensive lawyer, whom we certainly could not afford, and after a month's negotiations we learned that my father was being charged as a spy. The charge originated from the fact that a farmer who had stayed overnight in our home on the eve of market day had been identified as a member of the Lithuanian underground movement. As Lithuania had never given up its claim to this area, though it had long rested in Polish hands, the Lithuanian freedom fighters were under constant surveillance, and it took little to fan the flames of hatred between the two nationalities. As a result, my gentle father had been caught between two factions. For three months he shared a damp cell with the Lithuanian with whom he had been accused, the two becoming close friends. In the meantime, my mother travelled back and forth from Eisiskes to Vilnius, supervising the family enterprises and attending to my father's needs. Then just as suddenly as he had been arrested, and without explanation, the Polish police released him and allowed him to return home to us.

CHAPTER TWO

Eisiskes: September 1939–September 1941

On September 1, 1939, Hitler's armies and his air force attacked Poland from the north, the west, and the south. Within two weeks, all resistance by the Polish army had been smashed, Warsaw was under siege, and German troops were approaching the city of Lvov. On September 17, Russian troops entered Poland from the east and, encountering almost no resistance, rolled westward to meet the German army near the Bug River. The whole world was shocked by the defeat of the Polish army because it had a reputation as a precise military organization. But Poland had fielded a World War I army prepared for sabre and cavalry charges, not the tanks and sophisticated weaponry of the Nazi onslaught. Many Polish soldiers carried weapons they had never been trained to use, or ones that were thirty years out of date. In addition, the whole of the Polish defence system and government were so thoroughly riddled with German Fifth Column agents that all communications simply collapsed at the outbreak of war. On October 5, Poland was formally divided between Germany and Russia. The German Reich annexed the area which included the cities of Poznan, Gdynia, Bydogoszca, Katowice, Lodz, and Plock; from here all "undesirables" were deported and in their places more than half a million Germans settled. The four districts around Krakow, Warsaw, Lublin, and Radom were organized as occupied territory and policed by the German military. A partition line was drawn from the Czechoslovak border northward to follow the Bug River to Brest; beyond this the line curved northwest, then northeast, to the southern tip of Lithuania. The Russians took possession of the territory east of this line.

There was general rejoicing among the Jews of Eisiskes that we had fallen into Russian, rather than German hands, for although the Russians had no love for the Jews, the Germans' hatred was legendary. Eisiskes had even escaped damage during the invasion, and after a brief period of tension, life went on in much the same fashion as before. We were very curious about the mighty Russian soldiers who were our conquerors, and we had only three weeks to wait before they arrived. We had been told to expect troops that were invincible, worldly, and intelligent, but those who arrived in our town were incredibly simple farm boys, their uniforms ragged, and their boots cheap and often filthy. Most of them carried in their pockets the first rubles they had ever earned and they couldn't find enough to spend them on. For their girlfriends back home they bought nightgowns, which they thought were dresses, and enough wristwatches to cover their arms from wrist to elbow. We quickly learned never to tell a Russian the time, for the moment we looked at our wristwatches, they would be confiscated. A story was told of one soldier who confiscated a beautiful grandfather clock and took it to a watchmaker to have it made into ten small ones to carry home to Russia. Another story concerned a farmer who put an upright stick into the ground so he could mark the passing of the hours by its shadow across the field where he worked. A passing Russian soldier, seeing this, confiscated the stick! The soldiers' naïveté was easily explained. For years, all Russia's resources had been poured into the manufacture of military equipment because her leaders had long recognized the inevitability of war in Europe. As a result, luxury items were completely unknown and many of these young fellows had never before seen a watch or a nightgown. The Russian troops who entered our district were quickly accepted as part of the surroundings, and we managed to live fairly peacefully under their rule. From the German zone to the west came stories of brutality and ghettoization that daily made us grateful to be in Russian hands.

Within a month after Russian occupation, however, the province of Vilnius, which included Eisiskes, was ceded to Lithuania. While Lithuania was itself under Russian control, the new status meant the Lithuanians immediately installed their own people in government positions. Fortunately, for the most part, they were not extremists. For example, Ostrauskas, the chief of police, treated us quite fairly and we found no fault in his administration. Many Jews escaping from German-occupied Poland toward Lithuania passed through Eisiskes on their way, stopping to tell our family horrendous stories of life under the Germans. As my father spoke perfect Lithuanian, he was called on many times to bribe the Lithuanian border guards to help them escape.

Under Lithuanian rule, we carried on in Eisiskes much as we always had. In fact, our financial position actually improved at this time. My father had heard that the Lithuanian he had shared a cell with in Vilnius three years earlier was now an important official in the city of Kaunas. He went to visit him, was given a warm welcome, and also a document testifying that he was a Lithuanian freedom fighter who, by his imprisonment, had suffered for the cause of his country. Then my father was asked what special favour he would like. He did not have to think about this for long. For years, he and my mother had toiled to repay their debt on the disputed land; he asked for a liquor vendor's licence so he could have a decent livelihood. These licences were a rare privilege as they were usually granted only to handicapped war veterans. But my father's friend said it could be arranged. In January of 1940 the licence was granted. Soon afterwards my parents gave up their other businesses to concentrate their efforts on the liquor store.

When our fortunes quickly improved, I was sent off for my second term of high school in Vilnius where I boarded with my grandmother's sister. This had been far beyond my father's financial capabilities in the first term and I had worried continually about the expense of my education. However, I still managed to enjoy myself as any normal fifteen-year-old would. I visited with friends, acquired girlfriends, went to concerts, and studied very hard. I loved the excitement of the big city and investigated every inch of it, as it was so different from our little town.

School itself was a marvellous challenge because I had a tremendous desire to succeed. I was the middle child of the family but that wasn't the only thing that drove me. My mother must have realized early that my brother Benjamin took after my father with his gentle nature and non-aggressive instincts. It would have been useless to force him into higher education, for he was only happy when carving and whittling wood or moulding leather. But she knew that she could get me to accept a challenge, and often she would deliberately test me. I remember when the first tomatoes appeared in the market of Eisiskes, most people would not eat them because they were said to be full of "blood." My mother would serve tomatoes sliced up in a dish of cucumbers, herring and onions. Then she'd say when my brother and sister refused it: "See, Leibke isn't afraid of tomatoes!" And I would eat the dish — tomatoes and all — although I didn't enjoy it at all.

In school I always felt that I must do better. Mother had earlier provided me with Polish tutors that we could ill afford, so naturally I had striven to be the best in Polish class. When my parents sent me to Vilnius to study, it cost them sixty zlotys a month for board and tuition fees, so I was determined to be a "straight A" student for them. Whenever my father came to Vilnius to stock up on liquor for the store, he stopped at the school to discuss my progress with the principal. After his interview he would visit with me, and although he never told me what the principal had said about me, I surmised that it had been good because I would find a few extra coins in my coat pocket after he had gone.

Returning home for vacations, I had a choice of travelling by bus or train. Since the bus trip was most direct but also the most expensive, I would catch the train to Station Orany (now known as Station Varena), where my father or brother would meet me with the horse and wagon. When they hadn't time to come for me, I would catch a ride with a neighbour who often travelled the twenty miles from

Eisiskes to deliver produce to the train. Reunion with my family was always an emotional occasion, for we were a close and loving family. Afterwards I was expected to visit all my friends and our neighbours to tell them of city life and my progress at school. Everyone took a special interest in me, and I soon began to understand that I had a unique status in our community. I was the town's proxy in the outside world, the local Jewish boy making good.

In August 1940 the Russians annexed Lithuania in answer to "a call from the Lithuanian proletariat" which, in reality, was just an excuse to allow them to roll into Lithuania in force and step up their preparations for the inevitable confrontation with the Germans. They brought in thousands of convicts to build airfields, railways and roads in the occupied territory. However, Hitler's timetable was far more advanced than Stalin realized, and the convicts never did finish their work in time to benefit Russia. The Russian takeover brought a few other changes to the local scene; some of Eisiskes' officials were replaced and our police chief, Ostrauskas, disappeared. We never learned the reason for this, but we were already used to the vicissitudes of war and had learned to accept the unexplained with equanimity.

The people who suffered most under the Russians were the wealthy, and in Eisiskes this included many Jews. The Russians stripped them of all their possessions and shipped them to Siberia to forced labour camps. At the same time, the Russians rounded up former officers of the Polish army, policemen, and many underworld characters and deported them as well. It was during these deportations that Eisiskes' first war casualty occurred. In our town, as in most towns, we had a number of "characters," individuals who were eccentric or a little mad but who belonged nevertheless to the community. In Eisiskes, one of these was a man we called "Nochem the Pope." His title had no religious significance. It had been bestowed upon him because he wore his hair very long in the style of the Russian Orthodox priests.

Suffering from shell shock, Nochem had wandered into our town some time after the First World War, and stayed on. Homeless, ragged and filthy, and completely withdrawn from society, he would walk the streets like some ghostly apparition. With every few steps he would shout: *"Ich feif auf de reiche. Ich feif auf de reiche!"* (To hell with the rich!), and he would shake his fist at some invisible enemy. Our community treated Nochem kindly. He was fed regularly and provided with a place to sleep at night. Most of the time he appeared completely deranged and out of touch with reality although some people claimed he was a highly educated man with a thorough knowledge of the Torah, and some even claimed to have had lengthy discussions with him.

Nochem was in the habit of appearing at our home every afternoon for tea, which my mother's mother would serve from our huge samovar. She reserved a glass especially for him and gave him his own spoon to stir it with; no one else ever had the courage to use this cup and spoon. Then, because of the stench from his unwashed body, he would be required to sit apart from the rest near the door. There he would drink his tea and depart without a word. Nochem was part of a great parade that occurred every day at our house where afternoon tea was a daily social event. Grandmother's samovar held enough tea for the entire block and neighbours came and went for half the afternoon with containers to carry tea home with them. Some would stay to drink a glass with the family and discuss the news of the town, and this of course was the real reason my grandmother made the tea!

Sometime before the invasion we acquired a German shepherd dog, which took an instant dislike to poor Nochem, who was obliged to drink his tea outside after that to avoid the dog. One afternoon I looked down from my bedroom window to see Nochem drinking directly below me. Impulsively, I put my head out and shouted at him: *"Ich feif auf de orime!"* (To hell with the poor!) With one swift movement, Nochem threw the scalding tea up into my shocked face and disappeared into the crowd gathered in the square. I raced downstairs to tell my mother and grandmother. Instead of sympathy, I received a scolding for teasing a poor crazy man.

Every Rosh Hashanah, a group of "toughs" would decide to clean up Nochem and dress him in new clothes for the holiday. This took a great deal of strength and ingenuity as Nochem was wily and powerful and he did not wish to be clean. Five or six men were needed to ambush him and hold him down. He would be dragged to the barber where his hair would be cut while he screamed and threatened to dirty his pants unless they let him go. Then he would be carried to the town pump, stripped of his filthy rags, and scrubbed spotless. Next, wrapped in a blanket, he would be taken to the haberdasher's where he would be completely reclothed. The new Nochem was barely recognizable, but it took very little time for his old self to re-emerge. I'm sure that Nochem never knew that anything had changed in Eisiskes after 1939. He continued to wander the streets as he always had.

In the fall of 1940, the Russians commandeered all the local transportation to carry their new deportees to the railway station at Varena, and having loaded these poor souls aboard, ordered the drivers to start off. From the trucks came cries of anguish and fear, terrifying those who stood by the roadside and filling the wretched drivers with distress. As they approached Varena, Nochem the Pope stumbled onto the scene. The sad cries of the deportees must have penetrated the fog in his mind, for he walked right into the roadway to stand directly in front of one of the trucks. He waited for it to stop, as trucks had always stopped for him in the past, but when the driver started to put on his brakes, the Russian guards clinging to the sides of the truck ordered him to move on or be shot. Nochem died in the dust billowing up behind the trucks as they drove into Varena.

On June 18, 1941, I returned home from Vilnius for my summer holidays, prepared to spend the summer fishing and swimming and walking far into the countryside with my friends. Four days later, Germany declared war on Russia and crossed the partition line, catching the Russians completely by surprise. The Russians fled from Eisiskes in an attempt to escape the Germans' lightning advance, but many died as they retreated, cut off by a German paratroop attack. The Lithuanians ambushed the remaining Russian force and completed the annihilation begun by the Germans. Happy to be on the winner's side at last, the Lithuanians welcomed the Germans as allies, in the process becoming even more right wing than the Third Reich.

The first Germans arrived in Eisiskes on June 23 to find a town of drawn blinds and locked doors. All of us were apprehensive, but those Jews who had become Communists and had helped the Russians were even more frightened because they feared the Lithuanians would betray them. The first group of Germans was a reconnaissance party. They set up machine guns on the rooftops in case of air attack and then awaited orders to press eastward after the enemy.

After calm had prevailed for a few days, we unlocked our doors and ventured out again. We learned that these soldiers were the *Wehrmacht*, the fighting men, who were not overly cruel or sadistic. My mother, who spoke fluent German, ventured into a conversation with several of them in order to inquire after the fate of the Jews in Germany. The Germans seemed surprised that she thought that our people might have been badly treated. "They're just fine," they said. "Nothing's changed at all for them."

Certainly the *Wehrmacht* was not unkind to us in Eisiskes. They pilfered from stores and from home storage lockers, but this had been true of the Russian soldiers before them and the Polish soldiers before that. Many families had stocked up on supplies and hidden them, so that some of the caches found by the soldiers were very rich. A lot of the time the treatment meted out to us by the German soldiers was in direct contrast to that given us by the Lithuanians who now ran the town for their German allies and conquerors. Although Jews owned the bakeries, the Lithuanians had forbidden the sale of bread to Jews. To families without bake ovens, this was a considerable hardship, but the Lithuanians justified their decree by declaring that Communists didn't deserve bread, and that all Jews were Communists. One day a German soldier came upon a Lithuanian policeman beating a Jewish girl. He commanded him to stop, and then asked the girl what had caused the beating. She explained that she'd been caught trying to buy bread. He took her by the hand, led her into the store, and gave her two loaves of bread.

My parents had closed their liquor store and buried the remaining stock at the first news of the invasion. This cache of liquor would be our insurance against future emergencies. When a number of the *Wehrmacht* arrived at our home one day demanding liquor, my father was hard pressed to convince them that there was none left. At length, however, they decided he was telling the truth and went away. A week later, four newly arrived soldiers came to our house on business. Each wore a swastika armband. One was a vicious German who had lived in Silesia; he threatened us with horrendous punishments. Another was a German who had lived in Czechoslovakia. My mother was able to speak with him. "If you think life is hard with us here," he told her, "just wait till the Gestapo and the SS come! You're in for a lot of suffering!"

After they had gone, Mother repeated this conversation to us, and despair settled upon the family. In the days that followed, the optimism that had been the very foundation of my mother's character began to slip away as if she understood, better than her husband or children, what lay ahead. She had a dream – one that recurred again and again – in which she saw shiploads of our people ascending into the sky. At last the dream became as real to her when she was awake as when she was asleep. For all of us it became a sign of an impending disaster. My own nightmares were quite different. Ever since I had been a small child I had been fascinated with the adventures of Tarzan, the Edgar Rice Burroughs hero of the jungle. Every coin that came my way was spent at the little newspaper kiosk beside the bus depot in the centre of the square. Often I would come to the kiosk clutching my money even before the bus had arrived from Vilnius with its bundles of newspapers and magazines on board. Anxiously I'd wait for the strings to be cut on the bundle and the beautiful Tarzan comic books to spill out onto the kiosk counter.

Back home in my bedroom I would read and reread the adventures of my invincible hero, free to roam wherever he chose in his jungle paradise. As the years went by, the stacks of Tarzan books in my room grew higher and higher. In time, I knew every story as thoroughly as I knew the town of Eisiskes. It is little wonder then that one day when the reality of the German occupation became too horrible to accept, I fled to my room and locked the door. For three days and nights I sat reading all my accumulated Tarzan books. Then I reread them. And read them again. I was sure that if I believed hard enough and willed it to happen with every ounce of concentration I could muster, I would be able to transport myself to Tarzan's jungle paradise. There I knew I'd be safe from the German and Lithuanian terror. It was my dear mother who finally persuaded me to come out and accept the truth of our situation, a truth that was becoming more terrible each day.

At about this time, Ostrauskas was released from prison, and returned to Eisiskes as police chief. But he returned like a wounded animal, wrapped in some secret agony. We never learned what had happened to him in prison, but it must have been cruel, for he was a changed man. We could no longer expect fair treatment; he had come back hating all Jews. He gave orders that Jews could only walk in the gutter. Any Jew seen walking on the sidewalk was beaten over the head with a club and thrown in the gutter. Then he ordered the Jews to show their inferiority by going bareheaded within ten feet of any German or Lithuanian.

One of the men he selected for his staff was a young man named Baderas, the son of a Lithuanian farmer who had been a frequent guest in our home. It had been our practice to let the farmers who arrived the night before market day to lay their pallets on the floor of our front room to sleep. To make a few pennies in the days when we were poor, my mother would then sell them breakfast from our dairy. In this way, we made many friends among the Lithuanian and Polish farmers. When he was young, Baderas had come many times with his father and unrolled his pallet on our floor. Later he found a job as a mailman, but remained our friend. Naturally, we were pleased to learn that Ostrauskas had enlisted him as a policeman. But in his new position, Baderas ignored us when we spoke to him and acted as if he had never known us. Then one day he saw my cousin, Leibel Bastunski, walking on the street instead of in the gutter as he was required according to the new law. Baderas threw him to the ground, beat him and kicked him in the groin, severely injuring him. We knew then that Ostrauskas had chosen his man well.

Ostrauskas kept company at this time with a man named Stankewicz, who was the clerk at the city hall. Although he was not on Ostrauskas' payroll, he appeared to be his chief decision-maker. The Lithuanians now had complete control of the town; new proclamations affecting our lives were posted daily. They did this with impunity, for they claimed that all Jews were Communists. I suppose it was not hard for people to believe this, since during the 1920s and 1930s the Jews in Poland had been easily drawn to an ideology that promised absolute equality for all. To a people such as the Jews, who had suffered discrimination and persecution for thousands of years, the concept of Communism seemed like the answer to all their problems.

One of the earliest decrees required that all jewellery and gold and silver ornaments be surrendered to the authorities at the police station. Then they ordered all furs to be turned in to make coats for the German soldiers who were pursuing the Russians. A week later they called for all copper utensils; this order meant the confiscation of all our cooking pots. So it went, until we realized that we would soon be stripped of everything we owned. Everyone tried to give the appearance of complying with the orders, but each family contrived to save some of their belongings. My father filled a sack with a few heirlooms such as our cutlery, valuables such as my mother's diamond earrings, and documents pertaining to property. Then he took it to the home of Mrs. Carolowa, a non-Jewish friend.

As young children, we had considered Mrs. Carolowa an extra grandmother. Short and round and dimpled, she would drive her wagon from her home in the hamlet of Lebedniki through Eisiskes' central square every Sunday morning on her way to the Catholic Church in the hamlet of Jurzdiki on the road to Vilnius. When mass was over and she had prayed for her long-dead husband, she would drive home again, stopping first at the shops in Eisiskes, then waddling up our front steps to share tea from grandmother's samovar. Over the years, Mrs. Carolowa had cried with us over our troubles and laughed with us in good times. She knew us better than anyone outside the Jewish community, and we knew we could place our trust in her now when we were in such desperate need.

As the Lithuanians gave orders for us to surrender more and more of our belongings, we carried more and more things to safe storage with Mrs. Carolowa. We hid feather quilts and pillows and linens, then bicycles and fabric by the yard. We knew we could reclaim them after this trouble was past or use them for bartering if times got worse.

It was a few weeks after the demands began that a permanent garrison of ten Germans moved into Eisiskes to take over the administration. They were men in their fifties, not career soldiers, but reservists. Though they were neither SS nor Gestapo, they were every bit as sadistic. We knew them as the gendarmerie. Having moved into the best house in town, they settled down to the task of organizing the Jews. The first edict required all of us to pin yellow Stars of David on the front and back of our clothes. Next, they commanded that a committee of Jews be formed to carry out the Nazi edicts to the people and to facilitate prompt obedience to orders. As in all the Jewish communities in Poland, this committee was known as the *Judenrat.*

Many shocking stories have been told of the men who formed these committees, but they can be considered only in the context of the times. Most of these men did the best they could at the outset, honestly believing they could be of service to their community. Unfortunately, as the inhuman demands of the conquerors, the hunger and deprivation, and the dehumanization increased, some of them lost all sense of perspective. Under these circumstances, one can come closer to comprehending stories of the *Judenrat* betraying brothers to save themselves, of camp kapos treating their fellow Jews with cruelty and abuse for the sake of a crust of bread. The Germans had systematically planned to reduce the Jewish people to the level of animals by pitting one against the other in their fight to survive. Sadly enough, they often succeeded.

The next edict forbade the Jews of Eisiskes to leave the town except in work parties accompanied by Lithuanian police. Disobedience was punishable by death. We were now effectively isolated because the Jews in all the other towns and villages were subjected to the same law. The Germans had introduced a new tactic: isolate and conquer, hoping that if we didn't know what was happening in other towns, we would be less fearful and more passive.

The world often asks why we didn't believe the stories told us by the farmers who tried to warn us. The answers are simple. We had always been separate from the non-Jews around us and had learned to be suspicious of their motives. We could not believe that "civilized" men could perpetrate horror on the scale that was described to us. Hindsight now tells us how wrong we were, but how could we know then that there were men who would treat their fellow human beings worse than beasts in the market place?

A few people who were disquieted by rumours coming from the farmers held a meeting to discuss the situation. They didn't think things were as bad as they were painted, but they decided that, because the Lithuanians were in control, they were allowing gangs of hoodlums to roam the countryside unchecked. Naively, they resolved to send an emissary to Trakai, the provincial capital, to buy off the chief of police who would in turn offer the hoodlums a large payment or "insurance" premium to leave Eisiskes alone. Since Mother was articulate and could communicate easily with the Lithuanians, she was appointed emissary. For a bribe, she was to take a selection of valuables from the committee members' hidden stores. She began making preparations for the journey, but new events happened too quickly for her to leave.

In another part of the town, a sad event was unfolding. A German officer had stopped on the street to speak to a local man named Arke. The German asked his name and occupation.

"I am Arke, the housepainter," he said. Then he continued, "I know your Führer used to be a housepainter. You think maybe I could be Führer some day?"

Now the German was really intrigued with Arke, although he had only stopped him because he was dressed so strangely. The sleeve of Arke's shirt had been torn off and tied onto his arm. One pant leg had been ripped into strips and carefully wrapped around his leg, and the back of his shirt had been ripped away to make wrappings for his head and arms. In Eisiskes we knew him as "Arke the *Meschugener*" or Arke the Crazy One, for although he was often perfectly intelligent, he would have spells of irrational behaviour. At these times, Arke's family would send him to the village of Selo where a group of farm families took care of the mentally deranged. There, Arke would sit ripping his clothes up, and then tie the strips onto his body in some bizarre fashion. The German, upon learning of Arke's problem, decided to cure him. Taking Arke into the tailor's shop, he had him outfitted in the best clothing on the racks. He then warned Arke, "Now take good care of your new clothes, or I shall punish you severely!" In a matter of days, Arke had reduced the beautiful new clothes to shreds. When the German saw him again he was outraged, but after calming down he decided to give Arke another chance. Once more he took him to the tailor and clothed him. Then he said, "You rip one strip off these clothes, Arke the Führer, and I am going to shoot you! Do you understand?"

Arke nodded, but he must have known the inevitability of his fate; when his irrational spells overcame him, he was powerless to fight them. For several days the clothes remained whole, then one day Arke appeared in the streets in his torn-and-tied costume again. The German was coldly furious this time at Arke's disobedience. He led him to a spot behind the mill on the edge of town. A passing labourer was ordered to dig a pit, and Arke was told to stand in the pit. Arke could not fight what was to happen next but he turned to the German.

"May I have one last cigarette?" he asked, and having been granted this he smoked it to the end. Then he stepped into the pit. "I'm ready now. You can shoot me." And the German did. Arke was the first victim of the Germans in Eisiskes.

My uncle, Abraham Kaplan, had been elected head of our *Judenrat*. He and the six members of his committee had to deal with the Germans' constant demands. First they had confiscated the newest beds in the town and threatened to shoot a Jew for every louse discovered in the mattresses. After that, they wanted our linens and all kinds of household items to make their lives more comfortable. But one day a demand came from the gendarmerie, which my uncle refused to fulfil. A wounded German soldier, being taken home from the eastern front, had died in the ambulance near Eisiskes and was buried near the Catholic Church at Jurzdiki. As reprisal for his death, the Germans demanded from my uncle ten Jews to be put to death. My uncle refused. "You can have four Jews," he said. "My two children, my wife, and myself."

The courage of his reply impressed the Commandant and he withdrew the order. A moment later he had thought up another one. He wanted twenty Jews to work on the house and grounds of the building occupied by the gendarmerie. When Uncle Abraham sent for one member from our household, I volunteered. I was now sixteen years old, curious about what was to happen, and because of this, not really frightened. The next morning twenty of us were marched to the headquarters of the gendarmerie and set to work on household chores, gardening, and splitting wood.

After only an hour of this, we were herded together again and marched out of town in the direction of Jurzdiki. About seventy-five feet from the grave of the German soldier, we were commanded to drop to the ground and crawl past it on our bellies. To make sure we stayed on our bellies, the guards struck us with clubs and fired over our heads. After passing the grave we were forced to crawl for another seventy-five feet. Then with our hands, arms and elbows bleeding from the crushed rock that had been used in the road paving, we were ordered to link arms and march into the river flowing nearby. When the water was chin-high and we expected to drown at any moment, we were allowed to come out. By this time I was terrified, but I can remember experiencing a feeling of wild pride in refusing to allow the Germans to break me as this terrible day unfolded.

From the river we were marched to the city hall which for some long forgotten reason was located in Jurzdiki, although it held the administrative offices for Eisiskes. Here, a unit of Germans had been garrisoned and they had prepared further "games" for us. One of my father's friends, Faivel Epstein, and I were ordered to clean out the outhouses. This was not a task which either of us relished, but we certainly knew how to do it. The Germans ordered us to leave the outhouses in place and transfer the contents of the pit to a distant hole, rather than using the easier method of relocating the outhouses over a new pit. For our task we each needed a bucket fastened to the end of a pole, but the Germans had a better idea. They tossed us both into the pit full of excrement where we stood in it up to our waists. Then they handed us pails and ordered us to go to work.

We were wearing light summer clothes and open sandals, and this disgusting slime sucked at our bodies. Having already learned that we would be punished if we didn't get on with the job, I told Faivel to stand at the edge where he could take the pails from me and empty them. It couldn't make any difference to me whether I was in or out, for I was already covered in filth. After a half hour of this work, two Lithuanians who were passing by decided to investigate the source of the Germans' laughter. When they discovered what was happening, they took down their pants and sat down in the out-house directly over the place where I was working. I attempted to get out of the way, but the Germans ordered me to stand where I was and in a little while my face and my hair and shoulders were covered in excrement. The Germans and Lithuanians hooted with laughter.

An hour later I was ordered out of the pit. "Go wash yourself, you stinking Jew!" and I was sent to the river to wash. Then they added, "But see you get back here or we'll hunt you down and shoot you! Understand?" Down at the river, I scrubbed myself with sand and leaves, but it was impossible to clean myself. Filth clung to my hair and clogged every pore. My clothes were stiff with it. When I rejoined the group, we began to march back toward the house of the gendarmerie. The whole group was barely alive, for while I had stood in the pit, the others had been the victims of other sadistic games. But the Germans had one final piece of fun in store for us. A little distance along the road, we were halted and once more lined up. They ordered us to link arms and bend over till our pants were stretched tight over our buttocks. Then they whipped us till the blood ran down our legs. When at last the Germans could take no more pleasure in the game, they ordered us to run home, all the while firing volley after volley over our heads. We stumbled and fell, and stumbled again, but we ran all the way to the safety of our homes.

My mother stared at me as I stood in the doorway. I must have looked a mess, but in spite of everything that had happened I still felt this fierce pride in myself. It must have been written on my face. My mother tore the remains of my clothes off me and burned them.

In a short time she had a hot bath ready for me and I soaked and soaked until at last I began to feel human again. And as I told them the story of the awful day, I laughed. Part of it was hysteria, but part of it came from the pride of being a winner.

My mother comforted me, "If this is all the Germans intend to do to us, it won't harm us that badly."

And my father said, "Leibke, we have too much faith in God and in ourselves to let this destroy us. We'll outlive them, you'll see." And I believed him.

About a week later, twenty of us, including several girls, were ordered to the schoolyard next to the synagogue. A number of German soldiers had garrisoned there and had used the synagogue as a stable for their horses. Although we had managed to hide the Torah scrolls in a safe place in the synagogue, everything else had been ruined. In the schoolyard, the soldiers first tormented the girls, shouting obscenities at them, lifting up their skirts, and spitting on them. These soldiers were only ordinary fighting men, but they had already learned that when they were short of amusement it was quite all right to torment the Jews. They ordered us to clean and service the army trucks. I was ordered by one of the soldiers to crawl under his truck with a pan to catch the used oil when he released a plug in the engine. Carefully he directed me where to lie and in a moment the dirty oil splashed into my face. The Germans bellowed with laughter. When I tried to move away, the soldier who had invented this marvellous idea held me in place until the last drop of oil had fallen. When I was allowed to stand up, I took a rag and cleaned what I could from my face. I didn't protest; I knew better than that.

One of the soldiers then complained that his motorcycle wouldn't start and told two of us to push him until it started. But no matter how hard we pushed, the motorcycle wouldn't budge. The soldier, of course, was holding the brake down, but when we tried to stop this stupid task, the others threatened us. So we strained and shoved while all the Germans laughed. Next I was ordered to fetch some water, but as soon as I was out of sight I fled home to scrub off the oil and change my clothes. Apparently the Germans sent a search party for me, but since I hadn't given my name or address, I was fairly certain they would not find me.

Soon after this I was assigned to a road gang and sent to repair the highway outside Eisiskes. Our foreman was a Polish anti-Semite, but he could be bribed to be reasonably humane. Although the job was ten miles from home, I can remember walking all the way to work, putting in a full day with the road gang, and running home at night. During this time, my youth and my health served me well — while we waited for the axe to fall.

My next job was at a radio station where a group of young Lithuanians were in control. I was put to work cleaning, sweeping, and chopping wood. A few times when they were drinking they beat me, but other than that, it was not unpleasant working there. One evening when I had returned home from work, a Lithuanian policeman stormed into our house and shouted at my father in German:

"Where is the liquor? I know you hid it, you goddamn Jew, and you're going to show me where it is right now or get a bullet in your head!" He pointed his gun at my father.

Calmly, my father answered him in Lithuanian.

"There is none left. The Germans took it long ago."

The policeman was rather surprised to be answered in his own language and demanded to know how my father spoke Lithuanian. Father told him he had fought for Lithuanian freedom and produced the certificate given to him in Kaunas. When he saw it the policeman became very civil and invited my father to visit him some evening. My father then promised to see if he could locate some liquor for him. Several days later, father dug up a bottle of Lithuanian liquor and took it as a gift to the policeman's home. He stayed for a drink and the friendship was cemented. This same man, however, continued to mistreat other Jews in town.

Only a month had passed since the arrival of the gendarmerie, but our lives were completely changed. We no longer used the streets of Eisiskes, but skulked through back alleys to maintain contact with each other. We tore down the fences which separated our back gardens in order to pass more easily from house to house. We spoke in whispers. From time to time, groups of German soldiers and

Lithuanian police would surround a section of the town to terrorize the Jewish inhabitants. Dragging them from their homes, they would beat them savagely, and then invent games to further maim and humiliate them. Fearing these attacks, we all began to look for avenues of escape or places to hide until the danger had passed.

Remembering our childhood games of hide-and-seek, my brother and I returned to one of our favourite hiding places. Behind our neighbour Szewicki's home was a pair of stables built side by side which shared a common wall. Each of the stables had a ridged roof so that, head-on, they looked like a giant "M." The centre of this "M" formed a trough running the length of the building, and this is where we had hidden as children. No one ever found us there because the peaks of the two roofs were aligned along the width of Szewicki's property so we couldn't be seen from their house or from the house across the lane. The stables were long enough and too close to the next buildings for anyone to see us from the sides. For further security, we always lay in the centre of the trough. The "fortifications" were our final guarantee of safety. The building had been constructed of roughly squared logs, but on the end closest to our home they had been fitted too closely to climb. On the other end, the logs were just a little more irregular, making it possible to scale the wall using careful hand- and footholds. But what really stopped anyone looking for us was a swamp of animal and human excrement at that end. Many of the homes in that neighbourhood had no outhouses and their occupants used this rather secluded area as a toilet. Naturally, everyone else avoided the place. My brother and I weren't put off by it, for we had placed stepping-stones in the grass that grew rather lushly here and we had easy access to our hiding place.

As the summer wore on, more and more frightening rumours reached Eisiskes. Lithuanian and Polish people told us of truckloads of Jews taken to Ponar Mountain near Vilnius and never returning. They tried to tell us that these people had all been murdered there but we refused to believe them. We rationalized that it was only another trick to terrify us. One day, an elderly Lithuanian from Varena told my father that all Jews in that town and the surrounding villages had been killed.

"It's only a matter of days before they do the same to you here in Eisiskes," he said, and he grabbed my father by the arm. "Listen, since you're going to die anyhow, why don't you give me your samovar now. Where you're going you won't need it."

We might have believed that old man, but we concluded that he had cooked up his story just to steal our prized family heirloom. Still, the rumours circulated. One thousand Jews butchered here, two thousand in some other place. The Jews of Vilnius, we were told, had been placed in a ghetto. We closed our ears.

September came. On the morning of the eve of Rosh Hashanah, a proclamation was posted ordering all Jews to assemble in the synagogues. No explanation was given, and although we remained outwardly calm, we were desperately frightened. On the outskirts of the town, nearly two hundred Lithuanian police had taken up positions. Our family had long ago decided what we would do in such an event. Mother was quite sure that this was simply a method of rounding up the men to send them to labour camps; she was equally certain that the women and children would not be harmed. As a consequence, she insisted that my father, my brother, and I should run away and hide, and that she, along with my sister and my grandmother, would go to the synagogue as ordered. Reluctantly, everyone agreed that this was a sensible plan.

On the day of the proclamation my father dressed in homemade felted-wool clothing like that worn by the Lithuanian farmers, took a length of rope, and headed for the meadows beyond the town.

"Hey, you! Where do you think you're going?" he was challenged.

"I've got to fetch my cow!" he answered in perfect Lithuanian.

They let him go, for they knew that Shavel, the cowherd, would not be bringing home the cattle that day, and the non-Jews of the town would have to bring in their own cows. My brother and I filled our pockets with food and a few things we thought would be useful and went to join our friend Gershon, who lived across the lane behind our house. From his house we started across the meadow and had almost reached the river, which formed its furthest boundary, when shots cracked out over our heads. Then as two Lithuanian policemen ran towards us, we stood debating whether or not to run.

At that moment, I recognized one of the men. "Hey, remember me?" I said. "I worked for you at the radio station! Give us a break, eh?"

Just for a moment he stared at me, and then helped his partner search us, taking everything we had in our pockets. When he was finished, he struck me with his rifle butt and ordered us home. We ran toward Eisiskes, expecting a bullet in our backs at every step. At home, Benjamin and I mulled over ways to escape, determined not to be imprisoned in the synagogue with the women. Obviously the trip across the meadow was impossible, so it seemed logical to hide someplace within the town instead. We remembered the barn. Ignoring all the delicious things that our mother and grandmother had prepared for Rosh Hashanah, we each put an apple into our pocket and left the house. With enormous caution, we crossed our neighbour's yard, went behind the stable, and climbed up, wedging ourselves silently side by side in our hiding place on the roof. It was now Sunday afternoon. Through the evening and all that night we lay there. Since the weather was still warm, we were not too uncomfortable. The next morning, all of the animals belonging to the Jews were taken from their stables and driven away. Below us, some Lithuanians tried to break into Szewicki's stable, but it was locked. They pounded on it with their axes, but it wouldn't budge.

Then one of them called out, "Go up on the roof and chop a hole, eh? You can open it from the inside."

Benjamin and I forgot to breathe.

"Hit it just once more, eh?" There was a crash and they all cheered. The lock had been broken. My brother and I lay shaking in silence as they looted the stable below us.

From our vantage point that afternoon, we could see some of the Jewish homes being systematically looted by the Lithuanians and Poles. Their children, boys and girls we had played with, boys who had sat beside me in Polish school, ran from house to house taking everything they could carry. I listened as two Lithuanian boys who had been my friends argued over the division of the spoils they had stolen from our home.

On Tuesday the looting continued but we scarcely paid any attention, for now we could hear the sound of gunfire and screaming coming almost constantly from the direction of the synagogues. Because the synagogues were in a different quarter of the town, we could only guess what was happening. We lay in silence, refusing to speculate, even in whispered conversation to each other, on what was happening.

By Wednesday afternoon, we were weak from hunger and desperately thirsty. I was beginning to make plans to go down that night to investigate and find supplies, when we heard someone call: "Leibke! Benjamin!" We recognized the voice of a Lithuanian farmer who was an old friend. Carefully I raised my head and saw him; in each hand he held an apple, which he tossed to us. He then reassured us that our mother, sister and grandmother were all right. Apparently he had somehow contacted Mother in the synagogue and she had asked him to check the stable to see that we were safe.

But she should not have trusted him, for about two hours later we heard someone call our names again. "Leibke! Benjamin!" But somehow the voice was not the same. We lay without moving, puzzled because we could not place the voice. Then cautiously I began to raise my head to see who it was. On the ground below stood one of the cruelest of the Lithuanian policemen, a beast of a man who enjoyed persecuting Jews. But in the fraction of a second that I saw him, his own gaze had been distracted by two large black crows which had swooped low over my brother and me, and then flown away, cawing loudly over his own head. Fortunately, the crows had startled me too and I had ducked my head. Now the terror I felt matched the terror in my brother's eyes, as we waited to hear the man's departing footsteps. Had I ducked my head soon enough? Had he seen me? Then at last we heard him walk away.

In spite of this reprieve, we knew that we wouldn't be safe much longer on the roof. It was just a matter of time until someone found our hideout. Of course, if we stayed there we would have eventually died of starvation anyway. That night, as it neared midnight, we climbed down from the roof. Standing in the lee of the stable we listened to the sounds of carousing going on all over the town. Directly behind our own yard stood the house of a German laundress where a huge drunken party was in progress accompanied by wild laugh-

▲ Seated left to right: Sarah and Chaim Pacianko, uncle and aunt; paternal grandmother, Sarah; uncle Aarondon. Standing left to right: Ita Malka Pacianko, first cousin; Leon's mother and father, Miriam and Shael Kaganowicz; maternal grandmother, Liebe Gitl Rudzian.

▲ Left: Rebecah Bastunski, Leon's aunt; beside her,
Leon's mother, Miriam Kaganowicz.

▲ Leon Kahn's father, Shael Kaganowicz, as a young man.

◀ Leon's brother, Benjamin Kaganowicz, at eighteen months.

Kindergarten group in Eisiskes, 1933. Leon's sister Freidke Kaganowicz is seated in bottom row first on left. ▶

▲ Hebrew School in Eisiskes, 1932/33. Leon is in the first row, seventh from left.

▲ Leon's class in Polish school, 1938. Leon is in the second row from the back, third from the right.

▲ Marching band composed of members of the Fire Department in Eisiskes, 1930s.

▲ Left to right: Moshe Kaplan, cousin; Moshe Bastunski, cousin; Leon Kahn; Avigdor Katz, friend.

▲ Sarah Bastunski, Leon's cousin, in happier times near Eisiskes, 1938.

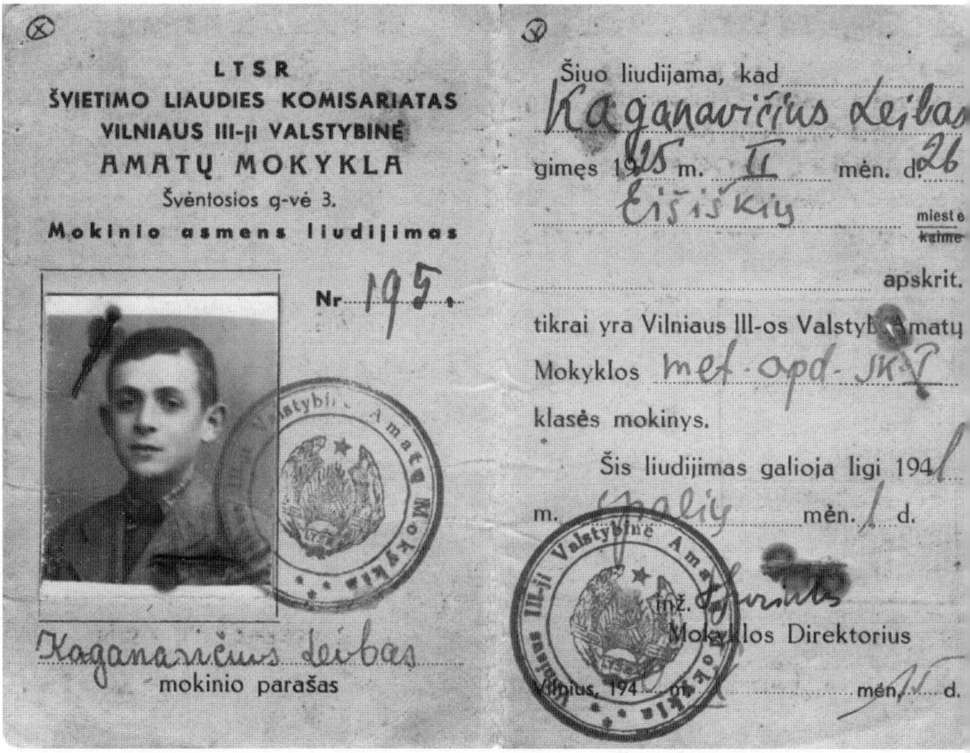

LTSR
ŠVIETIMO LIAUDIES KOMISARIATAS
VILNIAUS III-ji VALSTYBINĖ
AMATŲ MOKYKLA
Šventosios g-vė 3.
Mokinio asmens liudijimas

Nr. 195.

Kaganavičius Leibas
mokinio parašas

Šiuo liudijama, kad Kaganavičius Leibas
gimęs 19 m. II mėn. d. 26
Eišiškių miest e / kaime
apskrit.
tikrai yra Vilniaus III-os Valstyb. Amatų Mokyklos
klasės mokinys.
Šis liudijimas galioja ligi 194
m. mėn. d.
inž.
Mokyklos Direktorius
Vilnius, 194 m. mėn. d.

▲ Leon's school pass under Lithuanian rule, 1941.

ter, rifle shots and breaking bottles. A steady stream of Lithuanians came and went from the house so that the lane we had to cross was never empty. We had decided that our best route lay through our friend Gershon's property but this meant that we had to cross our own garden and the one beyond that in order to be in direct line with Gershon's home. Walking in absolute silence, we cut across our family's garden, stumbling a little over the place where I had dug potatoes the week before. From there we went to the back fence of the adjoining garden. Looters had already damaged the fence so it was easy to push a couple of pickets aside and slide out into the lane. Then it seemed as if we were flying across the lane, past the empty house, and into the garden beyond in search of a hiding place.

Just as we dived behind a gooseberry bush, a fusillade of bullets and flares exploded over our heads. Paralyzed with fright, I listened as footsteps pounded close to us. Thud! Thud! Thud! But strangely enough, they never came any closer. And then I realized it was the pounding of my brother's heart as he lay close to me. The shooting we had heard had just been part of the Lithuanians' celebration of the annihilation of the Jews. They had not seen us at all. For half an hour we lay there, terribly aware of the weakness in our legs from three days of fasting. When we had gathered our courage, we collected some fruit still hanging on the trees, climbed over the back fence and slipped into the meadow. We started toward the river, using the same route we had taken last Sunday morning. This time no one saw us. We pushed through the bushes that separated the meadow from the river, waded through the water, and climbed through the bushes on the other side. We found ourselves in a potato field and, exhausted, fell down between the rows. We must have slept for a while but suddenly I was sitting bolt upright, shaking my brother as he lay beside me. It was the middle of the night, but I was convinced we had been out to dig potatoes for Mother.

"Come on, Benjamin. You bring the basket of potatoes and we'll go home." I searched for the potato fork to carry it home.

"Be quiet, Leibke. Someone will hear us." He shook me to make me understand our danger. When I was fully awake, I knew that my dreams had only replaced the nightmare of reality.

We knew we had to find a better place to hide before dawn, some-place where we could remain until darkness could hide the next stage of our flight. It was then we remembered the old Catholic cemetery next to the gravel pit on the road to Jurzdiki, and we began stumbling through the fields toward it. Although it had been absolutely forbidden to us, we had played hide-and-seek there as children, for it was a jungle of commemorative trees and overgrown vines that clung to the gravestones and the fences. There was little likelihood that anyone would search for us there. Daylight was colouring the sky as we approached the cemetery, a desolate place some eight or ten feet above the level of the road and surrounded by a three-foot wall. A short lane led to the gate. Once inside, we found a place for ourselves in the tangle of bushes close to the wall in the old part of the cemetery next to the gravel pit. For a few hours we slept. Around ten o'clock we were startled awake. In the distance, we could hear the rumble of field wagons approaching and the voices of a great number of people. Some seemed to be crying, and some were shouting orders. And over all this were shots and screaming, and screaming, and more screaming.

As the sounds came nearer, we held on to each other, uncertain whether to run or hide. Then we shrank lower into the tall grass as we realized that the sounds came from the roadway leading to the cemetery. The terrible procession was coming here. When it passed the gates, we stood up among the bushes to peer over the wall at an unbelievable parade.

The Lithuanian police were herding the women and children of Eisiskes along the road, whipping and beating them to make them move faster. Farm wagons were loaded with children and with the dead and dying bodies of women who had rebelled at their captivity. As we watched, the whole grisly procession turned in at the farthest entrance to the gravel pit.

Then began a day I can never forget, for every detail is drawn on my memory as if it had happened only yesterday. Over the cries and moans of this mass of defenceless creatures, the Lithuanian police barked orders, then pushed and prodded to separate the women from their children. Benjamin and I desperately scanned the lines of women to find our mother, grandmother and sister but we could not see them. There was my aunt and my cousin, and that neighbour lady, and the woman from the newspaper kiosk. But we couldn't see our own family. We were afraid to hope that they had escaped. "What are they going to do?" Benjamin hissed in my ear. But we both knew in our hearts what was going to happen.

The women were taken in groups of a hundred or so down the path into the gravel pit. Once they reached the point where the bushes would hide them from the sight of the others, the women were made to strip naked and pile their clothing nearby. Then many of the younger ones were separated from the others and dragged into the bushes to be raped and raped again by soldier after soldier and policeman after policeman. At last they were dragged off to join the others, marched to the bottom of the gravel pit, lined up and coldly shot to death by the Lithuanian killers.

I clung to the edge of the cemetery wall as horror welled up within me. I wanted to hide, to run screaming from the cemetery to make this hideous thing end. Didn't they know what they were doing? These were human lives. These were people, not animals to be slaughtered.

My mouth opened to scream, but I could not. I wanted to close my eyes, but they wouldn't close.

"Don't look, Leibke! Don't look!" Benjamin sobbed, and pulled at me to make me leave the wall.

I didn't want to look, but I couldn't stop looking. I saw the Lithuanians shoot the breasts off some of the women and shoot others in the genitals. I saw them leave others with arms and legs mutilated to die in agony, and some to smother as the next load of bodies fell upon them. I saw my aunt die in a volley of gunfire. I saw my beautiful cousin raped and raped until death must have been the only thing she longed for.

My fingers slipped from the wall and I fell beside my brother, retching and sobbing. He clung to me. "Don't watch anymore, Leibke," he pleaded. "Stay here!"

I wanted to, but I couldn't. It was as if I had no will of my own, as if I had to memorize every crime and horror, and the face of each murderer. Weeping, Benjamin sat on me, trying to hold me down.

"No," I whispered and fought to get up. "I've got to . . . I've got to!" I returned to the wall.

Still the nightmare went on. Each group of slaughtered women was followed by another group. Hopeless screams for mercy. Shrieks of terror and agony. And gunfire. I felt each bullet enter my brain.

At last only a mass of terrified children milled about at the entrance to the gravel pit, and the Lithuanians made no move toward them. I saw Ostrauskas, Eisiskes' police chief, stride up to the Lithuanians, give orders, and point to the children. Then angrily he moved to the gendarmerie to give orders there. Someone handed him a coat and helped him put it on to cover his uniform. Then Ostrauskas and a few of the Lithuanians murdered the little children of Eisiskes. Some they shot, others they dashed to pieces by smashing their heads on the nearby granite boulders, until one by one they had killed them all, and Ostrauskas' hands and clothing were covered with the blood of his tiny victims.

Just before nightfall, he took off his blood-spattered coat and rode home to his family in Eisiskes. The Lithuanians were left to pour lime over the bodies and shovel gravel onto the forlorn grave. Finally even they went home, and only Benjamin and I were left to mourn. We stood dry-eyed in the darkness for a long time. Sometime before midnight, we left and made our way to the home of Mrs. Carolowa in Lebedniki, a two-hour walk from the cemetery. We knew she would hide us.

Lebedniki was on the far side of Eisiskes, but we didn't dare take the most direct route by road. We kept to the safety of the grain fields, moving silently between the stalks with the ripe heads of grain nodding above us. Near dawn, we reached Mrs. Carolowa's home. She held us close and cried, and then told us the first good news we'd heard in a week. Our father had been at her home before us and had only left a short time before for Radun where he had distant relatives.

Mrs. Carolowa fed us warm milk and big chunks of bread dipped in honey, then led us to the barn to sleep in the hay hidden from the eyes of curious neighbours who might betray us. We lay there unable to sleep, and unwilling to talk. Suddenly my brother doubled up in pain. He fought to keep silent, holding his abdomen tightly with his arms. I ran to the house to bring Mrs. Carolowa. She came running to the barn with home medications and ministered to him there in the hay. For a time, it seemed as though Benjamin was having an attack of appendicitis. As I watched over him that night I suddenly realized that our only chance for life lay in our ability to stay healthy. We could no longer go to a doctor to cure our ills. Nor could we evade the Germans if we weren't physically fit. I was terrified that Benjamin's illness might cause both our deaths, but in an hour the pain had subsided and Benjamin could sit up again.

After this crisis had passed, Benjamin and I put in a day of fitful sleep in the hay. When darkness fell Mrs. Carolowa provided us with food and we set off into the night with her thirty-year-old son, Stasiuk, to guide us part of the way toward Radun in the southwest. Radun was ten miles from Eisiskes along this road, but we were forced to stay in the grain fields that paralleled it. It was after dawn when we arrived at our relatives' house.

A distant cousin opened the door for us, and we looked past her to see Father standing in the centre of a group of relatives. He was in a state of shock, for he believed we were all dead. Then he turned toward us when he heard the commotion at the door. His face was blank. Someone shook him and said:

"Shael, it's Benjamin and Leibke!"

His face crumpled, and he began to weep uncontrollably. Benjamin and I embraced him and tried to comfort him, but he still wept. When I remember that day, I ache with pity for the poor soul who had taken the place of my strong and confident father. I had never before seen him cry or even lose emotional control. This could not be my father. Benjamin and I tried to convince him that Mother and Grandmother and Freidke were still alive. But he didn't seem to hear us, just as if he were on the verge of a mental collapse. We held him close and prayed that time would bring reason again.

In Radun, it was hard to believe that Eisiskes could have suffered such a hideous fate. Here the Jews lived almost as they had always lived, and it was nearly impossible for them to believe that things would ever change. But hundreds of Jews from Eisiskes kept pouring into the town, with tales of horror that could not be ignored. This one had escaped by hiding in a cellar, that one in an attic, and all had waited until it was dark to run away just as we had. Later that morning three truckloads of German soldiers arrived in Radun to round up the escapees from our ravaged town. They searched from house to house, checking everyone's documents, taking away the Eisiskes Jews, but leaving the people of Radun untouched. My father, who had left the house to buy cigarettes, realized what was happening and walked right out of the town and on to Lebedniki. It would have been impossible for him to return to our relatives' house, and useless as well, for he could not have helped my brother and me.

We ran into the back garden with a schoolteacher from Eisiskes called Persky, looking for some place to hide. The garden was untended and overrun with weeds, so we dove into the tallest patch we could see. Crouching here motionless while the Germans searched that block, we soon realized that we had hidden in a patch of stinging nettle. For two hours we stayed there burned and blistered by the vicious weeds, worrying all the while about Father, for we were sure the Germans had captured him.

Around noon, the Germans stopped for a lunch break and the three of us dashed from the garden, fled across the meadow and into the trees beyond. There we sat for the rest of the day hidden in the brush, anxiously listening for the sound of gunfire in the town. At nightfall, Persky left us to find his own hiding place, and Benjamin and I set off for Lebedniki once more. We didn't know where else to go. Besides, we were sure that if Father had escaped he would go back to Mrs. Carolowa's. Our return was difficult, as Mrs. Carolowa's son had guided us there, and now we stumbled along through unfamiliar fields. Twice we took a chance and stopped at the homes of farmers to ask directions. One of them told us that the streets of Radun were strewn with the bodies of Eisiskes' Jews. Benjamin and I hurried on our way with the knowledge that we had once more escaped death. We wandered most of the night, hoping we were still headed toward Lebedniki, but it wasn't until the first light began to show us a familiar bridge and a turn in the road that we knew we were almost there. It was too late by then to continue on to Mrs. Carolowa's, for the Lithuanians would have caught us in daylight. We thought we recognized the farmhouse ahead as the home of friends of the Carolowas', and risked knocking. To our relief, we had come to the right house. This farmer's son was a friend of Mrs. Carolowa's daughter and had been told of our plight. We were fed and hidden in the hayloft while the son cycled to Mrs. Carolowa's with the news that we had arrived. He came back with wonderful news! My father, mother, sister, and grandmother had arrived at Mrs. Carolowa's home the night before. It was nothing short of a miracle.

But what was to become of our family now? Eisiskes was finished forever, and now Radun, as well, was closed to us. Next morning we persuaded the farmer's son to cycle to Radun to find out what had actually happened there. We waited all day to learn the worst, but in the evening he cycled into the farmyard smiling. He had good news. The farmer's story of Radun's streets strewn with the bodies of Jews had been a lie, probably told to frighten us. The three truckloads of German soldiers were merely out to make a private profit from the Eisiskes Jews' misery. After arresting more than a hundred of them, they demanded that the *Judenrat* of Radun ransom them with jewels and valuables. Instead, the *Judenrat* supplied the Germans with a truckload of leather products. The Germans promptly released their victims and left the town.

Hearing this, Father decided that it would be safe to return to Radun. And so our family, once again reunited, came back to Radun quite openly without trouble from the authorities.

CHAPTER THREE

Radun: September 1941–May 1942

In Radun our relatives received us lovingly, and we thanked God that we were all together again. But the real joy of such a reunion was never ours, for all our relatives and friends had been brutally murdered, and we knew in our hearts that it was just a matter of time until Radun met the same fate. My mother now told us what happened in Eisiskes the day that Benjamin and I had gone to hide on the stable roof.

Five thousand Jews had been packed into Eisiskes' three synagogues so closely they had no room to sit. Then the Lithuanian guards posted outside the doors passed a bucket to them, and they were ordered to place all their valuables in it. Refusal was punishable by death. For three days they stood so tightly pressed against each other that they couldn't move an arm without striking someone else's face. Mothers tried not to weep, children whimpered in fear and hunger and thirst, and all of them were completely panic-stricken. They could not bear to contemplate their fate; it was too unbelievable.

On the second day the Germans had thrust upon them the Jews from the neighbouring town of Olkeniki, swelling the numbers imprisoned in the synagogues by half again. Finally as an added torment, they shoved into the synagogues the mentally deranged people from Selo. This was the small town nearby run by a group of Jewish farmers who took in the mentally deranged Jews of Eisiskes for a small fee to supplement their income. We knew many of the people who lived there, including a young woman called Luba who kept insisting she was pregnant and walked around with a pillow concealed under her skirt.

Once, my cousin Yankele and his friend Shepsel had visited Selo for the purpose of photographing the *mishugoyim* or "crazy ones." Yankele had approached Luba and asked her to round up a group of her friends to pose for him. Luba stared at him for a moment and then with great dignity she replied, "You, Yankele, can pose for Shepsel, and Shepsel can pose for you. Because you ought to know that no one can tell who is sane or insane from a photograph." Then she had turned away and joined her friends.

In the synagogues, the Germans gave these poor demented people clubs and hammers to use on the others. The Germans roared with laughter as the terrified creatures used the clubs to strike wildly at everyone imprisoned there. Among the prisoners was a man named Abraham Schwartz who owned a small inn in Eisiskes. At one time he had employed a young Polish girl to work for him as a chambermaid, but fired her when he discovered that she was selling herself to his customers. Now when the girl heard he was imprisoned in the synagogue, she bribed a Lithuanian guard to find him in the crowd and kill him as punishment for his treatment of her. The guard found Schwartz and, dragging him out of the synagogue, beat him to death. His screams of agony could be heard by everyone, but no one could help him. It was a blessing when at last his screams subsided, for at least they knew the Lithuanians could not hurt him any more. Now no one in the synagogues had any doubt as to what lay in store for them, but they still cherished the hope that some would be spared.

On Wednesday afternoon, the Lithuanian guards herded the Jews to the place that was used for soccer games and horse sales. Located on the outskirts of town just beyond the Polish school, it was a large field surrounded by a solid wooden fence six feet high. The transportation of the Jews was done in a systematic and orderly way. They were lined up, eight abreast, each one carrying the few possessions that he had left. They were told they were being taken to the soccer grounds only until they could be placed in a ghetto, which was under construction.

One wealthy man thought he could save himself and his family by bribing a policeman. On leaving the synagogue with the others, he approached the nearest policeman, promising him that if he allowed them to escape, he would give him all the money he had at his home. The Lithuanian agreed, and they went together to the man's home. After receiving the money, the Lithuanian murdered the man and all his family. Another man who hoped to save his life with a bribe was the shochet or ritual slaughterer. He also returned to his home with a guard, and after giving up all his wealth, gave up his life. The guard slit his throat from ear to ear with one of his own knives.

A young friend of ours whose name was Lubka escaped while the group she was with was being herded along. She ran to the home of a Polish veterinarian she knew. She had often minded his children and now, expecting help, she burst into his home. She pleaded with his wife to save her, but the woman only handed her a glass of water. "Here, Lubka, drink this. And just as the chickens are given water before they are killed to make their deaths easier, so it will be for you." And she threw her out!

But mostly the non-Jewish people of Eisiskes were too busy looting and celebrating to care what was happening on the soccer grounds. The few who did take an interest mounted their bicycles to round up the Jews who were trying to run away from the death march. Some of the escapees they killed; others were dragged back to their guards. The Germans and Lithuanians, hoping to lull the Jews into a feeling of false security, did not prevent them from taking some of the Torah scrolls from their hiding place in the synagogue to carry on their march to the soccer grounds. They set out with the cantor leading the procession. In one hand he held a Torah scroll and in the other, the small hand of his daughter. As they marched together, he led the throng that came behind him in a recitation of the *Vidui,* the last prayer before death. Thousands of Jews, walking behind their cantor, chanted in one voice the prayer of acceptance. They hadn't given up hope of survival but they wished to be at peace with God should death be inevitable.

At the soccer grounds they were herded inside and watched over by armed guards. They huddled in little family groups, sharing a last cup of water and the final crumbs of bread. Soon after, they were locked in. Faigl, the wife of Moishe Sonenson, went into labour and that night gave birth to a boy. A Polish friend came during the night and rescued Faigl and her infant by tearing loose two boards in the fence. From there, the mother and child were guided to Radun.

On Thursday morning, the Lithuanians asked for three hundred strong men to accompany them, on the pretext that they were needed to build a fence around the new ghetto. Three hundred volunteers, all young and strong, went with their captors. The Lithuanians took them to the old Jewish cemetery where, in the midst of the graves overgrown with grass, a huge pit had been dug by a group of Polish farmers who stood by watching. The Jews were told to undress, place their clothes neatly in piles, shoes in one place, trousers in another, and shirts in another. Naked, they were forced to lie face down in the ditch, side by side. At a command the guards raised their rifles and shot them all. Then the farmers were told to shovel a thin layer of earth over the bodies. But suddenly my friend, Leibke Remz, horribly wounded, stood up in the grave and shouted: "You didn't kill me! I'm still alive!" As was learned later, one of the Polish farmers hit him over the head with his shovel almost decapitating him.

The killers then returned to the soccer grounds for another three hundred volunteers. They took with them a letter from one of those they had executed, Milikovsky, who had been forced to write it. His letter said that the whole group was safe and that they were hard at work on the ghetto fence. However, he told them, another three hundred men would be needed to finish the job. When the letter was shown to the people in the soccer grounds, three hundred more volunteers stepped forward and were marched away. They met the same fate as the first group. As each group was murdered, the bodies were systematically layered into the pit. We learned that the Polish farmers never once protested against the killing. After the butchery of each group, they would descend into the pit and cover the bodies with earth. Then they'd go back to the edge of the pit to await the next macabre ritual.

The killers themselves were totally depraved and subhuman. Recruited by the Germans especially for this task, they were all young Lithuanians, many of them the very boys I had gone to school with. They were known as the *Einsatzgruppen*. With their usual efficiency, the Nazis trained them so well that they became extermination machines without the slightest degree of compassion for their victims. When the time came that only women and children were left in the soccer grounds, they clung together wretchedly, not daring to think about the fate of their men.

It was about that time that a Lithuanian policeman came searching for my father among the prisoners. This was the man who had come to our home demanding alcohol, but had gone away convinced that my father was a Lithuanian patriot. Everyone that he questioned about my father gave him a blank stare or denied knowledge of him. At last he spotted my mother. In fear, my mother told him that Father had been taken away that morning. The policeman then explained that he had come on his wife's insistence to save Father and his family, and he told Mother that she must bring her family and follow him. My mother tried to persuade her sister and my cousin to come with her, for the policeman was willing to save them, too, but her husband and two sons had already been marched away and she had lost the will to live. No amount of pleading from my mother and grandmother could change her mind, and they were forced to leave her behind. The policeman led them away from the grounds and accompanied them to our home where Mother "found" two more bottles of liquor to repay him. Finally he escorted them out of Eisiskes, pointing them across the meadow to the place where Benjamin and I had crossed before. Eventually they too found their way to Mrs. Carolowa's house.

Although my brother and I could have told them exactly what had happened to the women and children they left behind in the soccer grounds, we did not. Neither of us could speak a word about it, for the horror of it was so enormous that we were dumb. When others told us what they knew of their terrible fate, we listened in silence. A Pole named Juzuk Korkucian told us that Ostrauskas, who was a devout Catholic, went to confession on the Sunday after he killed all the children. How could such a monster hope for absolution? How could he return home to his own children with the blood of these innocents upon his hands? It is completely incomprehensible to me and I cannot make peace with it.

Many Poles and Lithuanians who came to visit wept with us, but for the most part these were only crocodile tears. They knew we had hidden articles of value and they looked only for ways to rob us. They would offer survival plans to us, such as suggesting we hide on their farms, paying what we could in return. But they only wanted to get their hands on our valuables. This type of offer was a lethal trap. Markel Koppelman, a wealthy man who had escaped from Eisiskes, accepted such an offer of sanctuary. Soon afterwards, the bodies of Koppelman, his wife and all his children were found hacked to pieces in a village ditch near Radun. The remaining survivors learned that the trick was to hide one's valuables at some distance, only paying the farmer with whom you were hiding on a weekly basis. Our family, however, decided not to go into the country but to stay on in Radun for the present to see what would happen.

The city was administered by a Pole named Kulikowski who had been a captain in the Polish army. When the Russians had deported Polish officers during their 1940 occupation, Kulikowski had eluded them, although his wife and children had been caught and deported. His first task as the Germans' administrator in Radun was to establish a *Judenrat*. For the head of this, he chose our kinsman, Noah Dolinski. Noah had once been the wealthiest man in Radun as he had owned a huge flourmill, but the Russians had confiscated it and ousted Noah from his home. As both Kulikowski and Dolinski had been victims of the Russians, a strong bond of friendship developed between them. Their alliance now had many advantages for the people of Radun. Whenever the Germans issued a particularly severe order, Kulikowski and Dolinski would sit down together to find a compromise which would be less disastrous to the Jews, but still acceptable to the Germans.

Outside Radun, the White Russian farmers who had settled in the district also suffered under the rule of the Germans. They were forced to supply huge quantities of food for the German army quotas that were far beyond the resources of their farms. The punishment for those who failed to meet their quotas was death for the farmer's entire family and the burning of his house and barn. Some of them, desperate to meet their quotas, would even buy supplies from their neighbours.

Shortly after our arrival in Radun, the White Russians were forced to supply two thousand sheep for the German army. In order to ship them to the eastern front for the use of the army, the sheep had to be herded to the nearest railway station, a distance of nearly twenty miles. For the Germans, the solution to that problem was quite simple: they demanded that the *Judenrat* supply ten men to act as sheepherders. Noah Dolinski first asked my father to go, but I volunteered to go in his place because I knew how his health had suffered from the recent emotional strain.

We marched from the town on foot, supervised by ten policemen on bicycles with rifles slung on their backs, billy clubs at their belts. To keep the sheep together, we wielded birch rods, which we had stripped from trees as we passed, but even so the flock was difficult to control. We were continually running after strays which headed for the fields beside the road to graze. Whenever we paused, we were beaten or kicked until our backs were covered in open sores. Since we were not given food or water, whenever the police stopped to rest, we would look for water, even in a drainage ditch where we could strain water through a handkerchief to quench our thirst. At night they locked us in some farmer's barn where we could take out the small caches of emergency rations we had hidden inside our clothing. Before we were allowed to sleep, the police would amuse themselves by forcing us to roll in horse manure. We didn't resist, of course, because they were too well armed. In the morning we were wakened again by kicks and more beatings, and so we carried on from day to day.

It seemed like forever, but the entire trip lasted little more than a week. My mother had been almost out of her mind with worry, for she felt sure that we would all be shot when we delivered the sheep to the railway. This was not an idle fear, since members of the Jewish intelligentsia had been lured from their homes by the Germans in much the same fashion in July 1941, and were not seen again. As I recovered from this episode, I marvelled at myself. I couldn't understand how I kept going. But I was young. At sixteen I could cope with the lack of food and water and the harsh treatment of our conquerors much better than the older men could. I also had the advantage of instinctively meeting a challenge head-on, something that had been encouraged by my mother. However submissive I was outwardly, I was always inwardly defiant, keeping a mental score of all the injustices.

Overriding these positive life supports, however, was a terrible fear. It wasn't a fear of death so much as a fear of torture. We had heard frightful stories that some of the Lithuanians had made a game of placing their victims one on top of the other to see how many they could kill with one bullet. I knew that if they caught me I would make sure I was the one on top so that I would be certain to die. I prayed that if I were marked for execution it would be over quickly. I promised myself that I wouldn't wait for death as so many others had done, but run for my life. Then if I were shot, it would be in the back and I would not have to see it coming.

After we had lived in Radun for six weeks, the Germans created a ghetto. Kulikowski and Dolinski had managed to postpone this day by various means, but now the Germans themselves intervened and we were forced into a segregated area. It was L-shaped and consisted of one long street and a short street where the synagogue was located. Our family was assigned to the house of the Chofetz Chaim, one of the most revered wise men of this century. He had died in 1930, and relatives now occupied the house. Noah Dolinski, his family and Persky, the young teacher, also came to share the house, which was on the short street near the synagogue. Each family was given one large room with two double beds, and we used the kitchen in common.

The problem of food supplies soon became acute. The only cow allowed in the ghetto was the property of Noah Dolinski, but it produced barely enough for his own family. Occasionally, Mrs. Carolowa's son would come to visit, bringing fresh eggs, butter and vegetables but these visits were not frequent enough to keep us healthy. Those of us with valuables or money could buy from the farmers who came to the ghetto, but their prices had become enormously inflated. Our family had almost nothing to trade by now and we were becoming desperate for food. I can remember my grandmother handing over her last valuable possession, a gold chain, for two bottles of saccharin.

My father then hit on a plan to obtain food for us. He asked Noah Dolinski to use his influence with Kulikowski to provide him a visitor's permit to a nearby village and permission to requisition a horse and cart. When this was granted, my father and I started out with the all-important permit, stopping on the outskirts of Radun to hire a horse and wagon. From there we travelled to the small village of Powielancy where Father felt we would be kindly received.

The village was composed of some forty houses strung out side by side on a single street. Each house was inhabited by Poles, but my father knew many of them and had done favours for them in the past. At each house, we knocked and explained our plight. Only a few turned us down or offered us ham or pork, which they knew we would refuse. Very soon our wagon was filled with butter and eggs, flour and fresh vegetables. My father and I wept both at their kindness and at the realization that we had been reduced to beggars. The people of Powielancy were so generous to us that I knew I must someday help to repay them.

One farmer in particular was a special friend of my father and he sympathized deeply with our situation. As we were leaving he promised to pray for our safety and we promised to pray for his welfare and that of his two young daughters. On our way back to Radun, we were intercepted by a group of Germans and two Polish policemen who promptly confiscated almost half of our provisions. But the food we managed to take home was enough to last the three families in the house for several months.

Life in the Radun ghetto was in many ways a rerun of the German occupation of Eisiskes. The German gendarmerie consisted of men in their middle years, demanding and sadistic. They had been small town tradesmen before the war: one had been a tailor, and another a carpenter. They ruled in the way that only men suddenly given power beyond their dreams will rule. It was as if they had to try out all their maniacal ideas at once. They confiscated beds, linens, furniture, and anything else they coveted. The ghetto Jews were marched off daily to do the chores at their headquarters and anyone refusing was shot. The cruelest and most feared was a man named Koppke who toured the ghetto with an unlit cigar clamped in his teeth. His eyes were as cold as agates and they seemed to see everything in the ghetto.

Not long after we had been confined to the ghetto, Koppke had invented an "entertainment" to intimidate us. He had a scaffold erected in the middle of the ghetto street. There, he ordered the public hanging of two accused thieves, one a gentile, the other a Jew. We were all ordered to watch. I stood looking from an upstairs window, horrified at what was happening. Rather than dropping the two men from a platform, Koppke ordered that nooses should be placed around their necks while they stood on the ground, and that their bodies should be raised slowly so that they would strangle in agony. They took a long time to die, gurgling and gasping for breath while the entire ghetto of Radun looked on. Koppke ordered that their bodies should hang there for three days so that we would not forget to follow orders.

A few days after the hangings, Koppke stopped my brother and me in the street. "Each of you go get a shovel and be back here in five minutes!" he barked. We did, and were led to a house where a beautiful young Jewish girl was living. She had been hiding with a Polish family as their maid, but her identity had been somehow revealed and she had been thrust into the ghetto with the rest of us.

"Wait here!" said Koppke and he left us in the street in front of the house. A few minutes later he returned with the girl and marched her to a spot behind the public bathhouse. Grabbing her by the hair, he shot her in the head. It all happened so fast that she could not have realized what was happening. Then, chewing on his unlit cigar and his expression absolutely unchanged, he ordered us to bury her.

As we dug her grave, we wondered what she had done to deserve this. Had she repelled his advances? Or had he simply followed out the orders of the District Commandant in Lida who also knew of her case? Or was this just one of the days on which he felt the urge to kill Jews? We never learned the answer.

In late autumn, the District Commandant arrived from Lida for an inspection tour of the Radun area. While there, he invited several members of his inspection party on a hunting expedition in a small forest northeast of the town. Although this forest was well known for its game, the hunting party had a disappointing morning. The truth was that most of the game had been killed or driven away by the local people as they became desperate for food.

The hunters returned at noon to Radun and soon, in the middle of a drunken lunch, they thought of a way to rescue the day from total failure. They went through the ghetto, looking for Jewish refugees from Lida, rounding up more than forty of them. These unfortunates were trucked about a mile and a half from town, unloaded and told to scatter. They did as they were told, and the Germans, using the trucks to fire from as if they were on an African safari, gunned them all down. The same day the Germans sent a group of us out to bury them. Benjamin and I were included in the burying party. The carnage was incredible. Heads and limbs had been blown off with the bodies frozen to the ground in pools of blood. We buried them in a common grave.

We had come to Radun believing that the Jews of Eisiskes had been the victims of the Lithuanians, but it now appeared that the massacre had been one small part of the overall German plan. We had little doubt now that extermination was in store for the Jews of Radun's ghetto as well. Each day was one day closer to violent death. I recall one tall, emaciated man who used to walk the streets saying,

"Our days are numbered. It is only a matter of time. We are walking corpses."

Radun's Jews began to take elaborate precautions to protect their avenues of escape. Each household posted a watch so that day and night someone was peering out into the street to watch for trouble. At night, those of us who slept would wake in an instant at the slightest noise. News of the smallest change in the ghetto's routine was passed from house to house, with everyone trying to interpret the change and decide whether our danger had increased. But life carried on day-to-day. The people of the ghetto were expected to work for their masters whether or not death waited around the corner. In midwinter I was assigned to a work party to cut wood in the nearby forest for the Germans. We spent seven days there, returned to Radun for a few days, and then repeated the cycle. As usual, the Germans assigned unreasonable quotas to each day; it was back-breaking work. We slept at nearby farms, bartering the few valuables we brought with us for food.

It was while working there that I first heard rumours of Russians living in the forest. They were construction workers brought in from Siberian work camps by the Russians, and then left behind when the Germans invaded. The realization that there were men somewhere in that very forest, perhaps even close at hand, who had escaped the Germans and had found a way to survive, excited my imagination. It was the old Tarzan dream again, but this time it was much closer to reality. When I returned to Radun and told my parents, they dismissed it as nonsense. About a month later, however, a friend told me of an encounter in the forest with one of the escapees. The Russian had invited him to join them in the forest.

"What do you have to lose? You're all going to be slaughtered anyhow," the stranger said. "Come and fight the Germans with us!"

My friend hesitated.

"You're crazy to stay here!" the stranger said, disappearing into the forest.

My next assignment was in the synagogue, which had been turned into a granary by the Germans. My job was to issue receipts to farmers bringing in produce to fulfill their quotas for the Germans. Many of them took a violent dislike to me, but I grew used to their insults; name-calling was the least of my worries. The winter wore on and the tension grew. Spring came and still Koppke prowled the ghetto chewing his cigar, and each household posted its nightly watch. On May 8, 1942, we awoke to find the entire ghetto surrounded by German, White Russian and Polish police. It was the beginning of the end. We were trapped once again.

Soon after, loudspeakers were blaring: "Stay away from your windows. Anyone coming near their windows will be shot!" During the day the woodcutting crews were returned from the forest. Noah Dolinski, whose status allowed him some freedom to disobey orders, opened our door a little to ask the German on guard outside our door what was happening. The guard was a short and chubby former tailor, but he was quite courteous and reassured us that we had nothing to fear. "It's a temporary measure," he said, "to give us a correct head count. There's nothing to worry about."

We were not reassured. By evening, the tension had become unbearable and some people ran from their homes in desperation. That's when the killing began. As soon as someone opened a door, gunfire ripped down the street. The screams of the dying were unbearable. Our neighbour was shot in the street, and in his death throes was dragged back to his house and flung inside the door. During the night we desperately searched the house for some place to hide. We examined ceilings, walls and floors. We even tried to find a way to excavate a hole in the cellar floor but it was useless. We had made this search many times before. We were simply petrified with fear now because we had always planned to run away from Radun when the time came.

Strangely enough, though we were terrified, we had tremendous outward control and seemed surprisingly calm. We were certainly not ready to give up. Perhaps our feelings were typical of the entire ghetto Jews, for it is a fact that suicides were almost unknown amongst us. The next day, when the chubby German tailor came by, Noah Dolinski asked him to join us for tea. It was rather bleak out that day, so he accepted and sat down at the kitchen table. Before sitting, he leaned his rifle against the wall several feet away. As he drank his tea, everyone joined in questioning him but his answers were always evasive. Persky and I stood to one side, tensely watching. Then under cover of the conversation at the table, I whispered, "Persky, do you think we could get his rifle?" He nodded. I continued, "One of us could put on his uniform, kill the guard outside, and we could all make a dash for it!"

He agreed. "We could be into the forest before they knew we were gone."

We moved over to where Noah Dolinski stood and in Yiddish and Hebrew outlined our plans. He was very angry with us.

"If you do this, everyone else will be killed! And you will be responsible! I absolutely forbid it!"

So we let the opportunity pass. One part of me had been ready to try anything to gain our freedom; another part of me wanted to believe that the little tailor was telling the truth. The truth, in fact, was quite different from the picture he painted. We had been imprisoned to await the arrival of the *Einsatzgruppen*. They'd been delayed and were not yet ready for us. It was simply a matter of waiting our turn. In the early evening, my father spotted a Polish policeman who had been on the police force in Eisiskes. He was an old friend and Father had no reason to believe that the friendship was no longer valued. Father called him over to the door. "Listen, Zalusky, we have gold and other valuables which are yours if you will come in the night and take us out of here. For the sake of our past friendship, Zalusky, please help us."

Zalusky gave his word but we waited all night and he never returned. On the morning of the third day, the Germans ordered all of us living on our short street to move to the houses on the long one. When we were told to choose any house we wished, my father chose the house of a woman called Musha, who was known as a firebrand and a fighter. He felt that she would not give up easily and that since she had always lived there, she would have prepared a hiding place. We crossed the street, and once inside our new quarters, stood watching the streets for signs of changes in the Germans' activities. But everything was calm. In fact, it was so calm that it was almost more terrifying. The farmers came and went delivering milk and butter and eggs to the Germans' dairy, apparently completely unconcerned with our tragedy. The Germans calmly supervised the traffic while keeping guard on our houses. It was totally unreal. Outside our window was freedom and a chance to live, yet we stood huddled behind the glass awaiting death.

Then suddenly in the peaceful traffic outside I recognized a boy I knew, Yudke Jurkanski. Somehow he had slipped from his house and begun walking behind the milk wagon of a farmer who was making a delivery to the dairy. Barefoot like a peasant boy, he had taken one of the milk cans from the cart and was carrying it as he walked slowly along. It must have seemed endless miles for him as he walked down that street, but at last he reached the corner at the end of the ghetto and disappeared into freedom. And we breathed again.

When another boy tried the same trick, we realized that others had been watching to see if this trick would succeed. This time an alert policeman spotted him and ordered him to drop his pants. Seeing he was a circumcised Jew, he beat him brutally and sent him back to his house. A young girl tried her luck. She was fair-haired and had tied her kerchief around her head in the style of the peasant girls. We watched in revulsion as the chubby tailor beat her viciously and dragged her back to the house she had just left. I thought how stupid I had been to obey Noah Dolinski the day before.

The Germans employed a Jew named Isaac Mendel Jurkanski as quartermaster because he had been an office manager and spoke German. Even during our confinement, Jurkanski had been taken each day to the Germans' headquarters and returned each evening. On the evening of the third day, as he passed close by the house, Father called softly to him in Yiddish:

"Jurkanski, what do you hear?"

Jurkanski slowed his pace, glanced at my father for a second, and shook his head slightly. "It's not good," he said, and walked on.

That night we went into hiding. As Father had suspected, Musha had prepared a place to hide. Adjoining her house was a concrete warehouse for grain storage. When looked at from the street, its roof appeared flat, but this was deceptive. If anyone had been able to stand back far enough, they would have seen that it actually sloped slightly with the high side next to Musha's house. Within the warehouse the ceiling was perfectly level so that a small, sloping attic space lay between the roof and the ceiling. Although this space had once been completely sealed off, before we had moved in with her Musha had placed a ladder against the outside wall and loosened a couple of concrete blocks in the wall of the attic.

Now under cover of night, we placed the ladder once more against the wall and removed the blocks. Then one by one we crept through the hole, packing ourselves into the tiny space. Finally more than fifty of us lay there in our dark prison-like sanctuary without food or water, breathing through the cracks in the concrete blocks. My father waited until we were all inside, then replaced the blocks, climbed down and took away the ladder. Quietly he returned to the house and hid behind a huge wardrobe, where he could act as watchman for the rest of us.

The waiting began.

Unable to whisper or shift our bodies in case someone entering the warehouse heard us, we lay with aching limbs and fought for air in the tiny space. As the hours passed and the morning came, we tried to imagine what was happening in the rest of the ghetto, but only distant sounds came filtering through the concrete. Then the second problem of our incarceration developed. As we had no means of sanitation, we could not deal with our normal bodily functions and the stench became absolutely unbearable.

I slept a great deal that day and so did most of the others. It was our only escape from the intolerable conditions and the terrifying spectre of death waiting below us. It was not normal sleep, but more like an extension of the paralysis of fear, or even a coma, induced by the lack of air and the warmth of the surrounding bodies. Unfortunately, in sleep we relaxed our vigil and left ourselves open to discovery with a moan or snore or movement of the foot.

Late in the day, we became aware that the Polish police were searching Musha's house. Then they entered the warehouse. Two of them, standing below us, took a moment for a cigarette break. One man related how he had helped to catch a friend of ours who had hidden himself in a huge basket suspended from the rafters of his barn. Laughing, he told how he had sprayed it with bullets so that it swung like a pendulum with its screaming victim inside. We lay helplessly above, afraid to breathe. Meanwhile, in Musha's house next door, the Polish police had found my father hidden behind the wardrobe. They marched him and a hundred other men, each carrying a pick or shovel, toward the Jewish cemetery beyond the edge of the town. Ten Polish police and five German gendarmes escorted them with the commandant or "maister" gendarme riding his horse at the rear of the column. As they marched toward certain death, my father walked shoulder to shoulder with a huge man, Meier, the blacksmith from Eisiskes.

"What are we going to do, Meier?" Father asked.

"We'll have to make a run for it!" the blacksmith said, and Father nodded in agreement. The big man went on, "Pass the word that when I give the signal, we all start swinging. Then we'll run for that bush up ahead!" They passed the word and in a few minutes they arrived at a huge rock pile at the edge of town.

"Now!" shouted the blacksmith.

And the men swung their picks and shovels at their startled guards. Horrified, the commandant whirled his horse around and raced back to town, leaving his men to fend for themselves. What followed looked like the combat between David and Goliath: the Jews with their picks and shovels and the Germans with their automatic rifles. Most of the guards who died were struck down in the first moments of the fight before they had a chance to fire; a few more died as they fled, struck by rocks hurled by the Jews. The fight was over in a matter of minutes but the consequences were far-reaching. Twenty-eight Jews died and many more received wounds; the remainder fled to the forest. In total, only three survived the war, since most of the others joined the partisans' fight against the Germans and lost their lives in combat or in ambushes. But their story gave others the courage to fight back. After this setback, the Germans rounded up a second group of one hundred men to dig the grave for the Radun people and employed one hundred police to escort them — in order to prevent another revolt from occurring.

The *Einsatzgruppen* were waiting impatiently to do their job, so the gravediggers were whipped and beaten with clubs to hurry them along. Once the pit was ready, the diggers were sent across the road to lie in a drainage ditch.

After a time, a tragic parade of men, women and children — three thousand of them herded together by police brandishing whips and guns — poured from the town. From our attic perch, we could hear the roundup and the terrified voices in the street. We heard the police enter Musha's house and shoot to death Noah Dolinski's aged mother, who could not climb the ladder, and his mentally handicapped daughter, who had little contact with reality. Later we found the two of them still seated, the girl holding a doll. Once all the Jews of Radun had been assembled at the cemetery, the gendarmes ordered the men who had dug the grave to stand up and call out the names of their wives and children. They were told that they and their immediate families would be spared. Many of the men would have called out the names of mothers, fathers, and sisters, but the Germans prevented them from doing so.

When Israel Sczuczinski's turn came to name his wife and children, he called out "Sosha Sczuczinski," and two women ran to cling to him. The gendarme demanded to know if he had two wives. Hoping for clemency, Israel admitted that one was his wife, the other his unmarried sister, both of them truly named Sosha Sczuczinski.

"You can only save one," said the gendarme without pity. "Make your choice."

Israel Sczuczinski was placed in the position of playing God. He stood there in torment in the roadway with the two women clinging to him, begging to be saved. At length he chose his wife, and his sister was shoved back into the ranks of the condemned. The son-in-law of the Chofetz Chaim, who had been one of the diggers, realizing that all the remainder were about to die, left the group of those who were to be spared and stood in the pit that had been dug.

"I wish to be first," he said quietly and the gendarmes shot him.

The ritual then continued as it had in Eisiskes. The victims were forced to undress, piling their clothes neatly. Dresses here, trousers there. Shoes over there. Then in straight lines they were marched to the grave's edge, forced to step in, hands clasped in one final union, eyes closed. Systematically they were shot to death. Layer by layer the bodies accumulated, a little earth thrown in on top to separate the layers. By noon all three thousand had vanished into the ground. Not all died instantly. Many suffocated to death as they lay beneath the weight of their brothers and sisters, their nostrils clogged with dirt. Others were burned alive by the lime poured over the grave.

While this was going on, my father returned to Radun. With great caution he replaced the ladder against the building and climbed up to a tearful welcome from his family. This time we pulled the ladder up inside our hiding place. When the digging brigade returned to town with the remnants of their families they were ordered to the city hall to register so that the Germans would have an accurate count of the survivors. As they entered Radun, one man ran ahead down the empty ghetto street, calling out in Yiddish: "Everyone, come out and register at city hall!"

From our attic we could hear him plainly but could not decide what to do. Finally my father and a number of the other men climbed down and went to city hall, hoping this was not a trap. Now a problem arose for Father because the survivors were expected to be just the gravediggers, their wives and their children. Father, exhausted by the whole ordeal, did not know what to do about registering my grandmother, as she didn't fit into any of these categories. In the end he simply did not register her at all. I guess he reasoned that we would simply find a way to hide her.

As he was about to leave the city hall, Father met Moishe Sonenson whose wife, Faigl, had given birth in the soccer grounds at Eisiskes. Moishe, Faigl and their children had hidden with sixty other Jews in another attic during this massacre and had escaped undetected. But they had paid a dreadful price for their safety. In the long wait in the cramped darkness, Faigl's child, now eight months old, had begun to whimper, endangering the safety of the group. Each time the house was searched they were all in peril for their lives, so a whispered conference was held and it was decided that the infant should die. One of the group then placed a pillow over the little one's face and smothered him. Moishe put his arms around my father and wept. "Shael, Shael, I have murdered my child! I have murdered my child!" He could not be consoled.

Once the authorities assured everyone who had come to the city hall that no further killing would be done, Father returned to the attic. That night a sombre little group returned to Musha's house. In the morning, the Germans ordered us all out onto the street and told us to line up on one side. The commandant's second-in-command strode out in front of us and produced the list of names that had been written in the register at the city hall the day before. My father's face went white. As each person's name was called out, the person was expected to walk across the street to the opposite side. When the whole list had been called, a hundred and fifty Jews were left standing on the wrong side of the street. They had not come out of hiding to register because they didn't trust the Germans. My grandmother stood among them. Koppke strode back and forth in front of this terrified group, chewing on the end of his unlit cigar and counting the "corpses" over and over again. But he had to wait to begin the next round of carnage, for the commandant had not yet emerged from his headquarters to give the signal to begin. Koppke, spying Noah Dolinski and his family, marched down the street to confront him. "You sly fox! You weren't out there digging that pit! Where were you hiding?" Dolinski pretended not to understand what he was referring to and, after a slight hesitation, Koppke walked away.

Suddenly, a Jew ran down the street, chased by a policeman on a bicycle. The man was overtaken in front of us. The policeman jumped from his bike and threw the man to the ground to kick and beat him. I heard my father's sharply indrawn breath. "Zalusky," he whispered in horror. The policeman was the "kind" Zalusky who had never before shown signs of cruelty. The very man we would have entrusted with our lives.

His victim crawled and dragged himself on hands and knees to the feet of the commandant's second-in-command, kissing the man's hands and feet. "Don't kill me! Don't kill me!" he pleaded. It was unbearable to watch. The German ordered him to stand up and go to our side of the street. Infuriated because his quarry had escaped, Zalusky scanned the faces of the Jews lining the street. Purposefully, he strode down the street and seized the arm of a handsome boy of about sixteen, nearly six feet tall.

"This man is a Communist!" he screamed. "He persecuted my son in Eisiskes!"

"All right, shoot him," said the German.

"Would you like to do it?" Zalusky asked the German.

"No," replied the German.

Zalusky looked around at the other police.

"Any volunteers?"

A young Pole stepped forward.

"Sure. I will." And he shot the boy to death. Zalusky remained unaware that the young man was the son of his spared victim.

Sixty feet away, on the other side of the street, my grandmother pleaded with us to save her life. First to my mother, then to my father she called, begging us to help her, but we were helpless. There was nothing we could do. Three hours ticked slowly by as we waited in torment. Israel Sczuczinski, quite mad since he had sent his sister to her death, ripped off his shirt and ran up to one of the German guards. We could see that his back was a mass of welts and bruises from the attacks of the gendarmes. "Make them take off their shirts!" he screamed, pointing at the rest of the men. "Then you'll see who dug the grave and who was hiding!" But the guard ignored him.

When we had lost all hope, the German commandant rode down the street toward us. We were silent, awaiting the latest edict of life or death. He took his time, and then announced that he had received word from Lida that the killings were now complete. "Go home!" he ordered, and rode off down the street again. Even the unregistered Jews were allowed to live. We ran to meet Grandmother in the middle of the street. Together we wept at this latest reprieve. We held each other closely and returned to the silent house of the Chofetz Chaim. It was empty now, looted while we hid in the warehouse attic.

Our emotional state was now even more desolate than the house. We knew that we would awake in the morning only if the Germans gave us permission to live. Like animals in a cage, we were helpless to determine our own fate. We were simply living at the whim of the Germans. But the most difficult thing for all of us to understand was how Poles and Lithuanians we had known all our lives could become ravenous beasts almost overnight. I thought of Ostrauskas and Baderas and Zalusky and became convinced that their crimes came from deep roots of ingrained anti-Semitism that had only been waiting for a chance to come to this terrible flowering. They seemed bent on a religious crusade to destroy all Jews. The ghetto was now eerie and unreal. With nothing else to occupy me, I would go from house to house, partly to look for food but mostly to satisfy myself that the others had really gone. I stood in kitchens where I listened to phantom women talking as they prepared meals; in the streets I heard children play as they always had. But these were the ghosts of Radun and silence was the only reality. I played a game with myself and imagined that they had only gone for a little while and would return, as if this would make the grave outside Radun a lie.

Several days after the reprieve, I was standing at the front window staring into the street when suddenly from the pharmacy on the corner burst a German officer dragging the son of the Jewish pharmacist. The young man had hidden behind a wardrobe when the Germans had rounded up the family. Unaware of what was happening outside he had remained there until a German in his search for hidden drugs had found him. Now the officer held a pistol to the youth's head while he debated what to do with him. Should he kill him or just thrash him? At that moment, Pietka Bartoszewicz peddled down the street on his bicycle. He was a policeman now but had once been the caretaker of the Polish school in Eisiskes. He was a kindly man and as a boy I had taken him wine and matzohs at Passover.

Now in the ghetto street of Radun he stopped beside the German officer and the pharmacist's son. There was a conversation between the two men. Then Pietka Bartoszewicz, the kindly caretaker, unslung his rifle and put a bullet through the youth's head.

It didn't take long after that day for the Germans to find chores for the survivors. Twenty of us were ordered to collect the bodies of those who had been killed while trying to escape. We were given a wagon and told to search the back gardens and alleyways for corpses and to bury them. The first we collected was the body of one of my teachers from Eisiskes, a rather large man named Botwinik. He had been shot as he fled by night across the back garden. His bloated body had been mutilated by the pigs that were roaming at will through the ghetto. I remember chasing them away as they devoured his face, and then standing by the fence, vomiting and weeping.

We collected more than twenty bodies and took them out to the Jewish cemetery and buried them in a common grave. Then we were promoted to the task of sorting out the clothing that the Germans had collected from their victims. With us this time was Jurkanski, the quartermaster for the Germans. The cook in the Germans' headquarters had hidden him, and although they apparently knew where he was, they let Jurkanski live. His family had not been so fortunate. As we sorted clothes, Jurkanski found the dress that had belonged to his sister. He held it to his face, weeping bitterly. The very men who had saved his life had murdered his family.

As was the case before the massacre, we were conscripted to chop wood and clean toilets for the Germans, although the system had become somewhat haphazard now, as the *Judenrat* no longer existed to supervise work parties. Noah Dolinski had survived, but was constantly questioned by the Germans to learn how he had managed to escape; apparently they were not really concerned, simply interested. To us, this was just another indication that we were being allowed to live only as long as it suited the Germans' purposes. Perhaps we were only there to lure other Jews out of hiding. We became convinced that our fate had been decided long ago.

At the beginning of June, the Germans announced that we were to be resettled. It made little sense, they said, to waste such a large ghetto on so few of us. Therefore, we would be taken to Szczuczin, a small town nearby where two hundred people had escaped massacre. After hearing this news, I found a place to be alone and think. I knew I could not face imprisonment in another ghetto, waiting from day to day to be killed, abused and degraded until I was no longer human. I was determined never to be caught again without some chance of escape. In my heart I was still convinced that the only refuge for us was the forest. Throughout the nightmares of Eisiskes and Radun, I had longed to flee to its safety, feeling that there at least I could find some means of defence. Even if I lived as the animals lived, I could die there with the dignity of a man.

Part of this feeling that the forest was the right place came from my boyhood idolization of Tarzan, of course. But we had also recently heard that groups of families were living in the forest just as the partisans lived. I was convinced that our family could accept the same kind of life if it meant living in safety. That night I sat down with my father to tell him that I had decided to go into the forest to find the partisans. Benjamin and Freidke came to listen.

"I've got to go, Papa! I can't wait around to be killed." I knew he'd been thinking about this too, so I pressed my advantage. "It's the only place we can be safe! Lots of our people are there now, whole families of them, and they're safe. They sleep nights and they get enough food so their stomachs aren't growling all the time. We won't escape from Szczuczin, father!"

My brother and sister nodded, agreeing with me, and then they urged Father to take the whole family there. Father was more cautious.

"We'll leave Radun," he said at last, "and we'll see if some of our old friends will hide us, at least for a time. After that, if there is no other way we'll have to go to the forest."

I had to accept his decision. We went to tell my mother. I believe she had always known that it would come to this because our family was so determined to live. But we were not prepared for her answer.

"No," she said. "You'll have to go without me. Grandmother could never make the journey, and she couldn't adjust to that kind of life at her age. I must stay here to look after her."

Although we begged her to change her mind, she remained adamant. Grandmother had no one left, only my mother, and Mother felt it was her duty to look after her. We all knew that Grandmother was too old to go to the forest, but somehow we had expected that she would accept the fact she had lived her life and generously tell Mother to escape with her husband and family. But my grandmother never opened her mouth.

"You go and save yourselves!" Mother told us. "This is my own decision and none of you is responsible. You must go and I must stay here to care for my mother. You have to understand. I can't come with you."

For four days and nights the arguments raged. We all knew that Szczuczin was just another trap, and that only our great good fortune had allowed us to survive both Eisiskes and Radun, but Mother persisted in saying that she and Grandmother would be all right there. She must have been terribly upset at the thought of parting with the husband and children she loved so dearly, yet she would not abandon her mother without her mother's permission, and she remained silent. Although my father must have been broken-hearted, in the end he realized he had to leave his wife behind and lead his children to safety.

Our parting will remain forever on my mind and my conscience. We hugged and kissed goodbye again and again. Then at the door I turned to look back, to take one last mental picture of my dear mother. I can still see her, her dark, wavy hair prematurely grey but her beautiful strong features unchanged. I was torn between my fear of dying and my conviction that I was betraying her, letting her down when she needed me. A hundred times I told myself to stay, a hundred times my terror forced me to leave my adored mother, the one to whom I had turned with my troubles ever since I was a tiny child. She had eased my bruises and scratches with a single kiss, made me whole again with just the right encouragement. She had set her own high standards before me. I needed her desperately. To this day, I still wonder whether, if we had insisted more or begged just a little longer, she might have relented. Somehow I feel certain that with Mother with us, my parents would have made different decisions and all of us would have survived. My only comfort is the prayer that, in those last moments before she and my grandmother were led into the gas chamber, she found consolation in the thought that her husband and children were still alive.

When dark thoughts possess me and I am torn with guilt and anguish, I am reminded of what Golda Meir once said to a group of survivors with the same feelings as mine. "You can get used to anything if you have to," she said, "even to feeling perpetually guilty. It is a small price to pay for being alive." We left Radun quite easily this time although we still took the normal precautions to avoid being seen, but for the most part, the Germans seemed almost indifferent to the ghetto survivors. It was almost as if, like leeches, they had become sated and had dropped off the carcass to digest their disgusting meal. Or perhaps, knowing that we were all doomed anyhow, they felt no need to stand guard, and could now spend their days and nights drinking. The day after we left Radun, my mother and grandmother were taken by truck to a ghetto in the little town of Szczuczin, a short distance away.

CHAPTER FOUR

Nomads: June–October 1942

We left Radun in the company of our old neighbours from Eisiskes, Yudel Szewicki, and his son, Shmulke. Unfortunately, Mrs. Szewicki had been caught and murdered, but the two men had successfully escaped. We made a party of five men and one teenage girl, each of us grieving for those we left behind. Of all of us, it was my little sister, Freidke, who felt the loss of the conveniences of Radun most deeply. It was very difficult for her to be the only girl in a group of men who did not understand her special problems. Time and again in the months that followed she would say: "Oh, I wish I'd stayed with Mother!" She was just fifteen when we left Radun, with the promise of great beauty ahead.

I was determined now to look to the future. There was one thing that I had been longing to do ever since the Germans had come to Eisiskes. As soon as we were outside the ghetto, I tore the yellow star from my shirt and threw it in the dirt. As the symbol of German oppression it had burned through my shirt to brand my soul. As I ground it into the dust, I felt strong and proud once again. The fear and subservience that had dominated my life in the ghetto were gone, and in their place was a new feeling of confidence coupled with an overwhelming desire for revenge: revenge for the bodies piled like cordwood in the ditches, revenge for the slaughter, the degradation, the humiliation. I swore I would make up for the thousands of innocent victims cruelly and senselessly butchered.

As we walked, I was more aware of the smell of the grass and flowers, and the song of the birds, than I had ever been. For me, the destruction of that yellow badge had wiped out everything that the Germans had tried to accomplish, for it had been intended to set the Jews apart like branded cattle so that we could never escape our identity. Then by daily humiliations and injustices they had reduced us in our own eyes, until we came to think of ourselves as an inferior people, only fit for slavery and eventual annihilation. As our estimation of ourselves fell and our oppression increased, the non-Jews who had once respected us as equals came to value us as we valued ourselves. This was exactly the Germans' intention. Now in my heart I knew pride in my people once again and I longed for the chance to seek revenge on our tormentors. I was on my way to join the partisans in the forest, to make the Germans and their accomplices pay for the humiliations, the savage beatings, and the pitiful dead of Eisiskes and Radun.

Our first task upon leaving Radun was to find a place to hide, and we went from farm to farm asking for help. This was risky, since any of them could have turned us in. And it was risky for any farmers who helped us; if they were caught harbouring us, the Germans would shoot them and their families. Under these circumstances we were fortunate that some of them gave us refuge for two or three days, providing us with good wholesome food which we had not seen in a long time. Others would give us food and ask us to go away, saying: "If it were up to me, there's no question, of course you could stay . . . but there's my wife and children. They'd leave me if I let you stay!" Others simply told us that they wouldn't take the risk for Jews. The ironic thing was that my father chose these farmers because they were old friends. Most of them had been quite happy to sleep at our house the night before market day in Eisiskes — and that had been only last year.

After several weeks of wandering, we came to the home of a

farmer called Babkin who agreed to take some of us while his brother-in-law agreed to take the rest. Babkin was not willing to do this out of friendship, however, as he really had no use for the Jews. In Eisiskes on market day, we were used to the sight of Babkin with his red face and Cossack moustache getting roaring drunk and beating up any Jew unfortunate enough to cross his path. Nevertheless, he had always respected my father as a friend, so we felt the present arrangement might work out. He hid Freidke in a loft above the house and found Benjamin a place in the barn. The rest of us went to stay with his brother-in-law.

Once settled, Father and I went to see Mrs. Carolowa to collect some of our possessions as payment for Babkin and his brother-in-law. Taking a roundabout route, we arrived at her house before midnight. We approached with caution and knocked softly at her window. Upon recognizing us, she opened the window a little, and we saw the expression of alarm on her round face.

"Go away!" she hissed. "The police have been here. They can't be far away and they'll catch you. Go away!"

Quickly we slipped away into the night. On our way back to the others we decided to beg for food at a neighbouring farm. The farmer obliged, and while he and his wife prepared something for us, my father remarked: "I hear the police have been giving Mrs. Carolowa some trouble." The farmer shook his head, obviously surprised. "No," he said. "The police haven't been out this way for almost a month now. It's been very quiet. Who told you that story?"

It was evident Mrs. Carolowa must have lied to us, but we could not understand why. She was our dear old friend; to her we had entrusted everything we had managed to save from the Germans. There had to be a good reason for what she had done. When we returned to Babkin and his brother-in-law, we told them that we had to return the following week to collect our goods as there had been police in the district. When the week passed, we returned to stand outside the window.

Again, she hissed, "Go away. It's not safe here!"

But this time, Father answered, "We'll just have to take the chance," and demanded several bolts of cloth to pay for our board. She left the window and returned a minute later, thrusting a small bolt of cotton cloth out the window to my father.

"This isn't enough!" he said. "I have to pay board for six of us!"

She insisted that the rest of our goods were stored far away and that she could not get them. It dawned on us then that our good old friend Mrs. Carolowa would probably turn us over to the police rather than surrender our possessions. Now that it was too late to do anything about it, we realized that we should never have trusted her. She had already come to regard our possessions as her own because she had been sure that, although we might have escaped death in Eisiskes, we would surely die at Radun.

When we handed the bolt of cloth to Babkin, he exploded in anger. "You think that's enough to pay for the chance we're taking? You expect us to feed six of you and hide you from the police for that little bit of cloth? You go back where you hide your stuff and bring me gold, and silver and furs. That's what I want." But the truth was that we had never owned such things. It would be impossible to satisfy him. And there was more trouble brewing. As Babkin stormed off, my sister began to cry and beg Father to take her away from Babkin's farm.

"Why, Freidke? We have no place else to go. And Babkin doesn't mean any harm. He'll calm down soon and be reasonable. You'll see."

But as Freidke continued to cry, we realized that her insistence had nothing to do with Babkin's temper over the bolt of cloth. He had apparently made "advances" to her when he was drunk. Poor Freidke! At fifteen she had had plenty of experience with terror and injustice but absolutely no experience with men. Once more we took to the roads, always moving by night in an irregular pattern around the countryside to forestall anyone who might send the police after us. By day we hid in cow barns. The farmers who gave us refuge developed novel ways to ensure their own and our safety. They would bring food to us in a bucket intended for animal feed, hoisting it to the loft on a rope. One of them gave us a small chalkboard so that messages could be exchanged among us in silence.

That summer of 1942 the weather was flawless. It felt good to leave our daytime prison to exercise our cramped muscles at night. Occasionally, we would take long walks, covering as much as five miles to beg food from farmers who could be counted on. The journeys were lengthened by the complicated routes we followed through the fields to make it difficult for anyone to follow us. But these hikes served the purpose at least of keeping us physically fit. Sometimes we would lie in the clover fields, with the earth beneath us still warm from the sun, and wish that the morning would never come. During the day we would peer through cracks in the barn to watch the farmer at work in the fields and his children playing happily nearby. How I envied those children and even the animals in the fields, for it seemed an eternity since I had run in the sunshine.

On one of these expeditions, a farmer dressed only in his underwear, a pair of clean cotton shorts and a snow-white undershirt, opened the farmhouse door. He looked beautiful to me. Royalty could not have been more finely dressed. I would have given anything in the world to be in his place, to wear those clean clothes, to sleep in his soft feather bed. I stood before him, my body filthy, my clothes reeking, feeling privileged when the hay allotted to us was deep enough to be soft. But the worst thing about my condition was the lice that covered me from head to foot. Whenever I passed a hand over my body, it came away covered with the dreadful beasts. My sheepskin coat was so full of them, we joked that it would march away by itself some night.

Occasionally, we would creep at night into the sauna of some Polish farmer. Because they were usually built some distance from the house, we could scrub at the layers of accumulated filth on our bodies in comparative safety. But the problem of the lice couldn't be solved in the sauna. Although we could wash the surface of our skins, the microscopic eggs embedded in our pores were in a constant state of reproduction and we could never rid ourselves of them. The lice problem was enormous for us because we had none of the usual means of combating them. In Eisiskes, although we had no running water in our homes, we used to carry water from the town pump until there was enough to fill the huge galvanized tin tub. On the day the laundress arrived, it was heated on the long kitchen stove. Each garment and piece of linen was first scrubbed on a board, using the strong soap prepared by my grandmother, soap that was used on our clothing, our floors, and us. Next the clothes were thrown into the big tub boiling on top of the stove. This, of course, killed any lice or larvae that were still hidden in them. Later the laundress ran a hot iron down the seams of every garment to destroy anything that might have the temerity to lurk there still.

In our home we had a special problem because of the farmers who slept there on the eve of market day. Invariably, some of them would be badly infested with lice and would leave some behind when they went to market in the morning. Every Thursday my mother and grandmother scrubbed all the floors in the house with soap and hot water to clean the crevices between the boards where the lice might be hiding. Thursday night was bath night for the whole family so that we would all be clean and shining for the Sabbath. Again we would bring out the big tin tub, big enough, in fact, for both Benjamin and I to bathe together, after it had been filled with water and heated on the stove. This accepted routine of cleanliness had left us completely unprepared for the filth and lice of our nomadic life.

The farmers had their own remedies for the lice problem and from time to time they would scrub their hair with kerosene, hair being a favourite incubation area for the creatures. In Polish school we had to submit to regular lice inspections, and many a child was sent home to be given the kerosene treatment. Unfortunately, we didn't even have kerosene to battle the lice that clung to us now. As we wandered, we scratched and scratched and scratched. Most of the farmers from whom we begged food or shelter were kind to us. Often they offered us the hope that the war would soon be over and we could live freely once more. They based their predictions on ridiculous things: an early autumn, the flight of the birds, old superstitions and beliefs that had no basis in fact. But they meant well and we needed to believe.

One farmer owned a crystal set and let me listen, using a set of headphones. It was tuned to London, but as I couldn't understand

English, I simply listened to the sounds. Suddenly someone was speaking Polish! He was a spokesman for the Polish government-in-exile and he told of the Allied battle to defeat Rommel in North Africa. The news was good, but Africa was too far away. How could that battle have any bearing on our situation? In general, all the European news was bad that summer. A couple of farmers seemed to enjoy relaying the worst of it to us. Many times they reported news that later turned out to be false. I can remember the terrible desolation we felt when we were told that Stalingrad had fallen, that the Germans were standing in front of Moscow. If the Russians were conquered, there could be no hope of liberation, and it would only be a matter of time before we met death at the hands of the Germans and their local allies. As time passed, the Poles and the Lithuanians, determined to be on the winning side, became progressively less willing to help us, as the Germans appeared more and more invincible.

One evening we sat with an old friend of my father's in his home. He was both a teacher and a farmer. Because he had lived in the United States and returned with wealth and an education, his opinions were respected. We had just been discussing the Japanese capture of Singapore, which our friend had read about in a leaflet dropped from a German plane. Although by now the news was four months old, it came as a fresh blow to us, another sign that Hitler and his kind would prevail. Our friend shook his head, and said cynically, "You know what I think? The way things are going, it won't be long before the Jews are extinct!" We stared at him in horror because this was our own constant nightmare. He went on, "The Germans, of course, will keep a few specimens alive, locked in cages like animals in the zoo. Then people can come to see what a real Jew used to look like." I could see myself, one of the preserved specimens, clutching the bars as people poked and prodded to see if Jews growled or barked or accepted peanuts. Please, dear God, I prayed, don't let me be spared for that.

Our safety was now becoming highly precarious. As the net closed on many of the others who had escaped from Radun, we began to lose heart as the stories of their fates were relayed to us. One farmer caught a Jew near the village of Paradun. He bound him hand and foot like an animal, threw him in his wagon, and took him to Radun. The refugee was immediately shot and buried at the site of Radun's mass grave. The farmer was given a year's exemption on his land tax. With such an incentive, how many other farmers would be ready to turn us in to the authorities?

We then learned of the horrible fate of a young woman from Eisiskes named Goldke, who had married a Polish Catholic farmer. At that time in Middle Eastern Europe, intermarriage between Jew and gentile was very rare and regarded as a family disgrace. Goldke added to her parents' horror and shame by converting to Catholicism. Thereafter, whenever she ventured into Eisiskes to visit them, she had been taunted in the streets with calls of "Goldke, the convert! Goldke, the convert!" Once the Germans began the massacre of the Jews, Goldke was protected by the Catholic Church and remained immune from danger on her husband's farm. When the Germans attacked Eisiskes, her parents and younger brothers and sisters fled first to Radun, but then when the massacres of the Jews began in Radun, her family fled to her for help. Of course, she hid her family, glad to have an opportunity at last to redeem herself, but a Lithuanian neighbour, hoping for a reward, betrayed them. The whole family was shot. For Goldke herself, however, a worse punishment was designed. The Lithuanian police tied her to a tree and set their dogs on her. Her screams echoed across the fields.

After that, wherever we went, the farmers whispered the story of Goldke to us, and closed their doors again. The risks were becoming too great for those who harboured Jews. Finally, my father decided that we would have to make permanent plans before we suffered the fate of Goldke's family. We prepared to move from that area to the other side of Eisiskes where Zoludzewicz, an old friend of my father's, lived. He kept house at his farm on the edge of the forest with his two sons and a daughter-in-law. In better times he had raised sheep in partnership with my father. On our travels Father had kept him in mind as a last resort. We had not come to him earlier because my father felt there might be a risk. Zoludzewicz's unmarried son was a deaf mute, and there was the chance that, since the young man couldn't really understand what was going on, he might give us away. It was a chance that we now had to take.

At about the same time, Yudel and Shmulke Szewicki decided they wanted to join a family group in the forest. We had already received instructions on getting there from a Polish recluse who lived at the edge of the forest and acted as contact man for the family group. Father was still reluctant to take the final step of accepting that kind of life, so we said goodbye to our friends and parted, hoping to meet again. For two nights we walked in a wide arc around Eisiskes, arriving at Zoludzewicz's farm as the second day was breaking. As it was now too risky to approach the house, we lay the whole day in the fields not far away, waiting until darkness came again. When we were certain it was safe, we went to the window of the farmhouse and knocked. Looking out, Zoludzewicz saw us and ran to open the door. He held my father, weeping in joy at seeing him again, then swept us into his house. He was so kind and generous that it was hard to believe that someone cared so much about us. We seemed to have found a home at last where we would be safe. Zoludzewicz took Father to see the sheep that had been their joint investment and told us that he would take care of us. He was a true Christian.

The days that followed were wonderfully carefree. We ate three times a day again instead of sharing the food that we had begged at one meagre meal. Zoludzewicz gave us food we had not seen in months: eggs, pancakes, cheese, milk, honey, fresh bread, vegetables and sour cream. We could not, of course, eat meat here but Zoludzewicz respected this. Everything tasted so good and there was so much that we felt we were wallowing in luxury. Each day we hid in the barn where Zoludzewicz would visit us, lying beside Father on the straw to talk of events in the outside world and make plans for the future when the war would be over. At night we walked in the fields, or sometimes sat with Zoludzewicz in his kitchen listening to the war news on the radio. It was still very bad, but Zoludzewicz would not allow us to be discouraged.

"It's always darkest before the dawn. It will get better soon, you'll see!" he'd say, and we listened eagerly, wanting to believe him. But by this time it was easier to be pessimistic. Deep down each of us knew that our present paradise was only temporary.

Two weeks later, Zoludzewicz came to the barn one night with tears in his eyes. "Shael, I have bad news. I thought it would all work out . . . I thought that in time . . . but it's no use!" He wept.

"What is it, old friend?" my father asked quietly, but I think we all knew. We had all seen his married son's anxious face and knew that he had been avoiding us.

"Shael, it's my son. He doesn't eat or sleep. He can't even work anymore. Ever since we heard about Goldke, he's certain he's going to be killed like that. He's certain the police are going to find you here. It's driving him mad, Shael. It's driving him mad!"

Then he brought his son to the barn, and the young man went down on his knees to beg forgiveness. It was a pathetic sight as he knelt there, accusing himself of cowardice and admitting he could not conquer it. Since all of us had known the terror that he spoke of, we could feel truly sorry for him.

Once again the dilemma: where to go now? My father was still reluctant to go to the forest, but there were simply no more options to delay the inevitable step. Even if there had been any more farmhouse doors open to us, they could only provide temporary shelter. Although life in the forest would be primitive, at least we could hope for a degree of permanence. Zoludzewicz bade us farewell tearfully. He had provided us with every possible thing to help us in our forest life, and now he gave us money to buy the rifles we would need there. Earlier, Babkin's brother-in-law had hinted that he could get guns for us if ever we needed them, and so we returned to his farm now. From him we bought two rifles, an old one and a new one. With these and our few possessions on our backs, we began marching in a southwesterly direction skirting the town of Nacha. After four nights of travel, we arrived at the home of the farmer Buczko on the edge of the Nacha forest. He would lead us to the family group. During the day we hid in the fields. When darkness fell, Buczko came to guide us deeper into the forest, crossing lakes and swamps, forcing our way through impenetrable thickets and miles of heavy forest.

We arrived at the camp just after dawn. It was an incredible sight. Almost three hundred people were living openly and apparently without fear in the middle of the forest. They laughed and called to one another, the children played noisily, and women prepared breakfast over open fires and cows grazed nearby. Terrified at first by what we saw in the camp, we had an awful compulsion to tell them to be quiet, to take cover before they were killed. What on earth were these Jews doing, taking such risks? Where were the sentries? What if we had been Germans or Lithuanians sneaking up on them?

Most of our fears were unfounded, of course, for they were much more aware than they appeared to be. The camp covered nearly fifty acres of high ground in the centre of a swamp, which could be crossed only by walking on semi-submerged logs. For miles around the swamp, the forest was thick and tangled. Few people would have guessed that any of this existed in its centre. The cooking fires that had alarmed us were, on closer inspection, very small, and since they burnt dry wood, almost smokeless. And, of course, in the early morning any smoke that did arise was indistinguishable from the morning mists rising from the lakes and swamps of the forest. What protection did they have? Many of the men carried guns and had learned how to use them. Sentries had been standing guard in the forest but we hadn't seen them. (If we'd been enemies, they would have dealt with us quickly.) In addition, the partisans were camped only a mile away, an added protection for the families on the island.

Our friends, the Szewickis, came to greet us and found a place for us to camp near them. On mattresses of evergreen branches we spread out the greatcoats that Zoludzewicz had provided for us. We then began erecting a lean-to of boughs for shelter. Later we were able to roof it with a tarpaulin to protect our beds from the rain. Other families had done the same, although some even acquired tents. In a short time we became part of the group, for many of the people here had come from Eisiskes and Radun. Others had fled here from Woronowa, Lida, and Waszelizki. At last we were among friends in a place of comparative safety. We were still vigilant, still careful to take precautions, but we began to relax a little for the first time in a year.

The partisan group nearby was composed of young Jews and Russians who had been together since May. Recently, other Jews hiding on farms near the forest had also joined them. All young, able-bodied Jews in our family group were encouraged to transfer to the partisans. This is what I had been waiting for, a chance to be one of the hunters instead of one of the hunted. With the partisans I could go out and attack, while the family groups were dedicated only to defence. And it was not much of a defence, since there were simply not enough guns among the family members.

Continual efforts were made to increase the number of guns by taking them from the neighbouring farmers, but this was a difficult process. The farmers were reluctant to part with guns that had been in their families for years; some of them even used guns for hunting that dated back to the Napoleonic Wars. And it was difficult to find out which farmers still owned guns, since they had learned to hide them well. But we desperately needed the weapons if we were to survive. Whenever we heard that a certain farmer had one, we would go in force to confiscate it. At first we would ask politely for it, but if we were refused, we became more insistent and threatening. Finally when all else failed, we were forced to beat him and threaten the lives of his wife and children. On one occasion we beat a farmer severely, but he still refused to give up his gun. Then we took his children, one by one behind the barn, slapped them to make them scream, shot a rifle into the air, then clapped a hand over the screaming mouths. The man was not convinced and refused to give up his gun. In desperation, we dragged his wife from the house. "All right," he said. "Take it!"

It was not a pleasant way to act, but we needed the guns more than they did. In such ways, the family groups began to build up the arsenal they needed for food-gathering forays. These expeditions always took place at night. On our arrival, a food-collecting group would consist of no more than five people, but only a couple of them would have guns. The remainder would carry sticks over their shoulders draped in tarpaulins to make it appear that they too were armed. To make the group seem even larger, we would enter the village in the dark from different directions, with our leader shouting orders that suggested the attack of an army brigade.

"Piat no levo!" (Five to the left!), the leader shouted, and one man ran to the left.

"Piat na pravo!" and one man ran to the right.

"Piat wpierod!" A man ran to the front.

"Piat nazat!" A fourth man ran to the back.

"Okroozhai!" (Surround!) and we all closed in!

All this violent activity was anathema to my father and for many of the Jews of his generation. They refused to support us.

"Leibke," he told me, "these farmers whom you're taking food from are my friends! I've known them all my life. I've eaten with them, done business with them. How could I hold a gun to their heads?"

"What are you talking about?" I asked him. "These are the men who helped to murder our people in Eisiskes, and in Radun, and . . ."

"No, Leibke. These men are my friends. I don't want them to call me a bandit."

We had the same argument again and again but it always ended the same way: my father didn't want his "friends" to call him a bandit. He seemed to live in the past, as if he could have his old status again and reconstruct the old life, simply by conforming to the old rules of gentlemanly conduct and friendship.

In August 1942, after we had been with the family group for three or four weeks, I moved to the partisan camp. There were close to thirty men in the unit at that time. We spent our time learning to defend ourselves and acquiring the techniques of guerrilla warfare. Although we had no specialists to teach us, our first encounters with the enemy were successful. They were only simple ambushes in the area of Radun, but their success was a tremendous boost to our morale.

Our most ambitious undertaking was the derailment of a train. We had no proper equipment for the job, and not one of us had the slightest experience with this kind of thing. The only explosive we had was a very large artillery shell which we placed between two railroad ties, its firing pin lined up so that it faced the barrel of a rifle propped up about five feet away. To the trigger we attached a cord that trailed down to our hiding place in a clump of bushes beside the tracks.

After setting up everything to the best of our ability, we settled down to wait for the train, not knowing whether our primitive bomb would work, but knowing that the consequences could be disastrous if it did not. If the gun went off but missed the firing pin of the shell, the German guards on the train would immediately start a search for the person who had fired the shot. If the shell exploded without damaging the engine, we were still likely to get caught.

Tense and terrified, we heard a far-off whistle. We looked at each other, suddenly doubting the sanity of our wild scheme. But it was too late to do anything about it, for the locomotive was already thundering down the track toward us. We could feel the ground beneath us trembling. "Get ready!" But the noise of the pounding engine drowned out our voices. I crouched down to peer through the branches of our hideout.

"Now!" The cord went taut and the rifle slammed its bullet into the artillery shell. The next thing I knew I was lying on my back, knocked flat by the explosion. But it had done the same to the train. The shell had exploded right under the engine, stopping it instantly, and the cars had toppled and folded like a broken-down accordion behind it. It was a marvellous, chaotic scene, and we were tremendously pleased with ourselves. What a sense of accomplishment! Never again have I felt such a surge of wild excitement as I felt that night.

It was not long after our train wreck that we received a delegation from another partisan group operating about half a mile away, asking us to amalgamate with them. Most of them were Russians who had been brought from Siberian prison camps by the Russians to build roads and airfields. Many had been sentenced to Siberia for political reasons but others were genuine criminals. For a short time after the Russian retreat, the Germans had employed them as road builders and carpenters; some were even put to work making felt boots for the German army's campaign in Russia. But the Germans miscalculated when they thought these men would collaborate with them. Even though they had been sentenced to cruel punishment in Siberia, they were still Russians. Sensing their underlying hostility, the Germans soon decided to deport these men to slave labour camps in Germany.

The Russians promptly vanished into the forest. Since they were used to the terrible hardships of Siberia, wresting an existence from the forests of Poland presented little challenge. At first, they merely hid out there, occasionally emerging to gather food. Such forays led naturally into small attacks on the Germans and their allies. It wasn't long before the Russians established a reputation as thieves, drunks, and rapists in the farm country surrounding the forest. They were a thoroughly reprehensible group, but they had one thing our group lacked — they were seasoned fighters. They were led by a Russian Jew from Gorki whose name was Elia Grace. A soldier in the Russian army, Grace had been stranded in the Nacha forest when the Russians retreated. The men from Siberia, untrained but toughened by hardship, looked to him for leadership. Grace named the group the Leninski Komsomol and taught them the skills of war.

Once the group was well established, they sent messengers east to find other groups that were already in contact with Moscow. They needed arms, explosives, radio equipment and sabotage experts to train the men if they were to be effective against the Germans. The first messengers never returned; it was assumed that they had been killed. The next messengers, however, returned with the promise of help from Moscow.

Some time during the winter of 1942–43, a group of partisans from the Naliboki forest joined the Nacha partisans. They were from a highly organized fighting unit carrying radio equipment from Moscow, and had been ordered by Moscow to make contact. Stankevitch, their leader, had been given the task of welding all the small groups in the forest into one big efficient force. Such a task was difficult, for there were many renegades in the forest who were a law unto themselves, and others who used the partisan life as a cover for their war against the Jews. A number of them refused to submit to Stankevitch's authority even after he talked to them at length, so he executed the worst of them and sent the others from the forest. The

Jewish partisans felt considerably more secure after this. Stankevitch organized the groups according to the jobs they were to do and established military discipline. Soon after, the Russians parachuted in a radio transmitter and a large supply of arms.

The partisans were not entirely happy with the nearby family groups of Jews because they did not contribute to the war against the Germans. They complained that they were little more than a nuisance. The family groups, on the other hand, made every attempt to be independent and self-sufficient. A tailor named Elke, who organized the members so that all necessary tasks were attended to, administered the group on the island. The biggest task was food collection, of course, and this was where the family group and the partisans constantly clashed. Both went to the farms to collect food. The partisans claimed the farmers were constantly complaining that Elke's people were bandits; Elke swore his group only begged for food. The argument, of course, was beside the point. If the family groups did not provide for themselves, the partisans would have had to look after them, for the families of many of the partisans lived with Elke's group.

The second difference between the partisans and the family groups was ideological. The leadership of the partisans was Communist and anyone joining their group was urged to become Communist as well. Elke and the family groups were firmly anti-Communist because the men of the families were mainly small businessmen and shopkeepers whose outlook was basically capitalistic; they were used to making their own way and could see no purpose in Communist doctrine. As the summer ended, the quarrel between the partisans and the family groups grew increasingly bitter. There were repeated delegations of partisans coming to demand Elke's promise that his people would stop taking food — food they believed should go to the partisans. Elke listened to them, then ignored them.

One day in mid-September when I had come to visit my family, a delegation of three partisans arrived to confront Elke once more. One was a Pole called Marusiak; the other two, Moishe Szmulewicz and Yankele Konichowski, were Jews. They demanded that Elke accompany them to a village that had complained bitterly of raids by the family groups. Elke agreed, hoping perhaps to reach some sort of compromise. Instead, the partisans held a mock trial in front of the villagers and then shot Elke to appease them. The following morning, the three arrived back at camp with Szmulewicz wearing Elke's hat. Then he assembled all the family group members and proceeded to harangue them. "You are not to raid the villages for food anymore," Szmulewicz said. "You are not fighters, and it is the fighters who must have the food. All of you will turn in your guns and ammunition. Only fighters need guns."

The partisans then took all the weapons that had been so laboriously collected by the family members. Against orders, I stayed on with my family after this and experienced with them and all the other family members the awful depression of fresh defeat. Just when we had begun to feel a certain degree of security, we were learning that the Nazis, Poles and Lithuanians were not the only enemies. The Communists were also out to get us, and they lived only a mile away. We elected a new leader after Elke's death. He was a man called Paisha. Formerly part of Grodno's underworld, he was much tougher and more devious than Elke, and we hoped to out-force the partisans with Paisha to lead us.

Within my own family there was talk of moving on again. The forest did not measure up to the sort of refuge my father had anticipated. Enemies were everywhere, but somewhere, we thought, there must be a place with somewhat less conflict. Shortly afterwards, on one of our expeditions to look for food, we visited a farmer whom my father had known casually in better times. He asked us why we continued to live in the forest with winter coming on.

"Where else can we go?" asked Father.

"Grodno," he said. "The Jews in that ghetto are doing fine!"

This was hard to believe, for we had assumed the Jews in Grodno had been murdered as all the others had been. But if they were still alive, this presented a new solution to our present problem. Still, Grodno was nearly sixty miles from the Nacha forest; it would be a very difficult journey. Back in camp we told the story to others, but they were all skeptical. "It's a trap," they said. "We've heard this kind of story before."

On our next visit to the village, my father called on the farmer once more. Again he told him of the Jews in Grodno, but now he added some details to his story. "As a matter of fact, there's a small community of Jews in Marcinkonys as well, and they keep in touch with their brothers in Grodno. If you want to go, the people in Marcinkonys will help you."

He told us that he had been doing business in Marcinkonys the previous day with some Jewish merchants. This astounded us, for both towns were in the area that the Germans had designated as part of the Third Reich. All Jews had supposedly been cleared from this "sacred" territory long ago. Still we hesitated. We had stood at the edge of so many traps in the past that it would be stupid to walk right into one now. We had agreed when we entered the forest that we would never set foot in a ghetto again. What were we thinking of now that we should consider going to Grodno? For hours we discussed the plan with the Szewickis, first agreeing to stay in the forest, then agreeing to leave. Finally it was decided that we should approach the farmer once more to find out how to make the trip.

"I'll take you as far as Marcinkonys myself," he told us.

"How much do you want?" my father asked.

The farmer shrugged and spread his hands. We knew that meant a lot of money.

"We've nothing left, my friend," Father said and turned away. Then he turned back, "Except, except leather."

The farmer tried not to look tempted. "How much leather?"

At Zoludzewicz's farm there was a large stock of leather, which belonged to my father; it was this that we now used to secure our passage. Father then wrote a letter to Zoludzewicz telling him to give the leather to the farmer to pay him in advance for acting as our guide. We arranged to return in a week, by which time he would have collected the leather and be ready to leave for Marcinkonys.

A week later, accompanied by the Szewickis, we returned to the farmer's house. He had collected the leather from Zoludzewicz and was ready to carry out his part of the bargain. For two days we hid in his barn, then on a dark moonless night we began our journey.

It was now late October.

CHAPTER FIVE

Grodno: October–December 1942

The journey to Marcinkonys took three days. We travelled in a westerly direction, crossing a small river by boat, and tramping through miles of forest. As we travelled we waited for ambush, unwilling to believe that our guide would deal honestly with us. But as we came closer to Marcinkonys, we realized that he was a trustworthy man and our confidence began to return. We entered the village by merely climbing over a small fence, and found ourselves in a situation so close to being normal that we were astounded. Although Marcinkonys was in the Third Reich and the Jews were ghettoized, we were aware at once of an enormous difference between their lives and those of the people of Radun or Eisiskes. Most of them were employed in the town's mushroom industry. Each day large groups of Jews went to the forest to gather the mushrooms. They could have slipped away quite easily, but instead they returned each evening with the day's produce.

In addition, they were allowed to trade freely with the local farmers; they seemed happy and well fed. We soon realized that their condition was due to the local *Judenrat* who were a particularly strong and protective body here, highly respected by both Germans and Lithuanians. But that did not really explain the enormous difference between this town and the towns of Eisiskes and Radun. After much discussion, we decided that the difference lay in the administration. The Germans administered Marcinkonys because it was part of the Third Reich, but Poles and Lithuanians had administered Radun and Eisiskes. Obviously the Germans here were basically kinder and more humane than the Poles and Lithuanians. It was an absurd rationale, but under the circumstances what else could we think unless we accepted the terrible truth that the time was not yet ripe for Marcinkonys? But we could not admit this if we were to sustain hope.

Marcinkonys seemed a paradise to me and I wanted desperately to stay there, but the *Judenrat* decreed that we could stay no more than a week or two. The village was too small for us to remain any longer without detection, and our party was only one of many that wanted to take refuge there. After a few days, we were placed in the hands of a guide named Yankele Kobrowksi, given money and food for our trip, and a permit that identified us as Marcinkonys Jews transferring to the Grodno ghetto. Then we boarded the train for Grodno. Without the permit we would not have been permitted on board, since normally Jews were prohibited from using transport. After an uneventful trip, we arrived safely at the Grodno ghetto.

The ghetto of Grodno was a tremendous contrast to that of Marcinkonys, or for that matter to those of Radun and Eisiskes. It covered an enormous area because it held nearly fifty thousand people and was isolated from the rest of the city by a huge barbed wire fence, with fortified guard towers at intervals. In addition, a deep ravine ran parallel to a great portion of the fence, further separating the gentiles from the Jews.

The inhabitants of the ghetto were supplied with approximately two hundred calories per day, hardly enough for a sparrow to survive on. Yet the Jews of Grodno were remarkably healthy and their morale was high. We soon learned of the ways they circumvented the Germans' restrictions. Since there were no sewers in the ghetto area, once a week the accumulated sewage had to be pumped into huge tanks and loaded onto wagons to be emptied far beyond the city.

The Germans were unaware that a false bottom in each tank provided a clean compartment the Jews used to smuggle food back to
the ghetto. They bought the food — eggs, flour, milk and vegetables — from the local farmers, and they sold any excess through the
fence to the people of Grodno. The money earned this way bought
more food. The bread baked with flour bought from the farmers
was also sold outside the ghetto.

The Germans used to have a saying that if you put a Jew in a
bottle and corked it, he would still manage to do business. I guess
Grodno was a perfect example of this enterprise. The Jews had many
other ways of outwitting the Germans. One example was the coffin
trick. As the Jewish cemetery was located outside the ghetto, burial
parties were allowed to leave the ghetto with the coffin on a covered
cart. The Germans guarded such processions from a distance and
never inspected the coffin because they feared contagion, so the Jews
used these mournful occasions to replenish food supplies by burying
the corpse but returning the coffin full of foodstuffs to the ghetto.

The girls returning from work in Grodno factories also carried
food into the ghetto. This trick depended on a conspiracy between
the pretty girls and their less attractive sisters. By dressing more dar-
ingly than the others, the pretty girls invited the Germans to search
them for contraband, while the less attractive girls, who actually carried forbidden foodstuffs, were ignored. Even animals were smug-
gled in and slaughtered by the shochet, then sold to the Jews of the
ghetto. Everyone knew that possession of contraband food meant
instant death but it was a risk that had to be taken. Otherwise they
would have died of starvation.

As we learned, the Grodno Jews were extraordinarily ingenious in
hiding the ghetto's food-gathering activities from the eyes of the
German patrols. While their ingenuity had not made them compla-
cent about the dangers, they apparently did not foresee any radical
changes in their situation. Our small group, on the contrary, was
most alarmed, for we could see many signs in Grodno that pointed
to the eventual massacre of the Jews by the Germans. We spoke of
this and our many escapes to the only person we found here that we
had known before. Although at first shocked and disbelieving, she

soon realized we told the truth and began inviting others to come to hear our story. Most of them refused to believe us; they even accused us of spreading rumours to create panic. Others said that the persecution we had suffered indicated that we were Communists and consequently enemies of the Germans. We protested that what we were speaking of was systematic genocide, but they turned a deaf ear to us. Finally we were ordered by the *Judenrat* to stop telling our fearful stories or they would hand us over to the Germans. They said we were causing unnecessary anxiety to the community. We soon became aware that in Grodno we had walked into the Eisiskes and Radun situations all over again. Still, we hoped to live out the winter in comparative comfort before taking our chances in the forest again.

Unfortunately, we found that this proved to be difficult. The Grodno Jews were different from the Jews we had known. In Eisiskes on a Friday night even the most ragged stranger was welcomed into our homes. No one was ever allowed to go hungry or homeless. In Grodno we were largely ignored. The Jews here were cold and inhospitable and never even offered us a place to sleep, though many had extra room.

For some time after our arrival we slept in the synagogue, but we knew we couldn't stay there during the really cold months of winter. After several weeks we found sleeping quarters in a carpentry shop, where at night we kept warm by creeping into huge piles of wood shavings on the floor. We shared this refuge with several other escapees. One Friday night after the synagogue service, the Shammes announced that there were strangers in the midst of the congregation who were homeless and had lost all their possessions. Would someone take these unfortunates home to share the Sabbath meal with them? We went to stand by the door so the congregation could see us easily as they filed out. Family by family they left, carefully avoiding our eyes until at last our little group stood there alone. My father was shattered. To be reduced to begging for food was bad enough, but to be publicly refused was a terrible blow to his pride. He had never refused hospitality to anyone.

Our damaged pride was not the worst of the problem. We were

quite desperate for food. In Grodno, food was provided only for people with ration cards. Since we were there illegally, we could not apply for them. This meant that we would have to obtain food illegally, and we devised many little ways to do this.

Once a day, the Germans provided a wagonload of bread for the *Judenrat* to distribute in the ghetto. Mingling with the crowd surrounding the wagon, we would arrange for one of us to steal a loaf or two to share amongst the six of us. Or sometimes Father was able to buy a little bread with the money he earned doing odd jobs in the ghetto. I remember his dividing it up carefully, saying, "My one prayer is to have bread enough for my family again one day, and no worries about tomorrow. Then I can give each of you as much bread as I want to." Tears would stream down his cheeks. Of course, this bread was not enough to sustain us, since we could not obtain it every day. Moreover, we needed some variety in our diet, and to obtain this, we took to breaking into the storage sheds behind the homes, helping ourselves to food kept there. Sometimes we saw cheese or butter that had been placed to keep cool between the inner and outer windows of a house. Creeping up in silence, we would smash the outer window, grab the food and run. Saturday we would have our one genuine feast of the week. This was the day for cholent.

Long ago in Eisiskes, my dear mother had prepared our pot of cholent every Friday morning. It was a dish made from a large piece of stewing meat, or brisket, and lima beans; over the top, to seal in the juices was kugel, or grated potato pudding. When it was all prepared, mother put her mark on the cast-iron cooking pot and gave it to us to take to the baker where it cooked very slowly till it was time to fetch it after synagogue on Saturday noon.

The purchase of the meat for cholent was a matter of great deliberation. The fatter its content, the higher its price; in our lean years, we could seldom afford such luxury. Often mother had to be content with soup meat called *Flanken* or one of the other cheap cuts. Of course, this was really more digestible but it was also the mark of poverty. Because the rich cholents were quite a strain on the digestive system, it was a joke amongst us that anyone who was foolish enough to take a nap after eating cholent was tempting providence and might never wake up!

Every Saturday at noon my sister, Freidke, and I were dispatched to the baker's with a pair of thick gloves to carry home the heavy pot. With a long wooden spatula, the baker would draw from the oven the pot we pointed out to him. Then the two of us would carry it home, the heat of its handle tingling our palms in spite of the thick gloves. Once in a while we would bring home the wrong pot by mistake, but everyone in Eisiskes took this in good humour. When the family sat down for the Saturday noon meal, the cholent pot, crowned by its crisp, golden-brown kugel, was placed in the centre of the table. Now, in spite of all the restrictions, the Jews of Grodno were still managing to prepare cholent for the Sabbath, taking it to the ghetto baker for cooking. Of course, our homeless little group was unable to do this, but we found a way to share the cholent that others had prepared. Two of us would go to the baker after synagogue on Saturday and claim the largest pot of cholent, then rush it back to our quarters where our whole group would literally gorge on it. A few times someone else claimed the pot I pointed out, and I had to acknowledge my "mistake" and claim another one. I can't remember feeling any guilt in doing this; I was just happy to find another way to stave off starvation. At least we ate well one day of the week.

For the people of the ghetto the daily routine was very similar to that of the Jews of Eisiskes and Radun, except on a much larger scale. Thousands of Jews were marched out the gates each day to work, some digging ditches, others building roads or working in factories. Each of them had a work permit issued by the *Judenrat*. Occasionally, when someone with a permit was unwell or unwilling to go to work, a substitute would be allowed to replace him, although generally everyone wanted to work since there were smuggling opportunities outside the gates.

A week after we arrived in Grodno, I replaced another man on a work brigade that was going to dig drainage ditches. I was wearing a pair of light tan breeches, the only pants that remained of the clothes I had taken from Radun. Naturally one of the Polish police singled me out for special attention because of my pants and forced me to work in mud up to my armpits, whacking me on the head with his rifle butt whenever he thought I was attempting to climb out. At midday, when we were given a short break to eat, I climbed out of the mud to share some bread with another young fellow. It was then that my first smuggling opportunity came along. A Polish farmer offered us four live ducks. As I had been given a few marks for working as a substitute, I used them to buy two of the ducks. My friend bought the other two, and we stuffed them into a canvas shoulder bag, the thought of eating them overcoming our fear of discovery. At the end of the day, when the brigade was marched back to Grodno, we prayed that the ducks would remain silent until we were past the ghetto gates. We marched along the road in silence, a hundred tired and hungry men and four bewildered ducks in the darkness of a canvas bag. We began to relax. Obviously the ducks had accepted the darkness and fallen asleep.

Just then, two SS men passed us on bicycles. As though a signal had been given, the ducks quacked in chorus. We kept walking, hoping that they hadn't heard, but at the head of the column the SS men stopped to speak to the policeman in charge. "Halt!" shouted the policeman. Then he paced past the brigade. "Someone is carrying *ducks* and unless he comes forward immediately, every one of you will be sorry."

I hesitated only a moment. I knew what the Germans' idea of punishment was and I couldn't jeopardize the lives of others just because I had behaved stupidly. I stepped out of the line of marchers; my friend came with me. I felt a hand grab me by the collar and I was hustled off to a nearby park. One of the SS men took the canvas bag from me and we watched as the two of them opened it. We waited to be shot. Instead, we were ordered to drop our trousers and bend over while they took off their leather army belts. Then with apparently infinite pleasure, they beat us with the buckled ends of the belts until the blood ran down our legs. When they grew tired of this, they returned us to the brigade where we hobbled back to the ghetto.

Once safely inside the gates the two of us clung together, laughing hysterically. The pain was excruciating but we were alive! For two weeks I could not sleep on my back or sit properly. Although I regretted the lost wages and the confiscated ducks, these were small tokens to pay. Father didn't even scold me for the chance I had taken; I'm sure he knew that I'd learned my lesson. Only a short time later, I was returning from work with a fellow named Liebke Rogowski. For some reason the guards chose this occasion to give us all a systematic body search and half a chicken was found in Liebke's possession. As an example to the rest of us, he was taken out of the group and shot. For weeks afterwards I could feel the bullets that had killed him in my own back.

Yudel Szewicki had by now left to live with a woman he had met, but he came running to the carpentry shop one day to tell us, "I've got a *Lebenschein!*" Tears of happiness and relief rolled down his face.

"Congratulations, Yudel!" my father told him warmly. But inwardly he had much less faith in the little piece of paper than Yudel had. A *Lebenschein* was a "life permit," a guarantee that the holder would be spared because he was in an essential service. Yudel Szewicki, for instance, was a bootmaker. Since the Germans needed a steady supply of army boots, it was not too difficult for him to persuade them to issue him a permit. Some Jews had given up all their possessions to obtain one. Those owning them guarded them with their lives, for there were many who would steal them. This was another ploy the Germans used to spread false hope and mistrust among the Jews of Grodno, but the sad fact was that the security guaranteed by the *Lebenschein* was as false as any other German promise.

At the beginning of November I arranged for a job in a rope factory inside the ghetto. Shortly afterwards, three SS men came to the factory to "request" a length of rope. From their shiny boots to the braid on their caps, they were the picture of polished elegance. Definitely very important people, I thought, as I watched the foreman measure out several hundred yards of our finest rope, handing it to them as though he served an emperor. The reason for the rope was made evident the following day. A proclamation ordered all of us to assemble in an open area on the edge of the ghetto where there was a large overhanging balcony. On a wagon below two men and a woman were standing bound hand and foot. One of the three SS men who had appeared at the factory announced, "These three Jews left this ghetto without permission. They were caught as all escapees will be caught. They are sentenced to die by hanging! Heil Hitler!"

Three ropes were thrown over the balcony rail and nooses placed around the necks of the two men, but when the German went to place the noose around the young woman's neck she spat in his face. Very deliberately, he turned the noose so the knot lay against her throat ensuring that she would die slowly by strangulation, instead of quickly by a broken neck. She was a beautiful and brave woman and we were forced to stand there until her agony was over. Then for three days, the bodies were left dangling from the balcony as a warning to the rest of us. Soon afterwards, a man and woman and their small son were executed for the same crime. The mother and child were shot first, and then a noose was placed around the man's neck to hang him. But as they hoisted him up, the rope broke and he fell to the ground still alive. Immediately he leapt up and demanded his freedom, proclaiming that international law forbids a man to be executed twice for the same crime. The Germans shot him on the spot.

I never forgot the injustice of this particular incident, and I swore I would avenge the senseless murder someday. Later on when we were again with the partisans in the forest, we captured a German gendarme who was well known as a sadistic Jew killer. We hung him on the nearest tree, but as in the earlier situation, the rope broke before it had done its job. The German insisted on his right to be freed according to the same international law. Immediately, the scene of the hanging in Grodno flashed before my eyes, and I remembered the sort of justice that man had received at the hands of the Nazis. Without further ado the German was immediately put to death.

Other "crimes" for which the Germans imposed the death sentence in Grodno were pregnancy and marriage. Since women appearing to be pregnant were shot on sight, it became automatic for the women of Grodno to terminate pregnancies by abortion. Whenever this was impossible, the woman was hidden until the birth and the baby then smothered because it was impossible to find adequate food for an infant, or to hide the young child from the Germans. Harbouring an infant meant a death sentence for the whole family. Anyone performing a marriage was also executed. In spite of this, rabbis continued to perform marriage rites in cellars and in other refuges, defying the Germans.

Every so often Polish farmers entering the ghetto on business would tell stories of the actual fate of the Jews who had been taken from their homes for "resettlement" elsewhere. But the Grodno Jews scoffed at their wild stories, believing of course that the farmers were only looking for ways to rob them. We could have told the farmers to save their breath; if the Grodno Jews wouldn't believe us they would never believe them. Probably they could not have carried on from day to day if they had acknowledged the truth. It is somewhat like a person who, although terminally ill, continues to function until the end by refusing to accept the truth. It is human nature to hope.

A similar example of this "false hope" occurred in Vilnius a year later, when a woman named Sara Menkis came to warn the remaining Jews of their impending fate. She had been one of the forty-seven thousand Jews taken by the Germans to Ponar Mountain for "resettlement." Every last one of them was shot and flung into a ravine. Sara, however, was only wounded and, after her murderers left, she climbed over the bodies of her family and friends to crawl to safety. She returned to Vilnius and entered the ghetto with a work party. She had come back to convince the rest of them to act now to save themselves, but they wouldn't believe her. At last she convinced two leaders of a new underground movement in the ghetto, Abbe Kowner and Israel Wittenberg, that she was telling the truth, yet even they could not convince the ghetto's president and were advised to stop spreading upsetting stories. Even when the two men published a leaflet to hand out in the ghetto, sharing Sara's story and warning people to resist the "resettlement" programs, they were still largely ignored.

The one beautiful thing that happened to me in Grodno was my meeting Bella Winicki. After Yudel Szewicki found his job in the boot factory, the rest of us used to wait outside for him as he was the only one earning regular money. The boot factory was located above the home of the Winicki family, and their daughter, beautiful Bella, would look out and see us sitting cold and hungry in the courtyard. She would invite us in and serve cups of hot soup. More than that, she gave us kindness.

In late November 1942, the first resettlement programs were announced in Grodno. The *Judenrat* explained that the people were being relocated. They were reassured that the relocation was genuine because the Germans had even provided the name of their destination. Those of us who warned the people were told: "If the Germans wanted to murder us, why wouldn't they do it right here? They're wasting a lot of time and expense this way if they've no intention of resettling us, aren't they?"

Extra guards appeared around the ghetto with heavier armament. Work parties were guarded and searched more closely. The Germans were now ready to deal with the Jews of Grodno. Five thousand people at a time were selected by the *Judenrat*, told to collect their belongings and assemble at a given place. They were then marched out of the ghetto on their way to resettlement and new jobs in the Third Reich. Unresisting, they left Grodno. Two or three days later this was repeated; in another three days another five thousand left, their possessions piled on trucks, small children held firmly by the hand, the whole group cooperative and apparently unsuspecting. For us, the sight of all this misplaced trust was terrible. We could have told them that their deaths were no more than hours away, but they would not have believed us.

We had been making plans all along for our escape from Grodno, and now we rushed them to completion. Shmulke Szewicki had already teamed up with a group who had arranged for a horse and sleigh to meet them outside the ghetto. Yudel Szewicki, with his misplaced faith in his *Lebenschein* and his new bond with his lady friend, refused to leave Grodno. Finally in mid-December, Shmulke left without him. He was taken to Szczuczin where he visited my mother and grandmother and attempted to persuade them to go with him to the forest. Again, they refused.

The four members of our family teamed up with a young man named Arke and his sister who knew the local countryside and could guide us as far as Druskieniki where they expected to find refuge. It was only a short distance from there to Marcinkonys. After that we felt we could find our way back to the forest with the help of several farmers we knew. But it was winter. There was deep snow and it was desperately cold. As we were not properly dressed for such a trip, I went around to the houses of the resettled Jews and found some abandoned clothing. By putting pants over pants and shirts over shirts, we added insulation. We had to make sure that the clothes we selected didn't look too unusual, however, for our escape route went right through the city. It was important to look inconspicuous.

A few days after Christmas we realized that we had no more time to waste. Another group was being taken for resettlement and we could not avoid attention much longer. Meanwhile, in spite of the heavy surveillance around the ghetto, we had found a weak spot. A bombed-out building, almost a block long, stood at a point along the line separating the ghetto from the rest of the city. My brother and I had reconnoitered it carefully. It provided a perfect opportunity to approach the fence line without being seen. At this point of the fence line there was no fence wire; the Germans relied on armed patrols to prevent escapes. One night, just after dark, our group went separately to the rear of the building, and then one by one we moved to a vantage point amid the rubble where we could watch the patrols. Only two soldiers were moving back and forth in front of the building. Slowly, throughout the cold night, each soldier would walk along his section of the sidewalk, stop at the end of this walk for a cigarette, and would then plod back to meet his partner and chat. This routine was repeated many times during a shift.

Was there time for us to escape while the guards stopped to talk? Could we do it soundlessly? No. We had to admit this couldn't be done successfully. One of us might escape — but six? Never.

"We'll have to kill them," Arke said.

"No!" my father said.

Benjamin shook his head. "That's impossible. They'd shoot before we got close enough."

"You brought your knife, didn't you, Leibke?" Arke asked. The others turned to look at me. "You were in the partisans — you know how to do it."

For two hours we discussed it. How to get close enough, how to use a knife effectively, and who was going to do it. In the end, there was no one to do it but me because Benjamin and Father did not have the stomach for it, and Arke was afraid he'd bungle it. The fact was, of course, that my month in the partisans had definitely not prepared me for this. Arke, Benjamin and I now set out along the side of the building, skirting in and out of empty doorways and windows until we neared the front of the building. At this point, we moved inside. We stepped carefully through the rubble and around the snow drifts where the guard took his cigarette break. Once again we settled down to observe the routine of the guards. It took ten minutes from the time they parted till the time they met again. If I were to escape before the other one reappeared from around the corner where his patrol ended, I would have to kill my man in absolute silence within moments after he stopped for his cigarette.

The coast was clear. I left Arke and Benjamin and hid in an "L" formed by the remnant of two adjacent walls. I was thirty-five feet from the spot where the guard normally stopped. I pulled my knife out of its sheath. It was the product of many hours of enforced idleness, a knife of perfect heft for me, with a steel blade I had honed until it was fantastically thin and sharp. I had fashioned a sheath for it and wore it buckled onto my side.

The guard reappeared on the sidewalk in front of me and stood clapping his hands together and stamping his feet to make a pattern in the snow. I was sure he could hear my heart pounding. Then he was gone again and I had lost my opportunity. I could have wept in relief and frustration. Ten minutes passed and he reappeared in front of me. He lit a cigarette and moved back and forth over the pattern he had tramped in the snow.

All right, this is it, I thought, horrified at myself. Then, with even more horror, I realized, *I don't know how to do it.* Obviously I had to stab him through the heart, but I could not let him call out. I'd have to put my hand over his mouth and stab him in the heart at the same time. Since I am right-handed, this meant coming at him from the rear, putting my left hand over his mouth and stabbing him with my right hand. But would I hit his heart on his left side if I stabbed him from the right? I might only wound him and he could still call out. I could use my knife in my left, but I knew that would be too clumsy. Finally, I decided to put my left hand over his mouth and draw the knife across his throat with my right hand.

By now the guard had gone back and forth several more times and the others, unable to share my horrible dilemma, must have wondered what was happening. At last I heard the guard's footsteps crunching once again toward me and knew that this time I would have to try. He stopped on his usual spot and fumbled for his cigarettes. Then, contrary to his usual habit, he walked right over to the building and lent his back against a narrow pillar, the remains of the partition between two windows, no more than three feet from my hiding place. He took out a cigarette. I stepped behind the pillar, clapped my left hand over his mouth, and sliced his throat with the knife in my right hand. He never made a sound, but slid down the wall into a crouching position, his head sunk forward onto his chest.

My ears pounded. I looked stupidly at him, then at my knife. I'd almost severed his head. In my terror and ignorance, I hadn't known how little pressure would be needed. I turned away amid the rubble, vomiting and vomiting into the darkness.

"Heinz!"

Along the sidewalk came the footsteps of the second soldier. Terrified, I pulled myself together and stepped back into the "L," clutching my knife.

"Heinzie!" He walked toward the building cautiously. "What are you doing there?" He laughed a little and reached out a hand to touch his friend. I took two steps and plunged my knife into his back. He moaned and fell across his partner. He didn't move again.

I leaned against the wall, knowing I was going to be sick again. I beckoned Arke and Benjamin to come, and sat down and cried. Cautiously they approached, saw the Germans, and continued walking across the street to disappear into the gentile side of Grodno. Five minutes later, the two girls emerged from the building and vanished into the city.

"Are you hurt, Leibke?" my father asked, coming up and seeing me doubled over, sobbing.

"No, Father," I lied. I wasn't bleeding from wounds the world could see. But I had just killed two men and I hadn't even seen their faces! I didn't know if they were good men or bad men or whether they had deserved to die. But I had taken their lives.

Father took my arm and together we left the ghetto. In minutes, we were back in a normal world. It was only 7:30 in the evening and Christmas was just over. The shop windows were still dressed for the season even though merchandise was in short supply. People walked casually in the streets, decently dressed and obviously decently fed. They called out to each other and laughed out loud.

Suddenly it occurred to me that perhaps we looked different to the other people on the street, and a terrible fear overtook me. If we were turned in, they would know I had killed the guards. What horrible punishment would the Germans demand for that crime? I wanted to run but I knew it would mean certain capture. I walked on, trying to reassure myself that the darkness of the night would hide us. Then a few minutes later the temptation to run nearly overwhelmed us again when we lost sight of the girls ahead of us because neither of us knew our way out of the city. We sighed with relief when we spotted Freidke again far ahead. The way out of the city seemed endless. As I walked, I thought about the Germans I had killed. Somehow my feelings changed as we left the ghetto behind. I gradually became aware of a tremendous elation; I had killed two men who stood in the way of our freedom. It was because of me that we'd made our escape! Then suddenly we were beyond the city limits, where Arke and Benjamin waited for us beside an old shed.

CHAPTER SIX

To the Forest: January–July 1943

We had over twenty-five miles to walk that night before reaching the home of a widowed friend of Arke's who would hide us. Whenever possible, we would walk on the road but when we heard anything coming we headed for the deep snow beside it. Although we were soon rigid with fatigue and cold, I knew we had to keep going. Then my sister began to cry and sat down in the snow.

"Get up," I hissed at her.

"I can't. Just leave me here." Exhausted, she sat in the snow and sobbed.

Benjamin and I pulled her to her feet and supported her between us to keep her walking. She had come on this terrible race with death wearing a pair of high-heeled rubber overshoes with no shoes inside them. The empty heels made walking nearly impossible; her feet were like ice inside the thin rubber.

Toward morning, my brother dropped in the snow, clutching his abdomen. Having seen this happen before at Lebedniki, I knew that it was another stomach attack, perhaps appendicitis, but this time there was no help available. I grabbed one of his arms and Father took his other one. "Walk," I said, and we propelled him along, though the pain must have been excruciating. Death was too close at hand to allow Benjamin's pain to delay us. "So you're sick," I said to him. "That's too bad. But we don't have time for it now. You'll get us killed if you don't get moving."

He dragged himself along, trying not to moan out loud. The night stretched on like a nightmare. I lost track of time and moved like an automaton, aware only that I must keep putting one foot before the other. Just before daybreak we saw the widow's home ahead. She welcomed us, clucking over our frozen hands and feet and poor Freidke's tear-stained face. She thawed out our frozen clothes on the oven, and then she made an herbal brew for Benjamin, and fussed over my poor sister until Freidke felt loved again. All that day she hid us in her kitchen; in the evening we had to leave.

We moved on past the village of Druskieniki to the farm of two bachelor brothers in the countryside beyond. We waited while Arke and his sister bargained with them. We could see that these men were very interested in Arke's sister, as she was a very beautiful girl.

"It's no use," Arke came back to tell us. "They'll look after my sister but the rest of us will have to move on."

Disappointed, we went out into the night. Arke led the way, for he knew another place, he said, that might take us in. The moon had disappeared behind clouds and we stumbled along after him on the twisted pathway. Then Freidke tripped over something, Father turned back out of concern for her, and the procession ground to a halt.

"Come on, Freidke." Benjamin helped her to her feet as she whimpered.

"Oh, I wish I'd stayed with Mother," she sobbed.

"Hurry up!" I whispered. "Arke's way ahead of us!" I ran ahead with Father.

"Arke! Arke!" Afraid to call out loud, my father was half whispering, half shouting. We stood in silence, listening.

"Arke!"

But we were calling out to the empty night. Arke had led us here just to be rid of us. We had no idea which way to go and the temperature had dropped far below zero. We plodded on, hoping we were heading northward, and I thought of Arke sitting in comfort in the bachelors' farmhouse and vowed I'd repay him for what he'd done to us.

After a time we realized we were only walking in circles, and Father decided to ask directions at the next farmhouse. It was terribly risky but fortunately it was another poor widow who felt pity for us who opened the door. Before leaving Grodno, a man who had shared our sleeping quarters had given Father a thousand marks, and so we were able to pay the widow for her kindness. We spent the day sleeping in the piggery; it wasn't deluxe accommodation but we'd slept in far worse places.

The widow carefully explained how to get to Linitsa. This was a village we had passed through on our way from the forest to Marcinkonys and Father hoped to find refuge for us there. Of course we could not travel through Marcinkonys to reach there because of the Germans, so we had to take a very circuitous route. This was the most difficult part of the journey. I walked in front now, making a path for the others to follow through the woods and across the fields. A freezing wind hit our faces and whipped the frozen snow into our eyes. Near collapse, my sister trudged behind me, sobbing pitifully. My father was not much happier. The events of the past year had so undermined his health that he had no stamina for this added hardship. Each step seemed as if it would be his last. Benjamin stumbled along at the end of our little procession, nearly out of touch with reality.

As the first touch of daylight began to lighten the sky, we were still more than a mile from Linitsa. We could not complete the journey in the daylight and there was nowhere to hide till night came again. Father decided that we should risk walking on the road. If anyone had been out that early we would have been caught, for there was no cover anywhere along that stretch of road. We had to take the chance. Besides, we had simply reached the end of our endurance. We set out along the road with an almost fatalistic attitude.

At sunrise that morning a farmer on the outskirts of Linitsa opened his door to find the four of us frozen and desperate, scarcely able to stand. For a moment or two he stared, unable to comprehend what we were doing there. In turn, we just stood staring back at him stupidly, having used our last ounce of strength to get there.

"Shael!" he cried at last, recognizing my father. "Oh, my dear man, what has happened to you?" He bundled us into the house. While he and his wife fed us and dried our clothes, the farmer continued to weep unashamedly, for he thought we had been murdered long ago. At last, as exhaustion prevented further talk, he sent us to sleep on top of the bake oven.

This oven was typical of those found in farmhouses throughout central Europe. Intended to cook the meals, bake the bread and warm a one-room house, they were generally big enough to allow six or seven people to sleep on top. Construction was quite simple with blocks of wood or piles of bricks arranged as short, sturdy legs for the brick oven to rest on. The front of the oven continued to the roof to form a chimney; behind this, the upper surface of the oven formed a flat table which, when covered in pallets, was an excellent winter sleeping place — as long as the day's fires had burned low. And down on the floor, the family chickens basked in the heat as they crouched between the oven's legs. The four of us climbed onto the farmer's oven and even before he had pulled the curtain, which enclosed our sleeping area, we were sound asleep. I remember thinking as I fell asleep that nothing, not even food, felt as good as heat.

I woke to hear unfamiliar voices beyond the curtain. Only three or four hours had passed since we arrived but I was rested enough to be instantly awake to danger. Beside me, Father's eyes opened and his gaze met mine. We listened in silence. It was a neighbour who had come to pay a New Year's visit. We relaxed and lay back to wait for him to go. At the end of an hour he finished his visit, and we climbed down from our overheated perch. We discussed with the farmer the possibilities of hiding in the barn but had to give up the idea as the temperature was dropping steadily. Suddenly there was a knock on the door. Hearts beating in fear, we climbed back on the oven and pulled the curtain. It was another New Year's visit. In the meantime, the farmer's wife began the day's baking, stoking up the fires. And so the day went — with the four of us hopping from the griddle in the brief respites between visitors. In the evening the real trial came, for a group of friends arrived to gossip and drink with the farmer. For four hours we lay there unable to decide whether being cooked alive by this friendly farmer was worse than some punishment dreamed up by our enemies.

At last, in the middle of the night, we were able to leave the farmhouse to go to Yureli, south of Eisiskes. My father hoped that a farmer there by the name of Danielewicz might take us in. He and his family were the only Lithuanians in a Polish district and consequently they were hated and ostracized. About four years earlier, Danielewicz's son had fallen in love with the daughter of a Polish landowner, a man who was considered to be a member of the aristocracy. The Pole refused to allow the marriage, but the young people, meeting secretly, were determined to marry. The young man told my parents his problem and asked help in finding a church which would post the banns secretly. Father found a church that would do this in a village on the road to Vilnius, and he paid for their six-week stay in a small inn nearby while they waited to be married. The Pole came to threaten Father, having guessed that he was involved with the lovers, but Father professed ignorance and the young couple was married. In his gratitude, Danielewicz vowed to help Father whenever the need arose. Now we trudged through the freezing night, planning to stay with Danielewicz until spring when we could return to the forest.

Father led the way as we were now in country familiar to him, but for some strange reason he seemed confused. We stood at a fork in the road while he debated which way to go.

"What's wrong with you?" Benjamin asked.

"Father, you've gone over this road so many times, you should be able to do it blindfolded," I shrilled at him.

"Sure I did! But it was summer then," he answered.

Every time he made a wrong turn, we scolded. Fear and fatigue and frustration confused him and made us harass him as we traced and retraced our steps in the freezing night, complaining and quarrelling until we arrived at the farm. Danielewicz was not happy to see us. He lost no time in explaining that since German inspectors were coming in the morning to count his livestock, we could not hide in the house or the barn. Just before daylight he led us to a small wooded plot on his property. Leaving us extra clothing and some food, he returned to the house. He promised to come for us as soon as the inspector left.

For more than twelve hours we paced in our little corner to keep warm. We jumped up and down and pounded our hands together. We rubbed each other's cheeks and ears with snow as we saw signs of frostbite coming. And all the time we looked in vain for Danielewicz. When darkness came, so did Danielewicz. By this time Father realized that it would be too dangerous to stay for long and announced that we would soon need to be moving on. The farmer insisted we stay the night and the next day, but he was definitely relieved that we would not be his responsibility for long.

The following night we moved on to the farm of another acquaintance named Rukowicz. He gave us a warm welcome but seemed somehow uneasy. We were poised ready to flee when the reason for his uneasiness became evident: he was sheltering another Jewish family — Sholem Levo, his wife, two sons and a niece. Nevertheless, Rukowicz invited us to share the Levo family's quarters, an unfinished wing of the house. Father gave him money, promising to pay him more as soon as we were able. The Levos, however, were not enthusiastic about our coming to join them. Sholem Levo explained that there was not enough food for two families and that the chance of being found by the Germans was that much greater with so many extra people at the farm. He asked Father to look for some other place to hide. Father refused. He told Levo that as long as Rukowicz would have us, we intended to stay, for the farm was safer than any other place we had been.

Father had an additional reason for being determined to stay. Sholem Levo's brother, Isaac, was a partisan in the Nacha forest. Sholem had told us when we arrived that Isaac was due to visit the farm in the spring and Father had decided that he could guide us back to the forest group when he returned there.

We could not enter the forest in the winter because we could die wandering in the deep snow before we found camp, and because our tracks in the snow would endanger the whole settlement. The forest groups were completely isolated at this time of year; none of them ventured out unless it was snowing enough to cover footprints. They were, therefore, almost entirely safe even though they lived an extremely primitive existence. Large pit houses were prepared late in the autumn by digging out an area twenty feet by fifty feet by four feet deep. The walls were lined with upright posts and the floor covered with boards split from logs. It was roofed over with rafters of peeled poles, a thick layer of pine branches, overlapping tarpaulins, and two feet of earth. The final layer consisted of autumn leaves, which fell to camouflage the whole job as soon as it was completed. Fallen trees and branches masked the two entrances of this pit house. Inside it, potatoes, onions and cereals were stored. Bread and meat were left in caches outside to remain frozen until they were needed. Snow was melted for a water supply. Cooking was done on a primitive version of the farmhouse bake oven, and this same unit heated the living quarters.

There was little privacy for the groups of families living in these pit houses but in all other ways life was normal. Romances flourished between the young, people made love, and babies were born. There was little serious illness. These underground families were decently fed and remarkably secure for Jews in the midst of German-occupied land.

Throughout the early months of 1943 we hid in Rukowicz's house by day and emerged to help with chores each evening. Anytime we weren't busy with chores we returned to our attack on the lice, which had clung stubbornly to us throughout the worst days of our travels. Freidke's hair was so infested by now that Father had to cut it all off and scrub her scalp with kerosene. At last she found some relief from the terrible itching but her new haircut certainly did nothing for her morale. The suffering those little beasts caused us was unbelievable. We found we could identify five different kinds by the number of legs on them, and four more by their colour. It's a wonder we weren't fainting from loss of blood the way they feasted on us. We dunked them in kerosene, squashed them with our fingers, stamped on them and mashed them into the walls, but still they marched over us. What we needed most of all was a big tub of hot water and a bar of strong soap. Since these were unheard of luxuries on Rukowicz's farm, we continued on with our losing battle.

Toward the end of March as the snow began to melt, Father made a trip to Babkin's farm again to arrange to buy guns. He came back with one, but a second rifle would not be available for several weeks. In the first week of April, Isaac Levo arrived to visit his brother and agreed to lead our family back to the forest. Sholem Levo, who was waiting for some more rifles to be delivered, was not yet ready to go. Isaac promised to come back for him in two weeks. One of Sholem's sons decided to go with us, but the rest of the family stayed with Rukowicz. Benjamin decided he would wait for Babkin to deliver our second rifle and then come to the forest with the Levos. I was pleased that he had volunteered, as I was very anxious to get back to the partisans. Spring was beginning to come to the forest when we returned, and we found it wonderful to be out in the fresh air and daylight again. I went directly to the Leninski Komsomol and re-joined, happy once again to be learning the techniques of guerrilla fighting. Father and Freidke moved into the family settlement to prepare a home while they waited for Benjamin.

In the third week of April, Isaac Levo left the forest again to bring the others back. He returned alone. My brother Benjamin and Sholem Levo's entire family were dead. Murdered. Sholem had quarrelled with Rukowicz a few days after we left, and the Levos had gone to Danielewicz's farm to wait for the rifles and for Isaac. Soon after, Babkin had delivered the guns.

"It was the Lithuanians." Isaac's voice was hoarse. He still couldn't believe it had happened. "Sholem and the boys fought back but they hadn't enough ammunition. The Lithuanians slaughtered them like pigs!" He sat down on the wet ground and sobbed.

My father was inconsolable. He blamed himself for allowing Benjamin to stay, even though my brother had made his own decision. He wept and wouldn't eat or sleep. He could not believe that after all we had been through together one of us had been killed. And neither could I. Just as I had done before when the pain and horror became unbearable, I refused to accept it. It's a ridiculous lie, I told myself. Benjamin's alive! He's in hiding, but he'll be back. It would be many weeks before I could accept his death.

During this time when I refused to accept reality, an argument raged among the other survivors. No one could be sure who had betrayed the group but everyone had a favourite candidate. Was it Rukowicz? Had he been so angry with Levo that he had informed on him? Or had Danielewicz become tired of them? Abraham Widlanski, whose sister was Sholem's wife, was convinced that Danielewicz was the guilty one. Or had someone casually passing the farm caught a glimpse of them or heard an unfamiliar voice in the barn and rushed to report them? There was no way to learn the truth until more was known, but everyone vowed to avenge the murders in time.

In May I met two young fellows from Szczuczin, one of whom was called Joshke Staniecki. They occasionally went back to the town to take messages or guide people to the forest. I asked them to take a message to my mother and grandmother, pleading with them to join us. I offered to give the boys the old rifle if they returned with a letter from Mother, and the new rifle if they brought my mother and grandmother to the forest with them. As the rifles were important to our lives, this was quite a sacrifice, but we needed Mother with us now more than ever before.

A week later the boys came to claim the old rifle. My mother's letter explained again that she could not join us because her mother was simply too old to survive in the forest. Life in the ghetto was not too difficult, she said, and food was in reasonable supply. They still felt comparatively safe. She ended her letter on a hopeful note. "The same God is over us all. If I am meant to survive, I will survive here as well as in the forest." In the months that followed, I always carried her letter with me, the only tangible memento I had left of my mother. In time the writing grew dim and the paper wore out, but the faint words served as my talisman.

The partisans that I returned to were much better organized and equipped, the members much more skilled than they had been the previous year. In Russia, experts in sabotage, guerrilla warfare, and radio communication had been specially trained to work with partisan groups like ours. By the end of 1942, thousands of these experts had been parachuted into the forest areas behind the German lines to mobilize the partisans into more efficient fighting units. The real importance of the partisans to the Russians was shown when a special ministry was created to deal with supplying and coordinating the partisans' campaigns. A number of Russian experts now trained the Leninski Komsomol, which included exiles from Siberia and many Russian soldiers who had been left behind at the time of the retreat. A few airmen who had been shot down behind the German lines and some Russians who had escaped German POW camps completed the Russian contingent of the partisans.

Local residents also joined us. As the war dragged on, the German regime in Poland had become more brutal, and treatment that had once been bearable became absolutely intolerable. The young men of the towns and villages began disappearing into the forest as the German scaffolds in the market squares became permanent fixtures and gunfire from execution squads became daily events. Men were also "encouraged" to join by the leaflets circulated by the partisans, reminding them who the eventual victors would be, and what would happen to people who collaborated with the Germans. Communists, who had gone underground when the Germans invaded, gradually found their way to the forest fighters. Many of them were members of the Communist Youth Party who had a long history of persecution and imprisonment for their cause.

One of the largest groups in the partisans was that of the Jews. Our people, of course, had only two recourses open to them — fight or die — and thousands of us chose to fight. We could not stay within regular society to fight the Germans with sabotage, as many non-Jews could do, so our fighting had to be done with the partisans. There we proved repeatedly that we were a match for any other fighting men.

Before they understood the size and strength of the partisan movement, the Germans had tried to use the local police and the gendarmerie to fight them. But the arsenal of the partisans had become far superior to that of the police. In addition, they had the advantage of fighting on their home ground. They knew their forest territory in intimate detail and could vanish with ease, their camps appearing and disappearing like dew on the grass. Trained in guerrilla tactics that neither police nor ordinary soldiers could match, they relied as well on a spy network that stretched across the farmlands and into the towns, a network that provided them with information on what the Germans would be doing next. In desperation the Germans tried to clean out "Stalin's Bandits," as they called us by attacking with troops en route to the Russian front. Our informers, however, always sent word in advance of these attacks, giving us time to retreat into the forest until the troops gave up. Assigning regular troops to fight against guerrilla forces was of course ridiculous, for they were burdened by heavy equipment and could not manoeuvre in the forest as we could. Finally the frustrated Germans attacked the farmers who lived at the edge of the forest, accusing them of being partisans in disguise or informers for the partisans. The Germans then claimed the murder of these innocent Polish farmers as a tremendous victory over the partisans.

From what we could see, there was one group of partisans who sometimes fought on the side of the Germans. They were Polish farmers by day and partisans by night, and they carried out the orders of the exiled Polish government living in London. We understood that these orders specifically stated that, in addition to ridding themselves of their German conquerors, all Poles were to see to it that no Jews remained in Poland after the war. Their slogan was *Polska Bez Zydow* or "Poland without Jews." These were the men of the Armia Krajowa or "Home Army," known to us as the AK. It seemed to us that the AK had a special status with the Germans because they carried on the work of exterminating the Jews and Communists. From 1942 to 1944 they concentrated on seeking out the hiding places of the Jews and the Communists and butchering those who had successfully hidden from the Germans.

Of approximately one thousand Jews who escaped from Eisiskes, only forty-two remained alive at the end of the war. Most of these murders stemmed from centuries of hatred nurtured by the Catholic Church and the Polish educational system. Despite what may have been heard concerning stories of help from the Catholic Church toward fugitive Jews, evidence points strongly to the fact that these were only isolated incidents. Basically, the Catholic Church was always anti-Semitic. Even before the war it turned a deaf ear and a blind eye to the pogroms, persecution and violence against Jews, common occurrences in the small towns of Eastern Europe. Even worse, the church sanctioned such treatment as just punishment for the "Christ Killers." Its influence on the illiterate, ignorant lower class was incredible. This group was composed of "church-goers" who from infancy had been nursed on anti-Jewish doctrine from the pulpit.

The local Catholic clergy was quite aware of the horrors which were being perpetrated by their parishioners against their Jewish neighbours on a daily basis. Yet, as far as we could see, not a single one of them raised a voice in protest against the destruction. Just a word from Rome could have saved thousands, but the Vatican, always in close touch with its deputies, never used its authority to stop the carnage. The silence of Rome was interpreted as tacit approval.

Even after the war there were incidents where the clergy could have protested. As an example, there was the incident at Kielce, a small town in central Poland, which occurred in 1946 after armistice had been declared. As a small remnant of returned Jews sat down to celebrate their first Passover after years of horror in concentration camps, they were descended upon by a group of Poles in the same town who systematically murdered them almost to a man. The Catholic Church ignored the killings as though they had never happened.

As for the schools, the educators deliberately taught the lower middle class youths of Poland to hate Jews. I can remember being forced to listen while my classmates in Polish school sang of the Jews who murdered Christ, and I recall the children who cornered me in the schoolyard chanting slogans in my face. "Christ killer! Christ killer!" The German occupation simply allowed the Poles who had carried these convictions to adulthood to kill without penalty the people they feared and hated.

As partisans we had to be constantly on guard when members of the AK were operating in our area. In contrast, most of the family communities, which had now existed for more than a year, were living in a relaxed manner. They felt secure and were oblivious to the dangers still waiting at the edge of the forest. It was almost as if the outside world had ceased to exist for them. My father worried about this constantly. He condemned them for their lack of vigilance and their failure to set up advance reconnaissance units. He felt that they could not rely solely on the contacts in the villages for notice of attack. He pointed out that anyone conducting a search near the swamp could easily find the clues to our daily lives. "We must be more careful," he warned. "Sooner or later, they'll find us and we'll all be butchered." His premonition proved to be correct.

On the morning of June 14, 1943, I was helping my father and sister prepare breakfast after spending the night with them. My sister stood with a pot in her hand waiting for Father to start the fire. All around us, small breakfast fires were readied and sleepy voices greeted each other. Then ZOOM! A group of planes swooped low over the forest, skimming the trees above our hiding place. Moments later, even before the roar of the engines began to fade, bombs exploded in the forest just beyond us. Desperately we smothered our campfires and looked for bushes that might hide us from the planes overhead. Crouched in our hiding places, we waited for an hour but the planes did not come back. As the bombing had been done at random, we emerged somewhat reassured to find that the Leninski Komsomol had already retreated, leaving the family groups alone.

"The Germans know we're here all right, but they can't pinpoint us. Why don't they come back?" we asked.

The answer was apparent a few hours later. The bombs had been intended only to flush us out to where a combined force of German and White Russian soldiers, Polish and Lithuanian police awaited us. When we didn't come running from the forest, they moved in to get us. As Father had predicted, our contacts in the village had failed us. We were at the mercy of our enemies now. As the enemy approached, we ran deeper into the forest until we came to a thicket of brush and young trees. About twenty of us lay there in silence, flat on our stomachs and praying we could outlast them. Between us there were only six guns, but even firing a single shot would have drawn the fire of ten times as many. It would be sheer suicide to try.

I lay almost paralyzed with fear. My breathing and the pounding of my heart seemed to echo from tree to tree, filling the forest until I thought it impossible that the soldiers couldn't hear me. For a long time it was so quiet that we might have been the only ones in our part of the forest. As the morning warmed we watched through a curtain of leaves as a group of soldiers came into view on our left and slowly advanced across the ground in front of us. Crawling between the trees, then lying on their bellies to fire their machine guns extended before them, they systematically sprayed the area with death, and the force of the bullets raised a cloud of soft earth in front of us. After each burst they waited for results, while our little group lay frozen in terror. I watched several soldiers crawl within fifty feet of us. Mentally I aimed my rifle and picked them off with ease, but I never moved a muscle.

Eventually they disappeared from view and only the periodic bursts of machine-gun fire indicated their direction. The day wore on endlessly until at last I became conscious of thirst and of the roots and fallen branches that were digging into my body, conscious of the fear that had blotted out everything else for almost an entire day. When the sun left the forest and the day began to darken, the enemy, fearing ambush in the dark, retreated. Cramped, hungry and thirsty, our little group emerged to confer in the last light of day. We felt sure that they would come back. We didn't know how many of our people had been caught, but we were sure the Germans had a fair idea how many of us were in the forest. We knew they'd return again and again until they finished us off. Father insisted we find a new hiding place. "All right," I agreed. "But no more ghettos!"

Just south of the village of Yureli, about nine miles northwest of us, was another forest, much smaller than this one, but young and incredibly dense with plenty of underbrush where it adjoined the fields. We agreed to move there. During the night I guided the group out of the Nacha forest as I had learned to do with the partisans. Skirting the village of Nacha, we entered our new forest just before dawn. For the next week we worked at preparing living accommodations for ourselves, and setting up lookout posts.

A few days after our arrival, I ventured out to buy food from several farms where I could count on a good reception. I learned from them that the partisans, realizing the stupidity of counterattack, had wisely retreated from the Nacha forest to set up again in the *Ruska Puszcza* or Russian Jungle about twenty miles to the southwest. The family groups, however, had suffered badly. The family group that had come from Grodno had returned to the island that night, thinking that the crisis was past, but they were wrong. The next day the Germans had pounced again, hunting down sixty of them and murdering them on the spot. Then at night when the soldiers had retreated, the farmers of the nearby Lithuanian village of Podemby had stalked the survivors, killing them as they hid in the underbrush near the edge of the forest or as they tried to flee across the rye fields.

The villagers of Podemby were not unique in collaborating with the Nazis in the destruction of Jews in the forest. Another village called Mostaika was responsible for the murder of hundreds of Jews from Marcinkonys who had escaped to the forest when the Germans began deporting them to death camps. In 1944, shortly before liberation by the Russians, four partisan groups including my own went into Mostaika and "selected" those villagers who were known killers of Jews. They were ordered to kneel and listen to a speech listing their crimes, which was prepared by a partisan who had originally come from Marcinkonys. The collaborators were then shot to death in the village square.

A week after our escape, a few of us returned to the Nacha forest to look for survivors. Cautiously we moved into the trees, then crouched to wait in case we were heading into an ambush. The forest was absolutely silent. Closer to the campground we stumbled over a body, and soon after, another one. Everywhere on the forest floor bodies were strewn. Most were naked. Many were mutilated. We dug a common grave using bayonets and several small spades we had brought with us. As we finished I realized that the emotion welling up in me was a terrible anger. As I buried each one it felt like I was burying my poor brother Benjamin.

The grim task completed, we searched further into the forest in case any of Paisha's family had survived. We found a few small groups who were determined to set up a new camp deeper in the forest, and they invited us to join them. I relayed this news to Father but he refused to leave the Yureli forest. He and my sister and eight other Eisiskes Jews, seven men and one woman, decided to stay where they were.

Surrounding their forest hideout were hundreds of acres of rye that often grew as high as eight feet tall, providing extra protection as the summer advanced. We had become extremely adept the previous year at hiding in the fields and had taught ourselves to walk between the stalks without disturbing them. This trick would probably be possible in modern machine-planted fields, but these fields were planted by hand in the old-fashioned way, so the stalks were placed irregularly.

We sent out food-gathering groups each evening to beg in the neighbouring villages where most of the people felt kindly toward us. One of the villages in this area was Powielancy whose people had filled our cart with food when Father and I had come from the Radun ghetto. They helped us again most willingly, for they sympathized with our plight. Before long I became restless in the small group; I needed to be actively fighting the enemy. I knew that most of the men from the Leninski Komsomol had gone to the Russian Jungle after the attack in the Nacha forest, but the Jewish partisans were being sent to the vast Lipichanska forest far to the south. This was because it was becoming difficult for the large groups to find sufficient food in the surrounding country, and because the partisan groups were continually plagued with internal conflicts based on anti-Semitism. I was reluctant to leave the Yureli forest as more than seventy-five miles would separate me from my family, but my father kept insisting that I go. Still I delayed from day to day.

Then one day our sentry alerted us that a stranger had come into the forest. His manner made it obvious that he was searching for us. From a secret vantage point I saw that it was an old friend, Lippa Skolsky, who was in the Yureli district on a train-destruction assignment. Skolsky was a cautious forty-five-year-old bachelor from

Varena who had been a member of an elite Polish cavalry unit until the invasion. He still wore his polished boots and spurs and endlessly parted and combed his hair, even in the primitive world of the forest. The farmer who was our local contact had directed Skolsky to the area where we found him. When I came out into the open he told me that he was now the quartermaster of the Otriad of Special Assignments, under the command of a man named Davidov. He invited me to join their company in the Lipichanska forest.

Even with this invitation, I might have still hesitated except for the terrible news that came to us now from a local farmer. It was what we had always feared would happen. The Jews at Szczuczin had been transported for "resettlement" to Treblinka. We tried to hope for the best but there was nothing in this news to encourage us. Thousands of Jews had been sent to Treblinka but no further messages had ever been received from them. I couldn't bear to look at my father. He had become an old man, almost resigned to losing us one by one. He wept inconsolably for days.

"Go with the partisans, Leibke," he told me. "You must fight for all of us now."

I knew this was true but I was reluctant to leave him when he looked so beaten.

"Do it for your mother, Leibke," he said.

I left the next night with two friends. For a week we walked south through rough country, some of it too hilly to be farmed. In the daytime we hid in patches of forest or in the fields, and we slept or just sat there thinking. Then my mind would search through all the horrors we had been through, trying to decide what we could have done differently. If only we had made Benjamin come with us . . . If only we had convinced Mother to come. If only we had gone straight to the forest from Eisiskes. But in the end, I always came back to the same thing: if Mother had come with us we would have known how to make the right decisions. I'd close my eyes and imagine myself as a child again, standing beside my mother in our kitchen in Eisiskes. I could see her examining the chicken that my sister and I had laboriously plucked in preparation for the Sabbath's chicken soup. Then, if she was satisfied with our work, we could sit nearby and watch while she made the soup and my grandmother made the twisted egg loaf or challah. Sometimes, when she could afford the sugar, Mother would bake a delicious light sponge cake or make compote of dried fruits simmered in sweet lemon syrup. She was so efficient that even in the years when we were very poor she managed to provide us with a splendid Sabbath meal. I would remember the tablecloth sparkling white, the flickering candles in their gleaming brass candlesticks, the scrubbed faces of my brother and sister, and my father's Sabbath dignity. But mostly I remember the candlelight on my mother's serene face as she placed the food before us.

She and her sister were the best-educated women in Eisiskes, for they had been the only children of a very wealthy man. The two had been born to his second wife when he was very old. He treated them like princesses, providing them with everything they wanted, even with tutors who taught French, German and Hebrew. My aunt had married a wealthy man but my mother had married my handsome father who had shown such "promise." Unfortunately, Father's promise was swallowed up in one bad business venture. But Mother was no complainer. She had set to work by his side as if she had always done these chores. She had been my father's strength; she had given him the courage to carry on.

And she had been my strength, too.

▲ Leon Kahn in Lodz, Poland, August 1945.

◀ Leon Kahn and several Russian friends, 1944.

Standing: Chaim (Pietka) Berkowicz. Seated left to right: Sophia Vivat, Russian-Jewish doctor; Leon Kahn. ▶

▲ Group of partisans after Liberation, 1945. Standing left to right:
Chaim Berkowicz, Benjamin Rogowski, Leon Kahn.
Seated: Yitzhak Sonenson.

◀ Dr. Sophia Vivat and Leon Kahn, while attending Russian military school 1944/45 in Vilnius.

Benjamin Rogowski and Leon Kahn on Leon's second visit to Lodz, 1946, to bring the Rogowski family to Austria. ▶

▲ Leon Kahn in Salzburg, Austria, August 6, 1946.

▲ A group of refugees, Parsch Displaced Persons Camp, Salzburg, Austria 1947. Leon is kneeling in the far right. The Parsch camp, a former German barracks, was located on the Salzburg River. The Von Trapp family home could be seen across the river. (Courtesy: Rita and Ben Akselrod)

▲ Leon (top left) with Ben Akselrod (top right) and Alter and Malka Rubin, at the Parsch Displaced Persons Camp, Salzburg, Austria, 1947–1948. (Courtesy: Rita and Ben Akselrod)

▲ Leon and his cousin Mort Rothstein, at Prospect Point, Vancouver, shortly after Leon's arrival in 1948. The Lions Gate Bridge is in the background. (Courtesy: Rita and Ben Akselrod)

CHAPTER SEVEN

Partisan: July–October 1943

By following Lippa Skolsky's instructions carefully we located the Davidov partisans in the Lipichanska forest and were accepted as members. There were now ten Jews in the ranks and, although he never acknowledged it, Davidov gave many signs that he was also a Jew. Several times he reminded us to speak Russian rather than Yiddish so that the non-Jews would not think we were plotting against them, and he always reprimanded partisans who discriminated against the Jews in the company.

Davidov's Otriad of Special Assignments was made up of units called "zwods" of about twenty-five men. Three zwods combined to form a "rota." Three of these rotas formed Davidov's Otriad, although some otriads combined as many as eight rotas. When a really big operation was under way, two or three otriads worked together as a brigade, a small army of dedicated and skilled fighting men. Most of the time the groups operated independently, maximizing their destructive impact by their ability to move undetected from place to place. Within the forest, the otriad's safety was maintained by lookouts and foot patrols. Approach was denied to anyone who did not have the password, and the chances of an unknown person re-emerging from the forest were very slight. All partisans learned to take scrupulous care to erase their own tracks, using branches to sweep away footsteps and covering excrement with moss. Nothing could be left to chance, for carelessness could mean the annihilation of the whole group. On the perimeter of the forest a reconnaissance group patrolled on horseback, stopping to talk to villagers and farmers who served as contact men.

These contacts were in constant peril of discovery by the Germans because of the number of partisans who arrived and departed from their homes under cover of night. Every person who contacted the partisans had to be treated with caution, as he might be a part of a German plot. In return for their services, our contacts were at first paid with the valuables that we had brought to the forest, but after we became part of the Russian organization, they were paid with counterfeit German marks, parachuted to the partisans by the bagful. The forgery was so expert that they could be used anywhere without fear of detection.

As soon as I arrived in the forest I began two weeks of training to learn to sabotage trains. I had had a brief experience with this a year earlier but this time, although our equipment was still primitive, the procedure allowed a much greater degree of safety for the saboteurs. The mines we now used weighed about twenty-four pounds and consisted of forty-eight pieces of dynamite (each of them resembling a rather large chocolate bar) wrapped in a big piece of burlap and held tightly together with heavy cord. Our training concentrated on preparing and setting mines quickly and efficiently. We could not, of course, do any trial explosions, as these would have been detected, so we wouldn't know how good we were until we blew up our first train, or got blown up ourselves.

When my training was over, I was assigned to the small mining detail of Michka Dubinsky. I was appointed assistant and four others made up the group. We were given six mines and a specific territory to operate in. Whenever we used up our mines we were to return for more. Our assignment was the stretch of rail line from Marcinkonys to Varena, and our base of operation was to be the forest that ran parallel to the railway just to the east of it. So once more I trekked northward, pleased to be back in the fight, and almost equally pleased to be somewhat nearer my father and sister again.

The railway line was patrolled by local people that the Germans had recruited, and they did their job very conscientiously because whenever trains were derailed or blown up they faced punishment. When these patrolmen could not stop us, the Germans sprayed the crushed rock on the railway bed with white paint. They thought they would be able to spot the place where a mine had been planted by checking for disturbed rocks. We out-manoeuvred them on this one because we learned how to collect the rocks, excavate a hole to bury our mine, carry away the excess dirt in our jackets and replace the rocks one by one, with the white side up. The soil was dumped in the forest and carefully covered in moss. Once the train approached, its weight set off the buried and camouflaged mine.

When the painted rock method proved no setback to us, the Germans began clearing thousands of miles of forest beside the railway track. Although we naturally preferred to have forest cover when approaching the track, we still carried on our work as usual, even where the forest had been cleared. Clearing the right-of-way proved a useless effort on the Germans' part.

At the end of the summer we received a supply of English magnetic mines. They looked like cigar boxes with a pencil-like timing mechanism sticking out of the top. By turning this device the required number of times, we could make the bombs detonate two to ten hours later. Attaching them to trains was simple, as they were almost impossible to separate from a metal surface once placed there. As an experiment, when the first supplies of the magnetic mines arrived, I placed two together and found that I could separate them only by sliding them apart with a great deal of force. At first, we took terrible risks in order to attach them to oil tankers on their way to the Russian front. Since the timing device allowed us to do our damage hundreds of miles closer to the front, the Germans had to give up their old trick of punishing the inhabitants of the area where the explosions occurred. Eventually, we found a Pole named Kozlowski who agreed to help us with this work. Although he worked for the Germans in the Varena railway station, he had been a

Communist party member before the war. His new job gave him access to all the armament trains passing through, so we supplied him with six magnetic mines at a time, and he sent word whenever he was ready for more.

We also made use of the trains for another method of sabotage. We supplied a very deadly, slow-acting poison to a young Polish woman named Josephine who cooked for the German gendarmerie in Varena, and sometimes prepared food for the troop trains. Josephine, who had worked as a domestic for Jewish families before the war, hated the Germans for what they had done. So when a large troop train passed through Varena, she was able to add the poison to their food supplies. Some time later we had a report of the mysterious death of a whole transport of German soldiers near the Russian front.

Our group leader, Michka Dubinsky, was a Radun boy about four years older than I was. Always calm and cool, he seemed to have nerves of steel. While the rest of us fussed impatiently, he would set the mine methodically and precisely, taking a little longer, but always doing the job right. On one occasion we had to approach our target in daylight and, since this was more dangerous than usual, we split into two groups to avoid patrols, with Michka, Cymbal and I setting off together. We carried the twenty-four pound bomb, a machine gun and extra ammunition for the gun. At length we came to a place where we disagreed on the direction to take, and Michka set off alone with the bomb. We agreed to meet at a bridge by a river. Eventually, Cymbal and I came to a field and spotted Michka on the far side of it. Although he didn't see us, we could tell from the path he was taking that he would come face to face with us in a few minutes. Impulsively, I grabbed Cymbal's arm and pulled him behind some bushes. As Michka approached, I shouted in German, "Halt! You cursed Jew!"

Michka spun around and dashed into the bushes and we heard his footsteps pounding off through the scrub forest! "Michka! Michka!" I shouted, "It's just me, Michka." But Michka wasn't stopping for anyone. We chased after him but couldn't catch up. Finally we set off walking toward our target location, hoping to meet him there again. It was evening when we sat down to wait for the others, and I took off my boots to bathe my aching feet in a little river nearby. I'd just lowered my feet into the water when an exhausted Michka burst into the clearing, his clothing torn and muddied.

Cymbal and I burst out laughing.

"What's so funny?" Michka snarled.

"I heard the Germans chased you!" I said, and we laughed again.

"How do you know that?" he asked tensely, and he looked from Cymbal to me.

"Halt, you cursed Jew!" I said, mimicking the command I'd given earlier.

Michka exploded with rage. "Why you stupid little . . . !" He had his rifle loaded, and in a moment it was aimed at me. Cymbal leaped at him and the two of them fell to the ground, Cymbal astride Michka, grabbing for the gun. When Michka had calmed down and I'd admitted to being a stupid fool, Cymbal let Michka up off the ground.

Now, however, we had a larger problem than just Michka's shattered nerves to deal with. In his fright, Michka had dropped the bomb somewhere in the brush. The loss of explosives by a partisan meant the firing squad. This punishment had been introduced so that partisans would not waste explosives on non-essential targets and claim credit for damaging the enemy. Since all explosives had to be carefully accounted for, we had no alternative but to find the missing bomb.

In the morning we set off to locate the spot where I had frightened Michka. Although we searched for hours, with Cymbal and Michka constantly reminding me that I had caused the problem, we were unable to find it. We could not rejoin the other three until we found the bomb because we couldn't carry out our mission without it. We sat down to figure a way out of the dilemma. Evening came and we were no further ahead, although by this time I was full of remorse for what I had done. Then a ridiculous turn of fate saved us. Just after dark, another partisan group moved into our territory, set a mine and blew up a train. It was nothing short of a miracle. Off we set at a great pace to visit our contact man to explain what had happened to us and to persuade him to give us credit for the other group's demolition. Only this would save us from the firing squad. But before we even got our mouths open, he greeted us. "That was terrific. A perfect piece of work. Congratulations!" What could we say except thank you?

Practical jokes, of course, were just about the only entertainment available to us, and we spent a good part of our leisure time dreaming up elaborate ones. Lippa Skolsky was one of our favourite targets because he was more cautious and more easily frightened than anyone else in our group. One day five of us were crossing a swampy area walking single file on fallen logs. Benjamin Rogowski was leading, with Lippa just behind him. Suddenly, the last man in the line shouted, "Germans!" The three of us behind Lippa began pushing as though we were frantic. Lippa, in turn, pushed Benjamin but he refused to budge so Lippa tried to wiggle past him and was knocked into the swamp. He stood there in mud up to his armpits while we laughed. When finally we pulled him out, he was ready to shoot us for ruining his clothes and shiny boots!

Losing explosives was not the only crime punishable by death in the partisans. Dereliction of duty also meant the firing squad. The Botwinick family of Eisiskes was particularly ill-fated. One, the schoolteacher, had died as he tried to escape from Radun. The next had been so badly wounded in a German ambush that his brother had shot him to end his torment. The remaining two continued as partisans with the Leninski Komsomol. Unfortunately, Isaac Botwinick fell asleep while he stood guard on the partisan camp and was discovered. He was reprimanded severely and warned that he would be shot if it happened again. It did. This time Isaac was court-martialled and sentenced to be shot with the entire company watching. Although we realized that we could have been annihilated if the Germans had happened on us, we still recoiled at the severity of Isaac's sentence.

Whenever we were not occupied with disrupting German transportation, we disrupted their communications. This job we learned only by trial and error. First, we scaled the telephone poles and cut the wires, but the German repair crews speedily replaced them.

After that, we cut down the poles, but the Germans would simply stick the shortened poles into the ground again and rewire them. Then we learned to saw each pole into short lengths when we had it down on the ground. We were only equipped with three two-handed crosscut saws, so our work had to be carefully coordinated for the greatest possible speed.

The Germans finally came up with a deadly device that should have stopped this kind of sabotage once and for all. They inserted a trip wire in each pole, attaching it to a buried mine which was detonated when the saw touched the wire. As we always worked in the dark, we couldn't be sure which poles were mined. We resolved this problem by forcing men from nearby villages to cut the poles. By choosing only those who had been hostile to the partisans and to the Jews, we forced the Germans to kill or injure their own sympathizers and collaborators, while we gained extra labourers to help in the fight. The Germans, as a result, soon stopped booby-trapping the telephone poles.

By the summer of 1943 there were at least 100,000 men and women fighting with the partisans in my area. One of the biggest problems was obtaining food for them all. The Germans themselves provided much of it. They had established collection depots at which the farmers were required to deliver their produce for shipment to the eastern front. The depot was guarded by the gendarmerie, who commandeered the nearest house, surrounding it with concrete and steel bunkers and gun emplacements, which overlooked the dairy. The house was connected to the bunkers with underground tunnels so that the guards could be rotated in perfect safety.

Several partisan groups operating together carried out attacks on these depots. First, we cut the communication lines between the depot and the German headquarters in the nearby town. Then we set up ambushes along the roads leading to the depot in the event that the gendarmes had had time to call for help. Next we began a small war on the gendarmes in the bunkers to keep them pinned down while another group raided the depot.

On May Day, my group took part in a raid on one of these depots loaded with butter, cheese and eggs, all packed in chopped straw. We took all we could use and destroyed the remainder. I can remember stomping over trays of eggs, smashing thousands of them till I waded knee-deep in egg yolks. Before leaving, we smashed all the machinery in the depot. On our return to the forest we enjoyed a fantastic May Day feast and celebration.

We had one other source of German supplies. During the Russian occupation the huge estates that had been the property of absentee Polish landowners had been confiscated and converted into collectives. When the Russians retreated, the Germans reinstated the owners so that they could supervise production and provide them with a steady supply of food for the German army. The partisans, who made the estates a prime target, continually interrupted this flow of produce. Farmers known to be German sympathizers were also raided, and sometimes the contents of delivery carts were confiscated while farmers were taking eggs and cheese to the supply depots to fulfill their quotas. In the later stage of the war, in places where the partisans had virtually occupied some farm territories, the farmers turned over their quotas to them in exchange for their protection. In some cases, partisans or family groups even provided the farm labour in exchange for a share of the produce.

Often we were ordered to set up ambushes when important groups of Germans were passing through. For these attacks, we chose positions on higher ground overlooking the road and waited for the reconnaissance group to pass. As soon as our victims reached the designated point we opened fire with our Russian machine guns and lobbed grenades onto the Germans below. This was usually effective in destroying the enemy, depending, of course, on the size of the force and the element of surprise. Units such as ours only took on small groups. But whenever our contacts could give us time to prepare, we teamed up with several other groups to take on larger convoys of Germans. It was very depressing to have to let a large group pass just because we had not had time to link up with reinforcements. We also set fire to public buildings, especially those used by the Germans. This was fairly easy as it simply meant entering a town by night while the people slept and the German patrols were less numerous.

Another type of assignment was destroying or capturing the enemy's arms and ammunition. Our group was sent to destroy an arms repair shop in a village outside Varena in August of 1943. The owner, a violently anti-Semitic man, supplied and repaired arms for the Lithuanians. He was alone in the shop when we arrived and we watched through a window from a distance as he worked. We could not enter through the only door because he was surrounded by an arsenal and could defend himself too easily. When he left for his evening meal I crawled through an attic window and opened the trap door that led to the room below. When he returned, I dropped on him and the others burst through the door. We confiscated all the arms and shot the man.

As a result of these events, I felt a new sense of direction. I now had a purpose again, a means of fighting the enemy that really counted. The partisans were a vital factor in destroying the Nazi machine, and I was one of the tools of destruction. It was not an easy life because we were never far from danger, and I knew such unrelenting fear that it made my old fears insignificant. But at last I was fully and completely alive, doing a job that had to be done. I still had the same fear of being captured and tortured to death by the enemy, but now I carried my own weapon of self-destruction: an anti-tank grenade. Each of us was issued a grenade or a gun to use to destroy ourselves in the event of capture. Partisans caught by the Germans or Lithuanians were not allowed to die easily. Some had limbs cut off one at a time; others were blinded and beaten to death. Two young female partisans were sent back to the forest, blinded by their German captors.

My grenade was always fastened to my belt, and wherever I went I felt its comforting bulk bobbing against my side. It left me feeling prepared for the eventuality of capture. But it was a misplaced confidence, as I was later to discover. It was just after the Russians had liberated our area in 1944, when a group of us went fishing in a nearby river. As we had no fishing equipment, we decided to use our grenades to stun the fish and make them rise to the surface. Happy that I no longer needed the grenade, I pulled the pin and threw it. Nothing happened. I had been carrying a dud grenade!

Because medical facilities were so limited, all the people in the forest communities feared being wounded or falling ill. The first groups had been forced to rely on old herbal remedies and medications. When our family first went to the Nacha forest, we were more fortunate as some doctors had already joined the partisans and a few of them gave help to the family groups. It was the medical student, "Doctor" Babisch, who showed us a remedy for pyorrhea, a gum disease caused by lack of vitamins. He had us collect a spinach-like plant that grew in the forest, boil it, and drink the water it was boiled in. It wasn't very appetizing but our gums soon began to heal. He also advised eating onions and garlic for extra vitamins, and these vegetables became highly prized by us. We suffered from many skin problems because of our poor diet and improper hygiene. Because we had to sleep in our clothing, our bodies were never exposed to the air. Even our boots never left our feet, for we had to be constantly ready for action. In addition, our skin was almost always filthy because we had no facilities for bathing.

In these conditions, even the simplest insect bite could become badly infected when scratched with dirty fingernails, and it was not uncommon for these infections to turn into boils. Other boils were caused by poor diet, as was the case with the huge boils I developed all over my back in the summer of 1943. I can remember the misery of riding reconnaissance on horseback with my rifle slung over my back, going bumpety-bump with every step taken by that horse of mine. I'd arrive back in camp with my shirt glued to my back with blood and pus. Finally I solved part of my problem by putting sheets of newspaper between my skin and my shirt, leaving them there for weeks at a time to act as a blotter. Eventually, the boils healed, but they left vicious scars in their place. Dr. Babisch prescribed eating large amounts of fat to rid ourselves of the boils; I swallowed great spoonfuls of butter, shuddering in revulsion as it slid greasily to my stomach.

Another source of annoyance was the rash of tiny pustules that erupted on our bodies, particularly in the sensitive areas. They spread like wildfire and itched almost as badly as lice infestations. This rash was directly due to our filthy condition and our malnutrition. One of the doctors prescribed an ointment consisting of butter or lard, axle grease, and sulphur. The first two ingredients were no problem, but we were at a loss for sulphur until we remembered our supply of dynamite. By grinding up a stick of it with some butter and axle grease, we had a good supply of a very effective ointment, with enough left over to sell to some of the farmers nearby who also suffered from the same rash. When the partisans' high command finally decided that camp hygiene had to improve if we were to be fully effective, new efforts at cleanliness began. Whereas before we had always stayed fully clothed, now I found myself sitting with my comrades around a fire, all of us stark naked while we picked lice from our clothes and bodies. Of course, we could not really win this battle because the lice have such an amazing ability to reproduce. In fact, I never got rid of them till I went to a delousing station at the end of the war and was sprayed from head to foot with DDT.

Doctors were badly needed by the partisans because, in addition to illnesses, there were always wounds and injuries to be treated. Most of the doctors who came to the forest were Jewish because Jews made up the majority of the Polish medical fraternity. In peacetime, even when the rest of our people had suffered from persecution, these doctors had been treated with respect. When the Nazis came and found themselves short of doctors, they invited the Jewish doctors to stay on in their practices even though they were exterminating the rest of the Jews. Many Jewish doctors chose, however, to escape to the forest to serve with the partisans.

At first they had to operate out of primitive quarters with almost non-existent equipment, but gradually the partisans found sources of medical supplies. During foraging expeditions, partisans raided pharmacies for bandages, thermometers and any medications in stock. Sympathetic farmers were sent to pharmacies with forged prescriptions for desperately needed drugs. Homes were raided for stocks of home remedies and cotton that could be made into bandages.

By early 1943, Moscow was parachuting in drugs and operating equipment, but it was still insufficient for our needs. Later that year, a small landing strip was cleared in the Lipichanska forest so that more equipment could be brought in and the most seriously wounded taken out to proper hospital facilities. The central hospital for the Lipichanska partisans was located in a corner of the forest that appeared to be entirely swampland. There was high ground at its centre, however, and just as we had done in the Nacha forest, the medical team built a small hospital on it. Logs were partially submerged in the mud so that they could be used as a bridge by the medical team and removed whenever danger threatened. This hospital provided facilities for surgery on the most seriously wounded partisans. Only the medical personnel and those who furnished supplies for it knew its location. Lightly wounded partisans were treated in emergency field hospitals that were constantly on the move.

Among the surgeons in the forest, one of the best known was Dr. Miasnik, who supervised the Lipichanska hospital. He was a remarkable surgeon, responsible for saving many lives with only primitive surgical equipment. Bulak, our brigade commander, was one of those he saved. The Soviet government honoured him for his outstanding work by parachuting a light machine gun and a pistol to him with a letter of thanks from President Kalinin. Dr. Miasnik was also very influential in the decisions made by the partisan leadership and constantly fought to prevent discrimination against the Jewish partisans.

All of the doctors in the partisan groups were not only skilled medical men but excellent partisans as well. It is sad to think that men trained in saving lives were forced to engage in destroying them. As physicians they were incomparable in their treatment of the wounded, but when involved in any encounter with the enemy they were as determined as anyone to avenge the suffering endured by their own dear ones who had died at the hands of the Germans. They fought savagely when the need arose. A particular incident occurred when a group of forty doctors and lawyers from Budapest and Vienna were liberated by the Russians and incorporated into a fighting unit. Despite their lack of experience in battle, the doctors insisted on joining the partisans in a confrontation with the Germans. They decimated an entire battalion, much to the astonishment of their Russian leaders. With rifles blazing and bayonets drawn, they charged the enemy shouting, "For our mothers, our fathers, our sisters, and our brothers!"

Many other great leaders emerged during those years. Usually they were men who would have gone unnoticed in ordinary times, men of courage and self-sacrifice who by their strength of character set standards for all of us. Two brothers, Tuvia and Zusia Bielsky, organized the Bielsky Otriad, which numbered several hundred partisans. Tuvya was my particular hero because he was the organizer of the family groups. The first time I saw him he was sitting astride his horse. He wore a leather coat with a rifle slung over his shoulder, the perfect picture of a fearless partisan. He was a powerful man with a reputation for playing fair and for always remaining coolheaded. The 1,250 Jews who owe their survival to his care still speak of him with love.

Another outstanding leader was Dr. Atlas, who had escaped to the forest in the middle of 1942. After leading a group of partisans in a series of daring raids, he became a legend in the forest. He was a tough and uncompromising fighter who was given Russia's highest military honour, Hero of the Soviet Union, before he died in a battle in December 1942.

Other partisan groups formed around men who showed obvious qualities of leadership. An outstanding example of this was the Itzkutzy Group, which was organized by the four sons of Itzik Asner of Radun. Their names were Yankele, Chaim, Abraham, and Aaron; Abraham's wife, Luba, was also a member of the group. After they had escaped from Radun, they headed for the Nacha forest because as children they had lived in the village of Nacha and knew the nearby forest well. The group soon developed a reputation for bravery and fearlessness that few partisan groups could equal. Because they were always in the thick of battle and took on such difficult assignments, only one of the brothers survived the war. Abraham Asner and his wife Luba eventually came to Canada to start a new life.

The leadership that men such as these brought to the partisan movement and the family groups made a vast difference to us all, because merely existing in the forest was far from easy. Those who were able to accept the filth, the inconvenience, the primitive conditions, the lack of security and the steady drain on health and endurance managed to say alive. The people from the villages and small towns fared best as they were more accustomed to hardships and could manage without the amenities. Few of the city people and the intellectuals could adjust to their difficult new circumstances. They lost the incentive to live.

CHAPTER EIGHT

The Yureli Forest: October 1943

A major advantage for me of being posted to the Marcinkonys-Varena area was being able to visit my father and sister just fifteen miles away in the Yureli forest. One of the partisans' contact men, a farmer named Tarashka, kept track of their little group and could always tell me where to find them. Usually I stayed overnight with them, exchanging news and enjoying my brief family reunions. Each time I rejoined my unit, I felt happier knowing that they were safe.

As fall came on, I tried to visit with them more often, since visiting would be impossible if they planned to winter there. Late in September, accompanied by a few friends, I returned to the Yureli forest and our usual welcome. That evening, a food-gathering party made up of half-a-dozen partisans and family members approached a farmhouse to obtain a supply of eggs. Since a light was on in the farmhouse, we crept up to the window to see who was inside. There sat Baderas! Baderas, the gentle mailman turned killer! There he sat with two Lithuanians, calmly eating dinner, not two miles from my family's hiding place.

After surrounding the house, two of us burst in with machine guns, ordering them to raise their hands. Chairs toppled and dishes fell from the table. They leaped to their feet, terrified that we would shoot even though they held their hands high in the air. Baderas was heavily armed and we took his guns.

"Well, Baderas, nobody's put a bullet into you, eh?"

"What do you mean?" he asked. "Who's Baderas?"

"You don't know, eh? He's the Jew Killer of Eisiskes! He's the murderer who showed the killers of Podemby how to do it!"

Baderas shook his head. "I never heard of him!"

We beat and kicked him, but he refused to acknowledge he was Baderas although the fear in his eyes told us that he recognized us. We would have killed him, but that would have touched off a search of the area by the Germans and they would probably have found my father's little group. We had to rest content with beating him up, then disappearing into the night.

On October 26 I decided to get in one more visit with my family before the snow fell, and since our demolition unit was on the move, the whole unit went with me to the forest. Most of them were well known to my father's little group, for we had all been together in the Nacha forest. Dr. Babisch, who was in command of our group, Cymbal the Ukrainian, and Isaac Levo were old friends. Even the two Russians who completed our group had been with us a long time. We had also teamed up with a group of partisans from the Leninski Komsomol whom we met at Tarashka's. Two of them were old friends from Radun, Benjamin Rogowski and Aaron Berkowicz; with them were four more fighters including a Russian pilot. The twelve of us entered the forest together, having stocked up on provisions beforehand so that we would not be a burden to the little forest community of eight.

It was evening by the time we arrived at the camp only a short distance within the forest and I had a loving reunion with my father and sister. We talked far into the night, going over their newest plans for hiding on farms again during the winter, discussing which farmers were to be trusted, and how soon they should go. While we talked, many of the others began to drink. This was commonplace amongst the Russians who were used to alcohol but it was very worrying to see that some of the Jews had taken to drinking. It was understandable, of course, as alcohol seemed to give the fighters courage and a feeling of well-being that blotted out the reality of the war and the dreadful insecurity of their lives. But the alcohol slowed their reaction time and often caused a fighter's death through over-confidence or misjudgment.

Obtaining liquor became such an enormous problem for some of the partisans that they took greater risks for this than for the cause of freedom. They would requisition a horse and wagon from a farmer and drive off to a distant town where they exchanged them for a few bottles of liquor. There were even cases of armed robbery just for alcohol. The partisan leaders tried all kinds of penalties for drinking — even executing a drunken fighter — but nothing stopped the real-ly determined drinkers. Almost all the fights that took place in camp were the result of the abuse of alcohol.

On this night in October, the Russians were drinking steadily and some of the Jews, including Isaac Levo, joined them. Isaac couldn't function anymore without alcohol. I suppose he would be classified today as an alcoholic. Sometime during the night the alcohol supply ran out and everyone slept.

About ten the next morning, the sentries posted on the edge of the forest brought a farmer by the name of Nowicki to us. He had been found at the edge of the forest where cattle often grazed. Since he owned the forest and the adjoining land, he had a perfectly logi-cal reason for being there, but there was something about his man-ner that made the sentry suspicious.

"I was just trying to find a stray cow," Nowicki protested.

My father looked worried. He told me he had a feeling that some-thing was wrong. "Let's hold him here until night," he said to me. "Then you'll be gone, and we'll move on as well. Maybe he's a good man, but somehow I feel there's something wrong."

Isaac Levo laughed. "You're being overcautious," he said. "No-wicki's a friend of ours!"

He turned to Nowicki. "Aren't you, Nowicki?"

The farmer smiled and clapped Levo on the back. "Why would I do anything to hurt you people?" he asked.

We let him go because Isaac Levo was head guide for our group and had the final say on all points of security.

"Nowicki," Isaac called after him, "Bring me back two bottles of vodka!"

Nowicki nodded yes. "And listen, Nowicki!" Nowicki stopped and turned to listen. "You be sure to bring 'em or I'm gonna come looking for you. And you know what I'll do to you if I find you, don't you?" Nowicki nodded, turned, and vanished from our sight.

Father was very worried. Even while we ate lunch, he started up at every sound. Then in the midst of a nap after lunch, we were startled awake by a cry of "Poles! Poles!" Immediately we went into action, setting up a line of defence along the forest perimeter. Our equipment was limited to one machine gun, several automatic rifles and a number of single-shot Russian rifles. Through the bush we could see at least a hundred and fifty attackers approaching. They were definitely not Germans as they were not in uniform. We soon realized these were the dreaded AK. To slow their advance, we opened fire, and they immediately dropped on their bellies a hundred or more yards away to begin firing. From behind me came the comforting bursts of our own machine gun's return fire. Then suddenly it stopped. It had jammed. With our machine gun useless and only a half-dozen guns between us, we hadn't a hope of fighting them, for it was clear that a well-equipped force surrounded the forest on three sides. My father crouched behind me. "Hold them back!" he shouted. "Hold them back!"

Relentlessly, they forced us back into the forest, chasing us from tree to tree. They had left us one avenue of escape, a field of stubble rye on the other side of the little forest, knowing they could easily pick us off there like rabbits. We had no alternative but to try to cross the field and outrun them to the next patch of forest. We had already lost the Russian pilot, one of the Russians from my group, and Aaron Berkowicz.

After a brief pause, we passed the word along to make a break for the next forest cover. I burst from the shelter of the trees, raced into the open field, and began firing at random to cover the flight of the others. Inching forward on my belly I fired, then ran a few yards and dropped to my belly again and fired. Behind me my father burst from the forest and fled across the field. "Run, Papa, run! Run, Freidke, run! No! No! Crawl on your bellies close to the ground where they cannot aim at you! Like me, Papa! Like me!"

He didn't listen to me, or perhaps he didn't hear me. I can still see him racing across that field as I carefully inched my way to the protection of the trees on the opposite side. I looked up for just a moment and saw him falter slightly in flight. He's been hit, I thought. Oh, God, he's been hit. But then as he continued on, I thought, it's just a flesh wound.

I looked for Freidke and saw her trailing behind the others, her pursuers inexorably closing in on her. "Poor frightened sister of mine, try a little harder! Hurry!" I whispered under my breath. By this time I was into the wooded area where my wounded father awaited me.

"Leibke! Leibke! I've been hit!" he said.

"Where, Papa, where?"

He undid his shirt and I almost fainted at the sight. The wound was enormous. I could put my fist into it and his lifeblood poured out of him in a river before my horrified eyes!

"It's nothing, Papa," I said. "You'll be all right. Sit by the tree for a moment and rest. Where is Freidke? Where is Freidke?"

I looked out and saw her. Three of her pursuers were almost upon her, bayonets poised as she fled in front of them. I raised my rifle, aimed and fired. "One down, Freidke!" I shouted. Then I fired again and as the next one fell, I screamed, "One more, Freidke! Run, Freidke, run!" Again I fired, but this time I missed. Her attacker was closer. I tried to fire again and my gun jammed. I saw her fall as her pursuer poised his blade over her. I cursed my gun and its impotence as the bayonet entered my poor sister's defenceless body. As in a dream, I heard my father shouting over and over, "Hold them back, Leibke! Hold them back!" But it was too late for Freidke, too late for my little sister. She fell like a wounded bird. As her life ebbed away, I wept with sorrow. "Goodbye, my Freidke. Goodbye, my little sister. . . . "

But there was no time for mourning in the forest. No time for prayers or tears as our pursuers closed in on us. Only the terrible need to run, to escape. And so we ran, my father, his flesh torn open by the bullet which had ripped his body apart, and me holding on to him.

"Faster, Papa. Faster. Here is a cloth to place over the wound. Run, Papa, run." And he ran, my near-dead father. How, I shall never know. The blood oozed in rivulets through his fingers as he clutched the crimson-soaked cloth to his chest. But it was soon clear he could not go much farther. On the edge of the forest we spotted a small farm, and racing into the yard we kicked open the door of the house. I pushed my father inside and he fell to the floor. The farmer and his wife clung together. "Take care of my father," I yelled at them. "Hide him and make sure nothing happens to him or I'll kill you both and burn your house to the ground!" I slammed the door. There was a chance one person could be hidden, but not three.

There was no time for anything more. Rogowski and I ran into a nearby meadow, jumped on the backs of horses grazing there, and rode off into another wooded area through the village of Powiel-ancy, and into another forest beyond that. As we rode I thought of the day the good people of Powielancy had given a whole cartload of food to us, and then I thought of Father lying wounded back there in that miserable farmhouse. "What am I doing, Benjamin?" I stopped my horse in the middle of the path we were following. "That farmer could kill Papa anytime. And here I am running away! If he's still alive, he needs me and I've got to go back to him! You'll have to go on without me." I retraced my steps, praying that I could avoid the Polish AK forces. Darkness had already fallen when I arrived at the farmhouse again. The farmer opened the door reluctantly. My father was not there.

"I could not keep your father here," he explained, "because the Poles are searching all the farms for you. I've taken your father to a spot I know in the woods. The trees are thick there and he should be safe."

He took me to where my father lay on the ground in a grove of trees. Although the farmer did not know it, he had laid him down close to the spot where friends had buried Benjamin and the Levo family, a spot that we had been taken to during the summer. Father's face was grey, and blood still seeped from the wound. I felt helpless. I knew the bullet couldn't have hit a vital organ or he would be already dead. I felt sure he could be saved if I could stop the bleeding and replace the lost blood. But this could be done only at a hospital and we were denied that kind of help.

Later, various plans for saving him tormented me. I could have held the farmer's family hostage and sent the man to town for a doctor. Or perhaps I should have sneaked into Eisiskes to the home of Dr. Lehr, the German who had long practised there. I could have held his wife and daughter hostage for my father's life. Perhaps if I had been brought up on a diet of television gangsters and kidnappers, I might have been more resourceful but at the time I had no models to suggest a plan of action.

The farmer and his wife brought bandages but the blood soaked right through each layer as I applied them. I sat beside him throughout the night waiting for the bleeding to stop. In the early dawn, I left him to go for help, noting that the wound was still bleeding. I went to a farm outside Yureli where a Polish friend from my schooldays lived. When I told them my story, my friend's mother announced that Father must be hospitalized immediately. It took some time for her to realize that this was impossible. She then advised feeding my father raw eggs so the protein would help the blood coagulate and start replacing the lost blood.

I hurried back to my father with great quantities of raw egg, literally pouring them down his throat in my desperation to make him live. It had now become extremely difficult for him to swallow, and between spoonfuls he protested pitifully.

"No, Leibke, no more," and he pushed my hand away, "I'm dying, Leibke."

I persisted, for I would not let him die. I decided then that he should be indoors because the ground was cold and damp. Nearby lived a Lithuanian farmer in an area predominately settled by Poles. Since he was poor, while his Polish neighbours were rich, there was little communication between them, and the Lithuanian seldom had any visitors. I went to him now only to find he was already harbouring seven Jews, one of whom was Abraham Widlanski who had also fled the Yureli forest with us.

The farmer was reluctant to accept Father because he was wounded and would increase the risk of discovery. However, when I offered him my father's gold wedding ring, he agreed to take us. I borrowed his horse and wagon, tying my confiscated horse behind the wagon. Even though it was still daylight, I had no alternative but to travel on the road. At the edge of the woods I lifted my father into the wagon, which I had filled with straw, and spread blankets over him. We began the awful journey back to the farm, expecting an ambush any moment. Every time we hit a bump in the country lane, my poor father groaned.

"Be quiet, Papa," I whispered. "We'll both be murdered if someone hears you."

"Why are you doing this, Leibke?" he asked softly. "Why not leave me in the forest to die? It would be better for both of us."

"Be still, Papa."

"You should have left me there. I was so close to Benjamin, Leibke."

"Others have been wounded and they recovered," I told him. "There's no reason to give up!"

But he was well aware of the seriousness of his wound and knew he had little hope of surviving. Upon reaching the farm I carried him into the barn and settled him in the soft hay. I stayed beside him until dark, then went to the farmhouse to prepare some thin cereal for him. When he had swallowed as much of the cereal as he could, we sat together talking.

"Remember I love you dearly, just as your mother and brother and sister loved you. Even though we're all gone, you're not alone. Someday, Leibke, you'll have a family of your own. Tell them about your murdered family and what became of us. Tell your children that they had grandparents who would have loved them if fate had allowed it. I know you'll survive, Leibke, and begin a new life. Never forget who you are and be proud of your Jewish heritage. Teach your children to keep their faith and practise it as part of their daily lives."

Then he asked me to make him a promise. "Leibke, you must make a solemn vow that you will avenge all of us. As long as you have breath you must look for the people who killed us and destroy them. Avenge your mother, your brother, your sister . . . me . . . and all the murdered Jews. Find Nowicki, the man who betrayed us all, and kill him!"

A little later he said, "When this war is over and we have time to reflect on what has passed, the true realization of our catastrophe will come to us. Only then will the questions come. Only then will we be forced to find reasons for the wholesale senseless slaughter of our people."

On the third day as I sat beside him, he talked of family matters that I was to attend to when the war was over. He asked me to find his half-brother in America and told me where I could find the remnants of our family possessions, those that had not gone to Mrs. Carolowa. Then he held my hand tightly and I leaned closer.

"Bury me beside Benjamin," he whispered, and I promised him that I would. That evening I went to the house and came back with a dish of cereal. The barn was large and in total darkness. I called softly, "Papa." There was no answer. "Papa?" Panic seized me as I groped my way in the darkness, one hand outstretched to find him in the soft straw. Then I felt the coldness of his face under my fingers and I knew he was gone. Carefully, I cradled his body, and holding him to me, I rocked back and forth, weeping.

"Papa, Papa, what shall I do without you? I am so alone. I don't want to live anymore. I have nothing left to live for. Don't leave me, Papa. Don't leave me!"

In the darkness, Abraham Widlanski found his way to me. "Leibke, I heard the Angel of Death come for your father. He is at peace now, Leibke. Be comforted."

So it was over. The last link with my past was gone, and I felt incredibly forsaken and alone. I was the only one left. I was now the mind, the soul, and the conscience of the Kaganowicz family.

I asked three of the men in the barn to help me bury my father. Under cover of night we placed him in a wagon and started for the forest again. Although it was extremely dangerous I had a promise to keep, the last thing I could do for my father. Beside my brother's grave, we dug a new grave. Gently I wrapped my father's body in several blankets and lowered him into the ground. He was so frail that it was hard to remember the strong, handsome man he had been only two years earlier. Tears streamed down my face as I held him for the last time. Beside the graves stood a tree blasted by lightning, its top sheared off. I thought how appropriate it was for a grave marker.

In an almost inaudible voice, I chanted the ancient prayer of bereavement. *"Yis-ga-dal, v'yis-ka-dash sh'may re-bo! B'ol-mo dee-v'ro hir-u-say, v'yam-leeh mal-hu-say. . . ."* I found no comfort in it.

As the others returned to the wagon, I knelt to place my hand on the earth that covered him. Then I rested my cheek on the forlorn grave and through my tears I whispered, "I'll be back, Papa. I'll be back." After the war I returned there with Abraham Widlanski. We unearthed the bodies of Benjamin and my father and all the Levos who were Abraham's kin and took them to Varena. There we interred them in the Jewish cemetery. It was one of the most heartbreaking tasks I ever performed but I knew that it was something I must do.

We returned the wagon to the farm, spending the next few days there in hiding. I was uneasy as I felt that our pursuers couldn't be far away and would eventually search the farm of the Lithuanian. Abraham Widlanski shared my feelings of uneasiness; we agreed to leave together and wander from place to place, staying only a day or two before moving on. We both knew from experience the danger in settling into a comfortable refuge.

We learned later that our premonitions about the Lithuanian's farm had been correct. A group of Polish partisans came to search the farm a week after we left. When the Lithuanian denied harbouring Jews, they set the barn on fire. Some who were hiding there died in the flames, preferring that to death at the hands of the Poles. Two of the others, Josl Michalowski and Shael Rogaczewski, were taken to AK headquarters where they were tortured to death. Abraham and I first took refuge with a farmer who was very kind to us. But after two weeks we left under cover of night when we sensed he was tired of us and feared he would turn us in. This reaffirmed in us our original intention to stay in one place no longer than a day or two, no matter how pleasant the situation seemed.

After that we moved from farm to farm, occasionally returning to one where we had been well received. At one farm there was an old farmer with a young wife who seemed interested in me. Abraham teased me about her, saying he wouldn't let an opportunity like that pass by. But she could have been a hundred years old for all I cared! We also stayed with two Polish prostitutes who were extremely decent to us. They plied their trade outside the village, and on their return would prepare dinner for us. They were compassionate women and never sought payment from us. Some farmers, however, were far from sympathetic or understanding. Although they never turned us in, they gave us chores such as feeding and cleaning the pigs, knowing full well our abhorrence of them. We knew enough to keep silent at times like this.

As soon as we felt it was safe, we returned to the field where Freidke had died. A farmer had told us that all the dead had been placed in a trench in the middle of the field, and we hoped to re-bury her beside Father. But in the interim, the field had been ploughed; it was impossible to find the site of the trench.

November, then December, came and went. Widlanski and I were always on the move. But we were growing restless and anxious, as we had no idea how long we could travel this way. I suspected that eventually we would be just a little careless. We would forget to check out some farmhouse and walk into an AK ambush. "Can we keep living like this until the war ends?" I would ask Abraham, and initiate yet another discussion about the future. Abraham was in his early forties then and had been a good friend to my dear father while they lived together in the forest near Yureli. Now he assumed the role of friend and tutor, filling in gaps in my interrupted education and doing his best to guide me. In the long days hiding in lofts and stables, we talked about life and prayed together, and I became aware of the breadth of his knowledge. I learned that he wrote poetry and translated Russian songs into Yiddish. He made a remarkable difference to the orphan youth I had become.

Early in the new year, Abraham and I contacted Tarashka, the farmer who lived near the Yureli forest, and he promised to let us know when any of the partisans from my unit came to the district. It was impossible for me to make the trip to the Lipichanska forest on my own as the way was infested with Germans and Poles. We would simply have to stay somewhere near Tarashka's farm and wait for the partisans to turn up.

During our travels, it wasn't always possible to get a roof over our heads when we lay down to sleep. Sometimes we slept on the snow-covered ground. Once we slept near an observation tower in the forest. When I awoke, I was disturbed and disoriented. I was so confused in fact, I couldn't decide where we were until Abraham pointed out the observation tower. Even then I insisted that we were to continue to the right of it.

"No, Leibke," Abraham said, "that's where we came from. This is where we're going." And he pointed to the left.

"What are you talking about?" I yelled at him. The argument reached the point where I was threatening to hit him. "All right! All right, I'll bet you my grandmother's gold watch that we're supposed to go this way!" And I pointed to the right. Abraham nodded. We gathered our bundles and set off walking. After a mile and a half, I had to concede he was right.

"Okay, Leibke, give me the watch!" But it was buried deep in my pocket and both of us knew that I wouldn't give it up until it was the only thing between total starvation and me. (To this day, whenever I visit my friend in New York, he teases me, "Don't forget, Leibke! You still owe me a gold watch!")

The next two months went by in a fog of grey depression. I lost track of the days and weeks as we trudged from farm to farm and through the forest. I became convinced this would go on and on until the Poles finally caught us. Because they roamed the forests and countryside by the hundreds, we would have no chance of escaping if we confronted them. Between us, we had only one gun. One rainy night, about the middle of March, we stopped once again at Tarashka's farm. He had good news for us. Partisans from my unit had visited the previous night and had asked him for news of me. Tarashka had told them I was in the district somewhere nearby, and they had promised to return for us in two nights' time. I felt an enormous surge of relief. Abraham and I went off to find a hiding place for the long day's wait.

It was still raining but we found a small thicket of young trees and settled down, feeling tremendously elated at soon being reunited with our comrades. As the day wore on, it began to rain heavily and the temperature dropped. Father's greatcoat, which I was wearing, was so wet that it had far more weight than warmth. At last darkness came again, and the two of us, soaked and shivering, went back to the farmhouse. Tarashka's wife prepared a bowl of dumplings and hot milk for us, which we ate gratefully. I have tasted many elegant dishes since then but none has tasted so delicious. When we finished, Tarashka sent us to wait in the hayloft for the partisans. The barn was warm from the body heat of the animals, and I put my arms around one of the cows, clinging to it to capture some of its warmth. As I rubbed my face on its rough hide, it turned its great patient eyes on me as if it knew how cold and miserable I felt. Then I crawled up to join Abraham in the hayloft where we fell asleep immediately.

I don't know how long we slept but suddenly we were both wide-awake. Over the sound of the rain on the barn roof we could hear Tarashka's dogs barking furiously; through the gaps in the end wall we could see an oblong of light stretching from the house across the farmyard. Tarashka had trained his dogs not to bark at our partisan group, and he made a point of never allowing light to show from his house at night. His windows were carefully covered to ensure privacy. Abraham and I turned to look at each other in the dark loft, tense and ready to spring into action. Before we could move we heard the back door open and people walking toward the barn.

"I don't know what you expect to find!" Tarashka said loudly in Polish. "I just keep cows in my barn. If you find any Jews in there they didn't get my permission!"

"Abraham," I whispered in the darkness, "I'm not running anymore. I'm going to pick them off as they come up that ladder, and then use the last bullet on myself. I'm too tired to run and I've got nobody left anyhow."

Below us the search party entered the barn with Tarashka still making loud comments. I felt Abraham grab me firmly by the wrist. We had been lying close to the gable end of the barn facing the field. Now in one quick move he smashed his arm hard against the woven straw that sealed the gable end and rolled us out. The two of us tumbled into the blackness of the field below.

It was a fall of at least fourteen feet and I was wearing wooden-soled pull-on boots. Since the soles had no give to them, I don't know why my legs didn't break when I hit the ground. Without a pause, the two of us went flying across the field in a hail of bullets. But Abraham was a fast runner and vanished into the forest ahead of me. I ran through the trees in the pouring rain. "Abraham! Abraham!" I called, but the rain drowned my voice. It didn't take long before I was completely lost in the thick underbrush. I was panic-stricken, for I had no idea how to find my unit now that Tarashka's farm was suspect. I couldn't make the journey to the Lipichanska forest alone through enemy territory. Nor did I know where to look for Abraham as we had made no alternate plans. My only hope was to begin searching for the miller who was to be our alternate contact man in case Tarashka ceased to be useful.

I returned once more to the old routine of hiding by day in the forest and begging for food from nearby farmers at night. It was a strange existence, for I was conscious only of rain and the alternation of day and night. Whenever I remembered my urgent need to find the miller I made discreet inquiries, but I'm not even sure that I was really looking for him anymore. Then sometime around the beginning of April I found the miller.

It was a miserable-looking, damp, underfed refugee who knocked on his door that night. "My name is Leibke Kaganowicz. I've been separated from my partisan unit and I understand they're looking for me."

The miller stared at me blankly.

"Can you tell me how to find my unit?" I asked.

The miller shrugged. "I don't know what you're talking about. I don't know anything about partisans. Go away!"

"Listen," I said, "I know you're the contact man for Davidov's. I was in the barn when Tarashka's farm was raided and I know you're the alternate to take Tarashka's place."

"Tarashka? Who's this Tarashka? I don't know anything about it. Go away!"

I turned to leave, and then tried once more. "Perhaps you knew my father, Shael Kaganowicz. He was killed by the Poles."

His face softened. "Yes," he said, "I knew him well." He promised to make inquiries for me and told me to come back the following evening. My reception was not only much warmer this time; he also had good news for me. My unit was nearby and would come for me the following night. The miller was also able to tell me what had happened at Tarashka's farm. The searchers who had fired at us were indeed Poles. They had been told that Tarashka was our contact man. The search was only a routine one, as they had no way of knowing we were there. Our unit, which was in the woods close by, was on its way to the farm when the firing began. The unit quickly disappeared into the forest again. Unfortunately, Abraham and I had run off in different directions and hadn't met up with them. The Poles, unable to declare Tarashka definitely guilty, had not punished him but were keeping him under surveillance. He was no longer useful to us.

The next night when I arrived at the miller's house, my old unit was waiting for me. I told them of the deaths of my sister and my father. They embraced me and tried to comfort me. In spite of the sadness beneath our reunion, I was happy to be with my comrades once again. Isaac Levo had survived the Yureli forest but was somewhat chastened after a severe reprimand from the high command for his carelessness there. Cymbal had also escaped. Michka Dubinsky once more headed the unit. Lippa Skolsky was still there, as cautious as ever, and still immaculately dressed. Two Russians completed the group. Despite earlier warnings and reprimands by the high command, the seven of us celebrated my return by drinking all night.

CHAPTER NINE

Return to the Partisans: April–June 1944

My life now entered an entirely new phase, but the change had little to do with any changes in the world around me. The partisans that I rejoined were the same people. They were perhaps more daring than before, encouraged by the news that the Germans were in retreat. The Russians had already swept across the southern Ukraine as far as the Pruth River in Romania, had entered Lutsk just inside Poland, and were approaching Minsk. The Germans' grip on Leningrad had been broken in January and they had been pushed southwest to Pskov. All this was encouraging, of course, but it made little difference to the work of the partisans. The big difference in my life came from within me. I had left behind the boy of sixteen who had fled from Eisiskes. My childhood had ended the day I buried my father. In three years all my illusions had disappeared.

I knew that what I'd said to Abraham in Tarashka's barn was true. I had no reason to fight for survival. I had no family and no future. More than anything else I looked forward to death so that I could be reunited with my family. The thought of seeing them again wiped away my fear. Another force had grown within me. Hatred. I was consumed by hatred for those who had murdered my family and my friends. I felt a lust to kill that almost drove me out of my mind. In the months that followed, I found myself becoming judge and executioner of any suspicious characters who crossed our group's path.

About the end of April, four groups under the command of Dr. Babisch embarked on a train derailment mission in the area near Varena. The Russians were preparing for a big offensive through Poland and it was vitally necessary to destroy the Germans' supply lines before the offensive began. Since the route to our target passed near the Yureli forest, we detoured to Nowicki's farm. I had no definite proof that he had betrayed us but every indication pointed to him. He was the only one who could have told the Poles of our existence because he was the only one who knew exactly where the family was camped.

We lay in the woods near Nowicki's farm all day, making certain that he was alone. By evening we knew that only he and his family were there, and we prepared to attack. In silence, we surrounded the farm, and then crept up to the house. We smashed open the door, guns in hand.

"I didn't do it!" Nowicki screamed. "I swear I didn't!"

"Say your prayers, Nowicki," I said, ignoring his outburst. I had waited for this moment too long.

"Kaganowicz, listen to me. I'd never betray your family. I loved your father. I loved him!"

"Say your prayers."

"No, listen, please listen to me. I wouldn't do a thing like that!"

Nowicki's pleas fell on deaf ears. Repeatedly, I stabbed him over and over again with my bayonet as I relived the scene of my sister's agony. In a blind haze of rage, I continued to attack him as my poor father's dying face returned to haunt me. "Avenge us Leibke," he had said. "Avenge us!"

"Die, damn you! Die!" I screamed, completely out of my mind with hate and grief. "This is for Freidke! And this is for my father . . . and my mother . . . and Benjamin. . . ." Tears streamed down my face as I relived the murders of my beloved family.

At last I fled from the house, feeling certain that I had killed the man responsible for my family's deaths. Although remorse might come later, for the moment I was glad. But Nowicki was not dead. I had inflicted something far more horrible on him: he was blinded and maimed. He lived out the rest of his life unable to see, speak, or function in any normal way.

We left Nowicki's farm to continue our train derailment mission to the northwest. We worked there for nearly six weeks, setting mines and destroying communication lines with so much ease that we began to look upon our assignment as routine, and became somewhat lax in attention to details. One night we set out to place a bomb near Varena, walking in single file, with our guide, Isaac Levo, leading the way. We'd all had a number of drinks, making us considerably less alert. Contrary to our usual method of approach, Isaac led us straight toward the railway crossing, a place usually guarded closely by the Germans. I marched directly behind him. There was a double set of tracks at this point, and we had just crossed the first set when a shot rang out.

A German patrol waiting for us on the other side of the track had shot Isaac and he fell at my feet. The rest of us dropped to the track with bullets screaming over our heads and the Germans' guard dogs barking furiously. I crawled backward through the darkness, cursing Isaac. It dawned on me then just how drunk he must have been to lead us into this mess and what a pack of fools we'd been to follow him.

The Germans began firing off flares to see us better. As each flare lit the night, I expected to be shot. But I kept crawling backwards. At last, my feet touched the outside track, and I slipped over it and rolled down the embankment into the bushes. Shortly after, the other five dropped beside me, and we dashed into the pine forest that we had left so confidently only a short time earlier. The Germans didn't give up easily, chasing us through the forest for half the night, setting off rockets and firing at us.

When they finally gave up, we set off for the miller's place, arriving before dawn. We sent him to Varena to find out what happened to Isaac; he returned with the sad news that Isaac's body had been strung up there to show the people that an important partisan had been killed. All of us had been worried about the consequences of

Isaac's drinking and had figured he would cause all our deaths sooner or later. It seemed to be only luck we had survived this time. Meanwhile, our most pressing problem was how to complete our assignment. Because that section of the track would be unapproachable for days, we would have to move our operation to the other side of Varena. I was elected to the post of guide to replace Isaac.

We stayed at the miller's the rest of the day, setting out again as soon as it was dark. As we neared the track, we could see that there were many more guards than usual. The German troops on the eastern front were in desperate condition and the railway was important to them for supplies. It was apparent that there would not be time for our usual careful bomb plant. We decided that we would have to race to the track when we heard the train, place the mine, pull the safety pin, and run for cover. We settled down nearby to wait. It was not long before we heard the whistle of an approaching train. While the Russians stood guard, Michka and I ran to the tracks, placed the mine, pulled the safety pin, and raced back to the woods.

It was only as we were preparing to make ourselves scarce that we realized our mistake. The sound of the locomotive engine was not growing any louder. It was actually fading away. The train we had heard had passed over our stretch of track before we had even arrived there. It had been stopped down the line and was now continuing on its way to Vilnius. We were in a horrible predicament. We knew we had to retrieve the mine before somebody found it, but we had already pulled the safety pin so that it was vulnerable to the slightest touch or vibration. I volunteered to go back to replace the pin; Michka offered to come with me.

Cautiously, we crawled up the slope to the rails and I eased over to the mine. Then for a long minute I held the pin in my hand, knowing that it could be my last one on earth. I could feel the sweat trickling down my back even though it was not a particularly warm night. Finally I stretched out my hand and eased the pin gently into its socket. I tensed for the boom that would end it all, but it didn't come.

I felt wildly excited at my success, but there was no time to celebrate. Calmly and silently I passed the mine to Michka, and we slid back down the slope and into the woods. Then it happened. Some dry twigs broke under our feet just as we reached the others. As the Germans' bullets sprayed out of the darkness, the whole group broke into a run, Michka in the lead with the bomb. Cymbal and I panted after him with the Russians following us. Then for some reason Michka suddenly changed direction. Too late, we realized we had lost him. We plunged on with the Germans firing wildly behind us. Some time before the firing stopped, it became clear that only Cymbal and I were still running together. The Russians had vanished.

At daybreak, Cymbal and I came to a village that had never shown us much sympathy. Since we were desperately hungry, we decided to take a chance. We knocked at the first door we came to. The villager who opened the door smiled warmly when he saw us.

"Come in, come in." he said.

His enthusiasm alarmed us, but I responded cautiously, "We need food."

"Of course, of course," he replied, and began putting dishes on the table while his wife scurried around preparing food.

"It's a trap," Cymbal whispered.

"I know. They must have sent for the police. We'll eat quickly and get out of here."

But we were wrong. The villagers had no intention of turning us in. Once the Germans had begun retreating, the villagers had decided it was time to build up their reputation with the partisans before the Russians arrived. After breakfast we were escorted to meet the rest of the people of the village who overwhelmed us with their friendliness. We spent the entire day there, walking about in broad daylight for the first time in years.

While there, we learned that the road from Eisiskes to Varena was jammed with truckloads of fleeing Germans. This good news gave us a fresh problem because we had to cross that same highway to return to the miller's place to meet our group. In the early evening we left the village and began walking east, staying in the woods as close as possible to the highway. The villagers had not lied about the truckloads of Germans; a continuous convoy was heading down the road away from the Russian front. It seemed obvious that we would have to wait until there was a gap in the convoy before we could dash across. When we decided to stop and rest for a time, Cymbal, being thirsty, reached for his canteen. It was empty, but we could see a stream running through a field nearby. It was impossible for either of us to approach it as the Germans on the road would see us. Fortunately a shepherd was standing there gawking at the convoy. Cymbal called him over. "Here," he said, "go fill this in the stream over there!" The shepherd took the canteen and headed toward the stream but instead of filling it, he ran to the highway to call out to the Germans. "Partisans! Partisans!"

Once again we were on the run, with the Germans firing at us from the highway. When we finally halted, we were back in the village where we started. Here we waited until it was dark before we set out once more, walking in the brush beside the highway with our eyes on the lights of the convoy, watching for a break. At one point we nearly tripped over a German soldier who was squatting to relieve himself. He was as shocked by the encounter as we were, but by the time he had pulled up his pants and pulled out his gun, we were far away.

Our next attempt was made a little further down the road. We crouched in the bushes till the right opportunity came, then dashed across between truckloads. Bullets whined overhead, but we raced into the woods unhurt and hurried on to the miller's house. There the rest of the group waited for us with some impatience. For a few days we stayed with the miller and relaxed, feeling confident that our troubles would soon be over because the Russians were so close. In the meantime, the need for caution was somewhat lessened as the local people had shifted their allegiances.

While we were still hiding at the miller's, a Lithuanian farmer came to him with a disturbing piece of news. He had encountered a group of seventy-two Ukrainians hiding in a small wood close to Varena. They were in German uniform and claimed they wanted to surrender. The farmer came to tell his story to the miller because he thought the miller would know how to contact the partisans. The miller denied this, but said he thought he knew someone else who might be in touch with the partisans.

"Come back in a couple of days," he told the farmer.

As soon as the man left, the miller came to tell us the story.

"Seventy-two?" I said, and looked around at my five comrades.

"Ukrainians in German uniform!" said Cymbal, the Ukrainian, in complete disgust.

I was worried about taking on this job. Not only was our group ridiculously small to be accepting the surrender of a group this size, but we could be walking into a trap. Outside of Cymbal, I knew few Ukrainians who did not hate Jews. After a long discussion, we worked out a plan that would guarantee us a certain amount of safety. We sent a message with the farmer that two of the Ukrainian officers, unarmed, were to meet us in a field near the forest. Two of us met them while the other four from our group kept the meeting covered from brush nearby.

The officers appeared sincere. They told us they had been forced into the German army. Now they wished only to escape before it was too late. We agreed to return the following day with our decision on their fate, and went off to mull over the problem. The next day we returned with surrender terms and some large burlap bags. We ordered them to surrender all arms and ammunition and deposit them in the bags. After that we carried out a body search for small arms. There was no way we could use so many arms, so we buried the bags in a large ditch.

Now we were ready for the long march back to our headquarters in the Lipichanska forest, six men in charge of seventy-two prisoners. The going was ridiculously slow because we had to stop and requisition food at every village. It took a whole steer to provide our prisoners with dinner; a cartload of potatoes and another one of bread just dampened the fires of their hunger. We had endless delays. Every time we stopped to eat, the roast of the day would have to be killed, butchered and cooked before we could move on again.

After six days of travelling through fields and forest, we were not even as far as Linitsa. We were well aware that the Germans were in desperate retreat with the Russians close behind them. When we camped each night we could see the Russians' flares drifting down to light the highways, and all night long we could hear the artillery and the bombing. But we were not sure how far the main Russian force had advanced. On the sixth day we emerged from the forest close to Linitsa.

What we saw less than a mile away was absolutely beyond belief. Our war had been fought in the silence and the dark of the night, forever sparring with a powerful enemy that we seldom saw. Here before us was a massive daylight battle. Thousands of men and machines were pitted against each other, the Germans fleeing, wheeling now and then to fight a rearguard action, the Russians pounding them with artillery and bombs. The air was black with smoke; here and there bright flames licked upward from burning trucks and tanks. And the whole scene was drowned in the roar of shells and planes, exploding bombs and the screams of dying men. We stood watching as if it were a movie on some gigantic screen. I could not believe that men were really dying and trucks were really being blown apart. I have seen Hollywood epics since then that have come close to replicating that scene, but they have never managed to capture that terrible picture of destruction.

The appearance of the Russians also resolved the largest difficulty in our trek with Ukrainian prisoners. Obviously it wouldn't be necessary to take them all the way to our own headquarters; we could now surrender them to the Russians. The only problem was how to accomplish this. We could not just march them into Russian headquarters, for the Ukrainians were still dressed in German uniforms and we might be mowed down. Two of us set off to reconnoitre and found a Lithuanian herdsman calmly tending his cows in a clearing at the edge of the forest. I could not believe anything so peaceful could exist next to that nightmare battle but it is human nature to try to carry on with day-to-day existence even in the eye of the hurricane. This schizophrenic quality of war only adds to its unreality. The herdsman did not seem at all surprised to see us and only nodded when I asked him to do an errand for us.

"I want you to go into the village and find out if it's in Russian or German hands. Understand?"

He nodded thoughtfully and then slowly started off towards Linitsa.

"And hurry!" I called. He nodded and continued on his way without the slightest change of pace. We sat down on a log to keep an eye on the cows.

In an hour he was back looking somewhat troubled.

"Well?" I demanded. "Are they Germans?"

"Nope."

We broke into grins and started congratulating each other.

"But they're not Russians either."

We looked at him open-mouthed.

"Then who are they?"

"I don't know. They've got things on their shoulders." And he gestured to show us that the soldiers he'd seen in the village were wearing epaulettes.

Now this was confusing, for the Russians considered epaulettes capitalistic symbols and never wore them. What we didn't know was that when the Russians had joined forces with the West against the Germans, they had adopted epaulettes on their uniforms. Suddenly I remembered another way to distinguish the Russians from other soldiers. "Go back to the village," I told the herdsman, "and see if there's a large red star on the soldiers' hats."

Dutifully, he trudged off to have another look at the soldiers in the village; then he trudged all the way back with the good news. "They're all wearing red stars!"

Happily, we spun him around and started him back across the field, yelling instructions at him.

"Now don't forget! Find an officer. Tell him that some partisans are holding seventy-two Ukrainian prisoners. Ask him to come back here with you. Understand?"

In half an hour he was back with a Russian officer. We must have looked like a very strange group to that officer: seventy-two prisoners and six ill-equipped guards standing at the edge of the forest. Yet he greeted us with great warmth. He told us that he was deeply honoured to meet us in the name of his country, and he thanked us for our help in driving the Germans from the country.

"Russia will be forever grateful to you for your sacrifices and your heroism. Your courage will never be forgotten and you will be honoured in our country for all time." When he finished his speech we hugged and kissed each other.

And then reality hit me. I had come through. After all the horrors of these black years, I was alive. The Russian officer standing before us was proof of it.

For days after, I wept whenever I was left alone. Awake or asleep, I found myself overwhelmed by terrifying nightmares, re-enacting all the horror of the past four years. As if my mind could only now face the reality of it all, I relived all the deaths, heard again the screams, saw the torn flesh and mutilated bodies of my people. Underlying everything was the realization that I was truly alone. I remembered clearly what my father had told me: the survivors would only understand the tragedy of what had happened to them once it was all over. He had been right. Later that morning we entered Linitsa in triumph. Russian soldiers hugged and kissed us, jumping down from their trucks to thank us over and over for what we had done in the war effort. The people of the town and the soldiers filled our arms with gifts and brought us food and liquor. We were simply staggered; the years of deprivation had not prepared us for anything like this.

Our Ukrainian prisoners in their German uniforms, however, received a far different reception. The local people jeered and insulted them as they were marched down the street; the Russian soldiers looked down on them with contempt. They were locked in a barn with Russian guards posted around it.

At Russian headquarters we were welcomed warmly by the ranking officers, then invited to go to the barn and take whatever valuables we liked from the rucksacks of the prisoners. When we asked the reason, the officer explained that the Ukrainians were going to face a firing squad in the morning. How could I walk into that barn and face the men that I had unknowingly escorted to their deaths? We had travelled together for a week, shared the same food, slept side-by-side, and had almost become friends, as strangers do in such circumstances. However, the Russians informed me that these same Ukrainians for whom I felt such sympathy had been staunch German allies. They had joined them on the promise that once the war was won, they would be given their independence, their own government, and considered heroes of the German Reich. They had changed sides simply to save their own skins once they realized that Germany was losing the war.

In addition, the Russians had evidence that many of the Nazi-indoctrinated Ukrainians were guilty of crimes against Russians and Jews. Some Ukrainian farmers, who had been forced to transport wagonloads of retreating Germans, had been overtaken by the Russian army and liberated. These men recognized some of the prisoners and submitted extremely damaging evidence, accusing them of committing serious crimes against their own countrymen. To substantiate their claims, the farmers explained where the prisoners came from, along with many other details of their lives. There was no doubt that some of them deserved to die, but I believed there were soldiers no older than myself who were innocent. I felt very sorry for them, but I could not alter their destiny. The next morning they were taken to the forest and shot.

For several days we stayed on in Linitsa, where we were royally treated. While there, I took time to visit the farmer who had rescued our little family from the cold on our flight from Grodno, nearly cooking us to death on his bake oven. The man and his wife welcomed me with tears and laughter, immediately asking after the rest of my family. They mourned with me when I told them I was the sole survivor, for they had felt great love for my father.

Before we left Linitsa, one of the Russian officers told me about a group of Poles who had been captured and interned nearby. Since Lippa Skolsky and I had quite a few scores to settle, there was always the chance that we might recognize one or two of these men. We decided to pay them a visit.

Within the stockade, the prisoners sat on the ground while Lippa and I walked among them studying each face. At last I stopped before one man who looked vaguely familiar. He was shaking with fear and babbling wildly over and over, "Save me! Save me!"

"Who are you?" I asked.

He then seemed to really see me for the first time. "My name is Yankele Stolnicki. Who are you?" And he clutched at me.

"My name is Leibke Kaganowicz."

"Are you Shael's son?" When I nodded, he held onto me pleading, "For God's sake, save me. Save me!"

"What are you doing here with these Poles?" I asked him.

It was a strange story that he told. Yankele Stolnicki was a Jew from Radun who had been a young Communist leader. When the Russians occupied the city he had been appointed secretary of the Communist Party, and in this post had compiled lists of affluent Jews for the Russians. Naturally this did not endear him to the Jewish community, for many of these Jews were subsequently sent to Siberia, losing both their families and their wealth.

When the Germans arrived, Stolnicki went into hiding with a sympathetic Polish farmer. For three years he remained there. Then, as the battlefront came closer and closer to Radun, the two men went to hide in the forest to avoid the conflict. While there, Stolnicki met another Jew and the two of them teamed up. One day they spotted a large group of Polish partisans hiding nearby, and they ran off to inform the Russians. Once the area was surrounded, the Poles surrendered. They were marched off to Linitsa accompanied by Yankele and his friend who were to explain to the officers in command who the prisoners were.

Unfortunately, on the way to Linitsa, the guards were changed and the replacements were not informed of the role being played by Yankele and his friend, so they imprisoned the two of them with the Poles. Yankele's friend, however, managed to escape in the confusion of the arrival at the stockade. Poor Yankele pleaded with the Russians in vain. As far as they were concerned, he was a traitorous Pole, and he would face the firing squad with the rest of them.

When he had finished his story I turned to the guard and explained the mistake. The guard ignored me. Yankele thought his only hope was gone and went back to crying "Save me! Save me!" I reassured him and went straight to Russian headquarters, explained Yankele's case, and was promptly handed a release order by the commanding officer. Yankele Stolnicki became a free man once more.

Our visit to Linitsa came to an end when we received new orders from Captain Davidov. By radio from a forest camp outside Grodno, he told us that the Otriad was being relocated to a village between the Russian Jungle and Grodno. Our job there would be to capture German troops who had escaped the Russian net at Minsk and fled westward toward Grodno. Our group's new location lay on the escape path they were using. We asked Captain Davidov about our comrades in the Otriad and learned that many had died in the Russian advance. Their position had placed them in the centre of the battle where they'd been caught in the German and Russian crossfire. Of the survivors, many had been conscripted into the Russian army. Only forty of us remained to fight as partisans. We set off to join the others at the new base, all of us somewhat bemused by this change of events. Now we were the hunters and the Germans were the hunted. We weren't quite sure how to play our new parts.

CHAPTER TEN

Mopping Up: Midsummer 1944

We quickly set up headquarters in the little village and began patrolling the area for Germans on the run. Our work was helped along by the local farmers who would take in the Germans, feed them, and then run to get us while their guests were eating. They were, of course, the very same farmers who had betrayed the partisans with equal enthusiasm to the Germans.

One day an SS officer was captured in this way and brought to headquarters. Captain Davidov established that he was the murderer of many Russians and Jews; this was verified by the documents that the man carried. Although many of our captives were sent to Grodno, this man was shot immediately.

Soon after, a farmer breathlessly rushed into our headquarters to tell us that several hundred Germans were hiding in a field between our village and Grodno. Twenty-five of us swarmed off to capture them. The Germans were concealed in a huge field of rye. As all of us had hidden in rye fields at one time or another we knew it would be impossible to spot the Germans from the ground. Michka Novikov, a Russian partisan, and I climbed onto the straw-thatched roof of a barn overlooking the field to see where they were.

Scrambling up to the peak, we scanned the field in full view of the Germans. The temptation was too great for them, of course. A bullet whined and I turned to see Michka's face and clothes covered in blood from a wound on the top of his head. I grabbed his arm and we slid from sight down the roof again. Luckily, although there was a lot of blood, the bullet had only creased his scalp; one inch lower and he would have lost the top of his head. Meanwhile the rest of our group was busy fighting it out with the Germans, killing twenty-five of them. The remainder escaped into the forest.

I took time after this fight to visit Danielewicz on whose farm my brother Benjamin and the Levos had died. Although Isaac Levo and Abraham Widlanski were convinced he had betrayed them, I still found this hard to believe. He welcomed me warmly and swore his innocence. "Now if it were you, Leibke, with your bad temper . . . maybe," he said smiling. "But Benjamin? Benjamin was always so soft, so gentle. I loved him like my own son! Why would I betray dear Benjamin?"

Although I was satisfied, a number of the partisans were not. About this time, there was a young orphan boy called Hirsche who roamed the countryside exacting revenge on farmers who had betrayed Jews to the Nazis. This boy accepted five thousand rubles and a month later eliminated Danielewicz and his entire family. The partisans were satisfied at last that they had been avenged. They reasoned that if Danielewicz had not been guilty, the Nazis would have killed him for harbouring Jews. And if Danielewicz really respected the dead, why had he let his pigs into the field where they could mutilate their bodies? To this day, I am not convinced that Danielewicz was guilty. But it hardly matters now, for they are all dead, and the truth will not bring them back.

I took the time to return to the village of Powielancy near Radun to pay my respects again. Because of their kindness to us when we had lived in Radun, I had exerted my influence to prevent the partisans from raiding this village in the closing months of the war. Now I went back again to see my father's friend and his two beautiful daughters, and to tell him that all my family had died. I knew the grief he expressed was sincere. When I asked after his daughters, he told me that a Russian tank commander had carried off the younger one whom I had admired so much. He asked if I knew of some way to bring her back to her family. I promised to try, but I didn't think I had much hope of finding her, since the countryside had been criss-crossed by Russian tanks. I set off, however, to find the headquarters of the various tank companies, always announcing that I was a partisan looking for my girlfriend. By this method, I located the right tank company, the guilty commander and, finally, the girl. I told him of her father's anxiety and suggested he return her to her family. His only reply was a threat to kill me.

There was no point in trying to take her from him by force so I went to his commanding officer to explain the problem. Luckily, he saw things my way and ordered the abductor to release her. She was relatively unharmed, although very frightened by the experience, and she retuned home to a grateful father. I felt then I had acted for my own father in repaying this generous man's kindness when we had been so desperate for help. In late summer I was granted permission to visit Eisiskes. Secretly, I had always nourished the hope that my mother was alive and waited there for me but I had not confided this to anyone, saying instead that I wanted to see if any of my friends had come back. Abraham Asner and his wife Luba also received permission to go back to Varena to look for friends and family. Captain Davidov issued permits to us, verifying our time served in the partisans, and giving us permission to carry arms. We were ordered to report to partisan headquarters in Varena when we completed our visits.

We caught the train at a nearby station and travelled toward Varena on a narrow gauge auxiliary line. From this vantage point we could see the remains of the main line, which had been destroyed by the Germans as they retreated. Demolition mines had caused some of the destruction, but an ingenious plough-like device that the Germans had used to rip up the railway ties caused most of it. The Russians were not stopped.

I arrived in Eisiskes almost sick with anticipation, only to find that my mother wasn't there. I felt my one shred of hope was gone; all my family was really dead. I looked for our house but even that was gone, demolished so that its bricks could be used to build a steam bath in what was once our synagogue. It was almost as if our family had never existed. Shmulke Szewicki, whom I had last seen in Grodno, came to stand silently beside me. We were both alone; there was no need for words. He helped me dig for the family possessions that my father had buried but it was an impossible task. Father had said they were under the middle support of the stable, but the stable had vanished just as the house had, and everything looked foreign. With my eyes closed I tried to imagine where the house had stood and how many steps I used to walk to the stable. I paced it off but it was no use. I consoled myself that our possessions had probably been taken long before, since it had been common practice for the Poles to dig up the earth around the homes of the departed Jews.

Before I left town I had another task: a visit to Mrs. Carolowa. It was early afternoon when I arrived and I stood with the sun at my back as she opened the door. She squinted and twisted her head this way and that to make out my face. At last she saw who it was.

"Leibke," she said and there was only shock in her voice. Her daughter, whom I respected, rushed to the door to greet me but the old lady mumbled and fretted, her eyes constantly shifting to the gun I carried. Had it not been for her daughter, I think I would have shot the old thief.

After a minute, she rushed off to find our family silverware, my mother's diamond earrings and a few clothes. She must have sold everything else. Next I went to the farmer and his wife who had stored my aunt's possessions. Apparently they too believed our entire family was dead, for they stood a long while staring in disbelief.

"I don't keep those things here," he said. "Come back tomorrow and I'll have them ready for you."

When I returned the next day, the farmer laid out three coats for my inspection: an eel skin, a broadtail, and a caracal.

"Which of these belonged to your aunt?" he asked.

"All of them," I said, and walked out with them, reasoning that, since they all had been stolen from Jews, none of them rightfully belonged to the farmer.

I walked through Eisiskes one last time and returned to the marketplace. The town was almost the same, yet nothing was the same. I strained to hear the voices of my people in the square, in the synagogue, in the streets. Instead, there were only echoes of my childhood clinging there — nothing that was real and alive. I was conscious of terrible waves of pain and longing.

In Varena I found myself reunited with many old friends who had also been reassigned there. Benjamin Rogowski from Radun, the leader of a crack squad of partisans, was there with his sister Chaya, who had also fought with the partisans. Benjamin was a little older than my brother would have been now, but quite different in temperament. The son of a wealthy hardware merchant, he had even had his own motorcycle before the war. With the two of them was Chaya's friend, Zlatella, a war orphan who had cooked for Davidov's group.

Young Chaim Berkowicz, the sixteen-year-old brother of Aaron who was killed at the Yureli ambush, was also stationed there. He was now nicknamed "Pietka." Another boy, about the same age as Chaim, was Yitzhak Sonenson, whose mother and newborn brother had been rescued from the marketplace at Eisiskes. Later, Benjamin Rogowski and I took these two young hellions under our wing, unofficially adopting them in the hope of keeping them out of trouble. This was quite a task because they delighted in practical jokes, especially whenever they spied Lippa Skolsky, who was also posted to Varena. As Lippa spent hours preparing his appearance, combing and re-combing his hair, these two would delight in ambushing him as soon as he had perfected his coiffure. Abraham Widlanski, whom I hadn't seen for nearly a year, and Abraham and Luba Asner completed our group.

Asner, Rogowski, Skolsky, and I had orders from the Russians to set up a police station in Varena. The new police chief was a Lithuanian and a member of the Communist party from before the war. Our assignment was to find the members of the *Einsatzgruppen,* all the Nazi sympathizers responsible for the murder of Jews, and all the civil officials who had collaborated with the Germans. We had lists of names to begin our search and more were added as time went by.

The work was risky and time-consuming because the wanted men had gone into hiding. We questioned their families but most of them claimed to have no information, and we spent hours preparing ambushes for quarry who never returned. Since we had no vehicle other than a horse and wagon, there was no question of high-speed chases to catch our man. Often, after receiving a tip that led to one of the men on our list, we would arrive too late to make an arrest. Naturally this didn't deter us, for we went back again and again until we caught him, but it was time-consuming and frustrating. Worst of all, our police chief freed our prisoners as soon as we had locked them up. He automatically released all Lithuanians. It didn't take long before we decided he'd have to go. We had no respect for him because he'd come through the war unscathed and got his job only because he was a party member. He was untrustworthy and uncooperative.

So we fired him. We had no authority to do this but that didn't matter to us. We were still operating with the minds of partisans; our instincts told us that he would only cause us trouble. We were reprimanded, of course, but that was unimportant since the man was not reinstated. After his departure, we really got down to work. We made bargains with some of the farmers who were guilty of lesser crimes in order to catch the big criminals. We promised them amnesty if they turned informer; many were quite willing to cooperate.

One of our big catches was the Lithuanian, Stankewicz, the friend of Ostrauskas, in Eisiskes. He headed our list of wanted men. One night an informer came to tell us that Stankewicz had returned to his farm. Four of us — Rogowski, Skolsky, Pietka, and I — went in our horse and wagon to capture him. Soon we had him locked in a cell in Varena. Stankewicz was no ordinary criminal, for there were witnesses to his murders who had survived the war. One of these was Abraham Widlanski's brother, who blamed Stankewicz for the deaths of his whole family. As soon as he heard that the murderer had been captured, he claimed the right to execute him and we granted it. He entered Stankewicz's cell with a two-by-four studded with spikes.

One of the criminals we never caught was Ostrauskas, the monster who murdered the women and children of Eisiskes. When we learned that his family lived in Alytus, we staked out the house for six weeks, but Ostrauskas never showed up. We questioned his wife, but she told us he was an insane murderer and that she had nothing to do with him anymore. We tried to force more information from her, but it was useless. Some of our group wanted to kill her for her husband's crimes, but such an action would only have lowered us to the level of Ostrauskas. Despite our youth and the horrors and suffering we had endured, we still retained our innate respect for life. Ostrauskas' wife was not responsible for the crimes committed by her husband. We could not punish her for them, so this was one murderer who went unpunished, and to this day Ostraukas has never been identified for what he is.

Another man on our list was a one-armed Lithuanian who lived close to Varena. He had lost his arm in an industrial accident before the war and made his living as a handyman for a number of Jewish families. After the slaughter of Varena's Jews, he took it upon himself to find the escapees and report them to the Lithuanian authorities. One day while driving his horse and wagon he recognized a ten-year-old Jewish boy dressed in farm clothes. He greeted the boy affectionately and asked where his family was hiding, claiming he wanted to help them. Trustingly, the boy told him. As neighbours recounted the story, the one-armed man lost no time in reporting them to the police and all of them were murdered.

When we set out on his trail, we found him very elusive, always managing to outwit us. At last we persuaded his neighbours to watch for him, and one day a man burst into our office to report that our quarry had come home. Twenty of us climbed into wagons to capture him. Only four of us were Jews. It was daybreak when we reached the house, and through a window we could see his wife baking bread in the kitchen. Her husband was nowhere to be seen. Some of the group surrounded the house and barn before the others burst into the house. The woman backed away from us.

"Where's your husband?" Frightened, the woman shook her head. Upstairs I roused a boy of fourteen from sleep. "Where's your

father?" I demanded. He stammered and finally said, "He's . . . he's
. . . he's in Varena."

We brought the whole family — two more sons and a grandmother — downstairs. We threatened to shoot them one by one and
burn their house down but they all denied knowledge of the one-
armed handyman's whereabouts. Finally we took the fourteen-year-
old outside and described all his father's crimes to him; still the boy
kept saying his father was in Varena. This loyalty surprised us, for the
man was known to have beaten his children and had been unfaith-
ful to his wife. Finally, when we told his son how the handyman had
tricked the young Jewish boy, he broke down and confessed that his
father was hiding in the hayloft with several guns for defence.

The next step required diplomacy because the Lithuanians in our
police force insisted that their countrymen be given full legal rights
and a fair trial in Alytus. Therefore, it would not do to simply attack
the barn and kill the man. Instead, we shouted at him to come out
of the barn.

"You're surrounded! You might as well come out!"

There was no movement in the barn.

"All right, you leave us no choice. We'll have to set fire to your
barn!"

Then one of the men walked slowly toward the barn with a lighted
torch. Just when we thought we would have to carry out our threat,
the barn door began to open cautiously and the handyman came
out. We started back to Varena with our prisoner but we worried
that he would convince the authorities in Alytus of his innocence
and gain back his freedom. As we were approaching a small forest,
Yacobovicius, a Lithuanian who hated the Nazis, leaned over to the
handyman.

"You better jump out and run when we get to the trees," he whispered. "These guys won't give you a fair trial! They're planning to
kill you themselves!" Naturally, as soon as we reached the forest, the
handyman leaped from the wagon. As he sped for the trees, we all
raised our guns and fired simultaneously. The handyman fell dead.

At about this time we caught a liquor vendor from Eisiskes who
was guilty of many crimes against the Jews. Unfortunately, we did

not have hard evidence of his participation, so we had to send him on to Russian headquarters at Alytus to which we were directly responsible. We were reluctant to do this. In the process of handing over our prisoners, we often lost them because the Russians required that we document the crimes of our prisoners in Russian, which was often beyond our capabilities. Although we had all the evidence for a conviction, we lacked the ability to write it up in Russian. I was the only member of the Varena police force who could write in Russian at all, and I was certainly not capable of reporting on a complicated interrogation. As a result, the Russians often could not understand why we had bothered to send them some of our prisoners, and criminals whom we had spent weeks tracking would be set free once they got to Alytus.

Many times we were aided by Aba Gefen, a Jew who was an assistant to the Russian colonel in command in Alytus. Aba became our liaison with the Russians, interceding when problems arose. All prisoners sent by us were interrogated and documented by him before the colonel processed them. Unfortunately, even Aba Gefen couldn't process documents that we couldn't provide. After we had stumbled along in this inefficient fashion for some time, we received a visit from a Russian general whose name, if memory serves me right, was Rudin. Hearing of our war exploits, he invited Rogowski, Skolsky and myself to dine with him. He complimented us on our record and our bravery and then suddenly, changing the subject, asked, "Do you like herring?"

"Of course," said Rogowski. Skolsky and I nodded in agreement.

"How much do you pay for it?"

"Ten kopeks," I said, completely mystified by the conversation.

"And where do you get it?"

"At the fish store."

"How is it sold to you?"

"The owner takes it out of the barrel, puts it in some newspaper, and hands it to me," I answered. "I take it home and somebody prepares it ready to eat."

The general leaned back in his chair. "Were you ever in Moscow?" he asked.

We shook our heads. "Well, in Moscow we sell herring in the Metro café. Do you know how much they'll cost you there? A ruble and a half. Do you know why they cost that much?"

We waited for the answer, still not understanding what Moscow's herring had to do with us.

"In Moscow, they take the same herring, arrange it artistically on a plate with onions and capers, and serve it with style. And that's why herring will cost you ten kopeks in Varena and fifteen times as much in Moscow. Because you have to pay for the service."

We got the message.

"That's what is wrong with your police department, you see. You keep sending us herrings but you don't serve them up with style. You need someone to write your reports so that your herrings come to us the proper way."

"We are trying," I said, "but between the lot of us we don't have enough Russian for the job. I write Russian a little, but I don't understand the legal procedures."

"Don't worry!" the general reassured us, and within a week a legal secretary arrived from Alytus to be a permanent member of our staff, take down evidence, document it, and then submit it to headquarters "with style." After that, we sent our prisoners to Alytus knowing that our documents would be read and given full credence.

On our fortnightly trips to report to Alytus we used to take a wagon filled with produce for Aba Gefen and his colonel. The food was welcomed, for in the first week of August the Germans had settled behind a new line of defence a hundred miles beyond the city, and there they held on for nearly six months. As a result, Alytus, thirty miles northwest of Varena, was close to the war zone and food was scarce. Since Varena was part of a rural community, it was easy for us to load up with barrels of honey, meat, bacon, and flour, and gallons of liquor. We also supplied them with boots for which Varena was noted just as Eisiskes had been.

Although we now lived our lives in the open, much of our work was extremely dangerous because the men we sought were desperate to escape from justice. We had to rely largely on ambushes and stakeouts to capture the men on our list. However, one of our biggest fish walked into the net himself. One afternoon, Benjamin, Chaya Rogowski, Zlatella, Pietka, and I were just finishing dinner when something made us look up. The dining room window overlooked the street and there walking calmly down the sidewalk was Baderas, the killer of Eisiskes.

Leaving the women behind, we dashed out of the house but we were too late. Our quarry had vanished. Furious at losing him, we searched all the shops down the street. Then suddenly there he was again, standing confidently in the wide foyer of the city hall talking to the Lithuanian who was secretary of the Communist Party. The three of us rushed in and began pounding Baderas with our fists, slamming him into the wall, while the tiny Lithuanian secretary danced around us.

"Stop it! Stop it!" he screamed.

I pushed him aside and smashed my fist into Baderas' face.

"Why are you doing this?" the little man howled. "Why are you hitting my friend?"

"Why?" I said incredulously. "You want to know why we're hitting this murderer? You want to know what your friend did to my people?"

We informed him of the crimes that Baderas was accused of, but the little secretary just kept shaking his head.

"No," he said, "you're wrong! This man isn't Baderas. His name is Markovicz. He is my old and dear friend. He's not the man you're looking for!"

Since it was useless to try to convince this man, we turned our backs on him and demanded Baderas' identification. Naturally he produced papers to show he was Markovicz.

I pushed my face into his. "Don't you recognize me, Baderas?" I asked him in Lithuanian.

"No! I've never seen you before in my life!"

"What about my father, Shael Kaganowicz? Do you remember him?"

"No!" he said, but his eyes were filled with fear.

Then Benjamin pushed me aside and grabbed Baderas and shook him. "Your name isn't Markovicz! It's Baderas! You don't fool us!"

And he shoved him roughly into the street. The secretary still hovered at my elbow yelling, "You're making a dreadful mistake! This man is my friend." I pushed him down and we left him sitting on the floor of the city hall foyer. The jail was only two doors away and we hustled Baderas along and locked him away in a cell. The three of us felt tremendously elated, for we had long dreamed of bringing this man to justice. Suddenly Pietka's eyes sparkled. "Did you see that guy's boots?" And he pulled up his pant legs to show us the remains of his own worn-out shoes. Baderas had been wearing a pair of soft leather riding boots that looked like they cost a fortune.

"No, Pietka! Keep your hands off the boots," I said, and we turned to the larger problem of making sure that Baderas got his due. We couldn't simply take the law into our own hands anymore because the Russians had sent a patrol of a hundred "Green Hat" border guards to Varena to help quell the Lithuanian partisans. These partisans had never operated during the German occupation but sprang into being when the Germans' retreat left the Lithuanians to atone for their crimes as Nazi collaborators. One of the reasons that we had been finding it so difficult to locate the men on our list was that these partisans were giving refuge to the wanted men. The partisans also made attacks on the members of our police squad to intimidate them.

The presence of the Green Hats made any summary conviction and execution of Baderas out of the question, but we thought their commanding officer, an NKVD man named Saffronov, might be approachable. It was now his responsibility to deal with our prisoners before they were sent on to Alytus. We were worried, however, that Saffronov might treat Baderas in the routine manner he used for all our prisoners and then send him on to Alytus. There the Lithuanian court would set him free. We decided to invite Saffronov to dinner; Zlatella outdid herself in the food she prepared for him that night. We plied him with delicacies and liquor until his mood was so mellow he just sat there smiling contentedly. Then we told him about our prisoner, who had now been transferred to the Russian jail, and the crimes he had perpetrated against our very own families.

"We want you to shoot him here in Varena," I said.

"No," he said. "That is contrary to Russian law, and I have no authority to execute anyone under these circumstances."

No amount of pleading would change his mind. Baderas would be sent to Alytus for trial where we knew he would be acquitted. "All right," I said. "We respect your position. However, we'd like your permission to interrogate him at our headquarters before he's sent to Alytus. Will you issue a permit for us to transfer him to our own jail?"

Saffronov must have known what we planned to do but he issued us the necessary permits. The three of us, Benjamin, Pietka, and I, came for Baderas the next evening and walked him back to our headquarters. As we walked, we told him that we'd decided to punish him for his crimes right there on the street.

"This is as far as you go, Baderas," Benjamin said. "This is where you get what you deserve."

Baderas fell on his knees on the cobblestones, weeping desperately.

"No, please don't! I'll give you anything you want! Anything! I've got gold and money! I'll give you anything, anything!"

We forced him to get up and walk again, prodding him along the street. Each of us carried an automatic rifle containing seventy-two bullets, and at a signal, coldly and methodically we emptied every one of them into his body. In minutes the street was full of Green Hats, demanding to know what was going on.

"He tried to escape," I told the Green Hats, but when I turned back to look at the body, I knew we were in trouble. His feet were bare. I glanced over at Pietka and saw that he was holding those beautiful riding boots. The officer of the guard who had surrendered Baderas to us only five minutes earlier pushed through the circle around us. His eyes lit on Pietka and the boots he held.

"You shot him just to get his boots?" he asked in horror.

"No, no," I said, taking him aside. "The boy took the boots after the man was dead. We shot the prisoner because he tried to escape. It had nothing to do with the boots."

"Come over to the house and have a drink while we discuss it," Benjamin said. Luckily the officer agreed, and in a little while Saffronov joined us. He convinced the officer that we were friends and had been heroes among the partisans. The officer then said, "You know, Leibke, all of us have been admiring those boots and trying to figure out how to get them!"

Not all the dangers in our job came from our enemies. One time we set out to retrieve seven Russian horses which had strayed onto the farm of a Lithuanian and been claimed by him. He became belligerent when told why we had come and refused to give up the horses. Abraham Asner, who was with me, became angry and hit the man, so the man got up and hit him back. Asner, furious now, struck the man with the butt of his automatic rifle and the rifle went off, the bullet zinging past my head. After the Lithuanian was shot and the horses retrieved, I rode home thinking how stupid it would have been to die at the hand of a friend when I had taken such great pains to avoid dying at the hands of the enemy!

On a number of occasions we combined forces with the Green Hats to halt the activities of the Polish renegades and the Lithuanian partisans. One day we received a call to go to the rescue of a small Russian garrison in Eisiskes who were under siege by the Polish partisans. In a battle with a large group of Poles, the Russians had captured forty or fifty of them and imprisoned them in the old Eisiskes post office, which had been converted into a jail. The Russians then retired to their own quarters directly across the street, but very soon the remaining Poles laid siege to these quarters. Under cover of the renewed battle, they released their comrades from the jail.

Once liberated, they roamed the streets looking for blood. Most of the people of the town were Polish and had little to fear from them, but some of Eisiskes' Jews had returned home determined to build their lives again. Among these were Moishe Sonenson and his wife Faigl. These two and their family had endured so much misery that surely no more could happen to them. Faigl and her baby had escaped from Eisiskes, only to have the child smothered to death in Radun to save their group from discovery. They had hidden in attics and pigsties and finally been given refuge in the barn of a man named Korkuc in Lebedniki. They had built a pit house below the earthen floor of his barn, covering it with hay for camouflage. In this pit, Faigl had given birth to another infant, but this time they left it on the doorstep of a kindly neighbouring farmer because the baby had little chance for survival otherwise. After the Russians returned, the Sonensons had retrieved their child. The farmer confessed he had always suspected the infant was Jewish. Although they had been robbed of everything they owned, they had still returned to Eisiskes with hope. For Faigl, the Poles rampaging through the town must have seemed like a continuation of the same terrible nightmare she had lived through for so long. Moishe grabbed the older children and ran. Faigl picked up her baby and fled to the attic but the Poles heard the baby's cry and dragged Faigl and her child downstairs again. Faigl recognized one of her captors, a pharmacist who had known her father, also a pharmacist. The man pretended not to know her. "Antony, please!" she pleaded. "You know me! We've been friends since we were kids!" As we learned later from one of the Poles, Antony turned away as the others shot her and the child.

Two truckloads of Green Hats and our police group drove the twenty miles to Eisiskes but we had been called too late. The AKs had fled. When we entered the Sonenzon house, I stared down at the floor stained with the blood of its poor victims. A large blotch marked the place where Faigl had died; beside it was a smaller one, that of her baby. A terrible rage came over me.

Young Yitzhak Sonenson, one of the boys Rogowski and I had "adopted," had returned to Eisiskes with us. He stayed now to comfort his father. The rest of us searched from house to house to learn who had helped the murderers. One man, a good friend to the Sonenzons, gave us information that led to the discovery of the Polish arsenal, but we never found the murderers, not even the pharmacist who had turned his back on a childhood friend.

During the winter of 1944 and the spring of 1945, the Lithuanian partisans were such an enormous problem that the Russians decided to open another police station in the area. They chose a village just four miles away also called Varena. In February 1945, I was appointed the police chief in the little village and given a number of police to command. Included in the group were the Nazi-hating Lithuanian, Yacobovicius, and the Polish Communist, Kozlowski. I had great faith in Kozlowski as he had taken such risks for us to attach magnetic mines to the German railcars. He was an exceptional machine-gunner and a great friend.

Our first task in the village was to bring justice to a Lithuanian schoolteacher who, like Ostrauskas, had organized the slaughter of the Jews of the village. He was not at his home when we arrived but we knew we could outwait him, so we lined up some informers and got on with the rest of our work. One evening, a farmer came running with the news that the teacher had returned.

We arrived at night, surrounding his farm on three sides, and settled down to wait for the dawn. The only avenue of escape was an open field, and Kozlowski and his machine gun guarded it. At dawn, I knocked at the door. "Open up! Police!"

The teacher jumped out the back window and fled. Immediately, Kozlowski's machine gun sprayed across the field, catching him in the leg. He fell, unable to escape any further. Now we had the problem of transporting a man with a badly shattered leg to Alytus for trial. If we took him by cart we would be targets for the Lithuanian partisans waiting in the forest. What we needed was a bus or a truck and an escort, but there was simply none to be had. We phoned the Russian police at Alytus who told us to keep him until they could come for him.

Shortly after this, gangrene settled in the teacher's leg. We phoned Alytus again. The Russians intimated that we should shoot him. Now this was certainly a reasonable solution since the teacher would eventually be shot for his crimes anyway, but it posed an additional problem. It was still winter and the ground was frozen solid. How would we get rid of the body? Meanwhile, the man was rotting away. About a week later, a Russian NKVD general on an inspection tour happened to stop at our headquarters. I explained that we had a murderer on our hands who would die of gangrene before the police in Alytus came for him.

"Shoot him," he said.

"Yes sir. But how do we dispose of the body? The ground's frozen solid."

"Throw him in the river," he said.

This had never occurred to us. That night we told the prisoner he was being transferred to the hospital in the town of Varena. The journey included crossing a bridge over a wide and deep river. We loaded him onto a wagon and when we came to the bridge, I stood guard at one end while Kozlowski guarded the other approach. One of the Lithuanians was given the job of taking the teacher to the middle of the bridge and shooting him. We heard a shot. Then another shot. And then another. But the teacher kept right on yelling! We ran to the centre of the bridge and there stood the Lithuanian with a smoking revolver and a look of panic on his face. "I can't kill him!" he said. I pulled out my revolver and shot the teacher between the eyes, killing him instantly. Moments later his body had vanished into the river, and we rode back to town.

We had received information that the Lithuanian partisans were actively recruiting in the area and decided to investigate. Their headquarters was a house nearly five miles away. Three of us decided to make a trip disguised as farmers who wanted to join the partisans. As my features would pass as Lithuanian and I spoke Lithuanian fairly fluently, I went with two of my policemen (Yacobovicius was one of them) who really were Lithuanian. We told the owner of the house that we wanted to join the partisans because we were tired of all the Russians and Jews running things. The man sent for three more partisans and all of us sat around the table talking politics, the three of us trying to convince them of our sincerity. By this time, I had begun to wonder what we were doing there, for they were all heavily armed. If they became suspicious we'd be done for. I was careful to speak very little in case I made mistakes in the language, but under cover of the table I held my gun ready. Just when I was beginning to break out in a cold sweat, Yacobovicius yelled, "Hands up!" He jumped to his feet knocking over his chair. It was too sudden for the Lithuanian partisans to retaliate and they surrendered without a fight. In our office in the village we interrogated them, and by slow degrees extracted the names of nearly sixty families in the area whose fathers or sons had been members of the *Einsatzgruppen*. All of them were now members of the partisans or collaborated with them.

It was an enormous task to round up all sixty of these men and imprison them in the cement basement of the police station. We refused them food, water, or toilet facilities, allowing them only the supplies brought by their families. After a week, the trucks arrived with armed Russian guards to take them to Alytus. It was a terrible scene. As the men were loaded onto the trucks, the Lithuanian women screamed and threw themselves on the ground or clung to the sides of the truck. I felt nothing. I was in Eisiskes again, lying on the roof of the stable, listening to the screams coming from the synagogue. I could hear my brother Benjamin's heart beating in my ears; I could hear the looters ransacking the house and breaking the barn door below us. Some women clutched at me. "How can you do this, Leibke Kaganowicz? What would your father think? He was such a fine man. He would never do this!"

At their words, I exploded with rage. "And what did you do to help my father or any of the thousands of my people your men murdered?" I screamed. "Don't you dare come crying to me about your fathers and sons. They killed us by the thousands, without mercy, without pity. Now they will be punished, as they deserve to be. At least they will get some sort of a fair trial. What justice was given to my people? Don't you talk to me about kindness or neighbourly responsibility. You are all animals! And I hope you die like animals!"

They cried out that they were innocent and their men wrongfully accused. As I walked toward my office, they followed, pleading. I turned in the doorway. "Tell me one thing you did to help my people when we were being murdered. You threw dirt on our bodies as we died. You shot my sisters and brothers who had only been wounded. Tell me one thing you did to help us. At least your men will get a fair trial! What court of law were my people tried in?" And I slammed the door on them.

After that day I was on the top of the Lithuanians' "most wanted" list. Since they even put a price on my head, it was only safe for me to go out to make arrests in the company of a squad of policemen. On one of these forays we found a completely deserted farm. We all felt uneasy and, fearing an ambush, I ordered three men to stay at the farm and the rest to follow me to a farm over the next ridge to make enquiries. As we approached the farm, a fusillade of bullets whizzed over our heads and we dropped to the ground. We fired back with all the guns we had, but we had left our heavy equipment in the wagon near the last farm. We were pinned down, unable to approach any closer, and our enemies would not show themselves long enough to become targets.

"Go get the others and the machine gun!" I yelled at one of my men. "And make it fast!" He dashed off while we sprayed the farmhouse and barn with bullets. We were well aware that if he did not return in a hurry we would be out of ammunition, and we would not have a hope of survival. The Lithuanians were now firing at us from the roof of the house and their aim was becoming more accurate.

Suddenly, the shooting stopped. From the rooftop the Lithuanians had seen Kozlowski running to our rescue with the machine gun; they had run out the back of the house and headed across the fields to the forest. Scarcely pausing after he arrived, Kozlowski started firing; a moment later the thatched roof of the barn burst into flames. Realizing they had escaped, we ran around the other side of the barn but they were out of range by then. The fracas was now joined by a Russian patrol, which roared into the farmyard, drawn by the noise of battle. I asked for their help to pursue the Lithuanians but they turned me down because it was too late in the day to begin hunting partisans in the forest.

That was my last battle. It was now the spring of 1945, and the country was beginning to return to some semblance of peacetime stability.

One afternoon, without any warning, a Russian police sergeant appeared in my office, produced documents naming him head of the Varena village police detachment, and told us we were fired. We refused to believe him. This was our police station and they could not kick us out, especially not by this NKVD man! We decided to ignore him and carry on as usual. Next Benjamin Rogowski and I received official letters from the Russian command ordering us to report to Alytus. This was real trouble, we knew, for a new colonel had replaced Aba Gefen's tolerant Russian colonel in Alytus, and

Gefen could not influence him on our behalf. The new colonel was already tired of listening to complaints from the Lithuanians that we had robbed them, or mistreated them, or taken the law into our own hands. He was not as tolerant as Gefen's colonel who had once, laughingly, said, "If I took half the complaints against you seriously, I'd have to jail you, your children and your grandchildren for life!"

When we appeared before him, the new colonel stared coldly at us and asked, "What do you have to say in your own defence?"

"We were partisans, sir! We fought side-by-side with the Russian people!"

"The day of the partisans is over," he interrupted coldly. "Take off your belts and hand over your pistols. You will face trial for your crimes against the Lithuanian people!"

We were speechless. I saw years of Siberia stretching before me and I had to check a wild impulse to shoot my way out. At that moment the phone rang. We waited while the colonel barked a few questions into it, listened, and hung up. Abruptly, he stood up.

"You two come back here directly after lunch and we'll decide what's to be done with you! Now get out!"

We did not need a second invitation. Out on the street, Rogowski and I commiserated with each other. Yesterday we were heroes, today we were outcasts, but there had to be a way to avoid Siberia. We could not run away because we would not get far with only a horse and wagon. Unhappy, we wandered into a restaurant to discuss our predicament over lunch and, looking around, saw what we hoped was the answer to our prayers. He was the tallest man I've ever known, sitting alone at one of the tables in the uniform of a Russian lieutenant. We asked to share his table in the crowded restaurant and introduced ourselves. We learned that his name was Kalinin and we bought him a drink. Then we told him our troubles.

He looked thoughtful, and asked a few questions.

"I think I may be able to help you," he said. He was the recruiting officer for an NKVD school scheduled to open soon in Vilnius. The recruits had to be partisans or Communist Party members. He thought he could clear it with the angry colonel for us to be accepted as recruits.

"There's only one problem. The school construction isn't finished yet so I can't take you for three months."

In three months we could be in Siberia.

"You see, I just came to Alytus to hire some more carpenters and mechanics," he explained.

"You're in luck!" I said, beaming with a confidence I didn't feel. "I'm a carpenter and my friend's a mechanic!"

It took only a few more drinks to cement the deal. Then Kalinin went off to make arrangements with the colonel. Of course, the colonel didn't mind because we would be as safe in an NKVD school as in jail, and he could put us on trial for our crimes once our training was completed. A half hour later we were in Kalinin's truck heading to Varena to pack our belongings. We then drove to the Orzeszkowa Gymnasium, a former high school in Vilnius, which was being renovated to house the NKVD school. We met a few friends from our partisan days and, among them, Bolke Maciekowski from the Leninski Komsomol. Bolke was remembered best by the partisans for his one continuing problem: finding boots to fit his unusually large feet. After one raid in which nine Germans were killed, he tried on all their boots but none would fit. He was reduced to the discomfort of tight boots or going barefoot. Finally, the problem was solved by lying in wait for farmers as they left church on Sunday morning, taking the boots of the one with the largest feet and leaving him a smaller pair in return. The farmers, of course, had larger feet than soldiers because they had gone barefoot as youths.

At the school, Bolke, Benjamin and I were the only Jews amid six hundred Lithuanians. We were always aware of the antagonism of the Lithuanians, but we led a protected existence, for Kalinin was the head of supplies and organization for the school, and he made sure we lacked for nothing. He even allowed us to carry revolvers, which were forbidden to all the others. In return we gave him the companionship he craved, all of us carousing and enjoying ourselves together. Meanwhile, our minds were always on the problem of escaping from the school. In the evenings and on Sundays, we explored Vilnius, looking for Jews who might have returned. Among them we found Benjamin Akselrod, who was now serving in the

Lithuanian Brigade of the Russian army. During the war he had been imprisoned in the Vilnius ghetto but, because he was a hat-maker by trade, the Germans had taken him out of the ghetto to a cap factory on the other side of the city. Until liberation, he had the dubious pleasure of making caps for the German army. When the Germans left, the Russians conscripted him.

Akselrod had no more love for the Russian army than the three of us did, and so all of us sat endlessly mulling over possible methods of escape. Then one day in April 1945, the Russians gave us one. The Germans had finally surrendered Warsaw in January, and now the Russians announced that all Poles in Russian-occupied territory could return to the area that would in future be designated as Poland. Provided, that is, they had the necessary identification papers.

Neither Akselrod nor I had Polish papers, but I contacted a friend in Vilnius to prepare false ones for us. Akselrod, who was in his mid-twenties, would pose as my brother-in-law. Once in Poland, we would find a way to escape to the west where we hoped our futures would be more promising. The only problem still unresolved was that of escaping from the school. We could not simply vanish because the Russians would begin searching for us immediately; we had to give ourselves ample running time, at least a couple of days' head start. We decide that we would have to find some way to get closer to the front, and thereby closer to Poland. At the school, Bolke, Benjamin and I approached the problem head-on by asking for an interview with the commandant of the school.

The head of the school held the rank of colonel, was a dedicated Communist, and spoke only Russian even though he was actually Lithuanian. The three of us stood before him with a brash plan in mind.

"Sir, the three of us wish to be transferred from the school."

He looked enquiringly at each of us.

"The students here, sir, are Lithuanian fascists and murderers."

His eyes widened a little, but he didn't speak.

"These are the same Lithuanians that collaborated with the Germans and fought against the Russian people. We had to fight them long after we had destroyed the Germans. They have the blood of thousands of Jews and Russians on their hands. Our own families died at the hands of these Lithuanians."

The colonel's face was completely expressionless. There was nowhere to go but onward.

"We request a transfer, sir."

His eyes travelled over us again, but his expression remained inscrutable. Finally, he spoke. "If you leave here, you have only one alternative: the army, and that will mean going to the front."

It was hard to keep calm because this was exactly where our friend, Kalinin, had suggested we go when we told him we were unhappy. "Well," he had said, "you could always transfer to the army and join the Allies in Germany!"

Now we looked straight at the colonel and said in chorus, "Yes, sir!"

This time his expression changed enough to show his surprise. He thought he'd called our bluff. Two Russian soldiers were detailed to escort us to the induction centre. On the way, we dazzled them with stories of our activities as partisans, and in no time we had become five old friends just out for a walk. We passed a tavern.

"How about stopping for a drink before we go to the induction office?" asked Rogowski. The soldiers exchanged a look. They'd just remembered they were guarding us.

"Oh come on, we've got plenty of time," I urged.

They grinned and we entered the tavern. One drink led to another and the second led to the third, and soon it was mid-afternoon and the induction office was firmly closed.

The Russians panicked. They couldn't return us to the school because they'd have to explain why we didn't get to the office on time.

"Never mind," I said. "It's nothing to worry about. You can go back to the school and tell them we enlisted and we'll do it on Monday morning."

"That's right!" said Maciekowski. "Remember we *volunteered* for the army!"

"And that's where we're going!" added Rogowski. "Now let's all have another drink since we're not going anyplace right now!"

Afterwards, they left us swearing eternal friendship. As soon as they were out of sight, we split up, with Rogowski and Maciekowski leaving on their own, and my setting off to meet Akselrod. We travelled to the small railway station of Pozeczy, near Varena, and stayed there with a friend of mine, Joseph Kaplan, awaiting the arrival of the railway cars that the Russians were providing for the Poles returning home.

Two weeks later, several boxcars were shunted onto the siding and we boarded an empty one with our false identification papers. In my pockets were ten thousand rubles saved from my policeman's salary. It was against the law to leave Russian territory with money but I knew the funds would come in handy for bribes. The real problem on this trip was Akselrod. He was now an army deserter and it was fairly easy to spot him, since his head was still shaved in the Russian army pig-shave given to all enlisted men. Besides, he still wore his army greatcoat although he had ripped off the buttons. Plenty of civilians were to be seen in similar coats these days, but his haircut and the greatcoat together were too much of a coincidence. However, it was autumn and he had nothing else to keep him warm, so he had to wear it and take the chance.

I had no problem with my haircut, for students at the NKVD school were considered officers and wore their hair longer. I still wore my army boots, but they were not different enough from work boots to be noticeable. When we arrived at the Polish border, the Russian guards entered our boxcar to find just the two of us, me trying to look nonchalant, and Akselrod sound asleep on the floor with his greatcoat almost covering his head. I showed one of them my papers, which he examined carefully. Then I handed him Akselrod's papers.

"My brother-in-law," I said by way of explanation.

The other guard asked, "Are you carrying any Russian currency?"

"Why?" I asked innocently.

"It's against the law to take Russian currency from the county."

"Oh!" I said. "I didn't know that! I've got ten thousand rubles on me," and I dug into my pockets for it.

"Hand it over. I'll give you a receipt for it."

"What for? It's no use to me in Poland!" And I waved his receipt book away. The guard smiled and pocketed the money. By this time, the first guard had finished examining our papers and he interrupted the conversation.

"Where's your brother-in-law?"

I pointed to the heap on the floor that was the sleeping Akselrod. "Should I wake him?"

"No, no, it won't be necessary. His papers are in order."

They climbed out of the car, the train moved on, and we were inside Poland. I shook Akselrod awake and together we celebrated in our private boxcar.

CHAPTER ELEVEN

Lodz: May–September 1945

The first stop inside Poland was the city of Bialystok and we left our boxcar to investigate. We found the office of the Jewish Committee and asked about survivors from Grodno. The woman brought out a list.

"Who are you looking for?"

"The Winicki family," I said, and stood silently praying.

She looked up from her list. "Yes," she said, "they survived."

By some miracle the entire family was alive and they were now living in the city of Lodz. More than anything, I wanted to see Bella Winicki again! I had never had the courage to tell her how I felt about her that winter in Grodno, but I wanted to tell her now. Before the war, Lodz had been an important Polish industrial city and it had remained virtually intact in spite of the terrible devastation in other cities. Now it was overflowing with nearly thirty thousand Jewish survivors and Russian refugees and humming again with industry. Through the Jewish Committee in Lodz we found the Winicki family without too much difficulty, and they urged us to stay in their home until we found a place of our own.

At last I could tell dear Bella how I felt about her and indulge in the innocence of a youthful love affair that ghetto existence had discouraged. Bella returned my love and I was in a state of complete bliss, at least for a while. The end of my idyllic state was not Bella's fault. It was the result of the circumstances around us, for young men were almost non-existent in post-war Poland and suddenly I had more than my share of female admirers. It was a delightful situation for any young man to find himself in.

In Lodz I returned to my search for my mother, haunting the offices of the Committee for information. But her name never appeared on any list, and none of the survivors ever recalled her.

Coincidentally, I met my future wife, Evelyn Landsman, and her family in Lodz. Their home was a centre for survivors searching for information about lost relatives from our area. At that time, Evelyn was a beautiful girl of twelve and she lived with her mother and grandmother, Hodl Shuster. I informed them I was on my way to a relocation centre from which I hoped eventually to go to the United States, and they asked to join me. I had to refuse, for I felt it would be too hazardous for Mrs. Shuster to undertake the trip, as she was quite elderly. Little did I know that a few short years later I would meet Evelyn again, and that she would become my dear wife and the mother of our children.

Benjamin Akselrod was also looking for his missing family; he was more fortunate than I in his search. He knew that he was the only male survivor of his family but he had always hoped that his sister, Malke, might also be alive. Again and again he returned to read the lists of concentration camp survivors and the lists of people that these survivors had identified in the camps where they were interned. When he had almost given up, he met a survivor named Reisel Rosenthal, who told him Malke Akselrod was alive and living on a farm outside Danzig, a town where Reisel had also lived.

We left as soon as possible to find her. Benjamin and his sister had an indescribable reunion — full of tears for the lost and happiness for those who had been spared. Malke and the man and two women whom she had been living with returned to Lodz with us. There, she was reunited with Alter Rubin, a man she had known in pre-war times, and the four of us — Benjamin, Malke, Rubin and I

— moved into an abandoned house on a bombed-out street of whorehouses. There was no furniture or utilities of any kind but it had a roof, and we were quite satisfied to sleep on the floor.

As the days passed and the weather worsened, however, we began moving our bedding over a little for other Jews who were homeless and in need of a place to put down their bedding. They, in turn, moved over for others. Finally, the house was wall-to-wall sleepers; anyone who didn't return home early in the evening had a difficult time finding a spot to sleep. Nevertheless, it was a wonderfully warm and friendly family environment.

In the meantime, the four of us had been busy making plans. We had no intention of staying in Poland, but we had to earn some money if we were going to leave. After a month, we rented an apartment where the living space would be less congested and where we could set up a workroom. Under Benjamin's direction, we organized an assembly line making cloth caps for sale in the streets of Lodz. My job was to make the peaks. We worked hard, for we were desperately afraid of settling into the old pattern of second-class existence as we had known it before the war in Poland. Already we could feel the old prejudices against Jews returning as peacetime stability returned. Jews who attempted to regain their old homes and possessions were found murdered. Others returning to Poland were thrown off the trains and beaten by hoodlums. I had not forgotten the stories of my wealthy uncles in America; I felt that if only I could go there, I could escape this unreasonable hatred and discrimination.

There was another possibility. Although it was still illegal, many Jews were finding a refuge in Israel because an escape route, or "Bricha," had already been organized by the Zionists and financed by Canadian and American Jewish organizations. Branches of this route extended into every country in Europe to bring the survivors together in displaced persons' camps, and then transport them to Israel. The movement of Jews along this route was camouflaged by the flow of non-Jewish refugees, many of them from slave labour camps. We made contact with a representative of the Bricha in August 1945, and once the investigating committee had cleared us we were told to prepare to leave Poland. The four of us were to travel to the town of Katowice on the border between Poland and Czechoslovakia with our few possessions. We were to pose as Greek Jews and, as such, would have to learn a sufficient number of Greek phrases to escape suspicion from the other train passengers. That journey turned out to be both hair-raising and hilarious, for we found that for some perverse reason people wanted to chat with us. We answered them in halting German, Hebrew, or our limited supply of Greek. One Russian officer who tried to strike up a conversation with me became furious when I kept saying in German, "I don't understand!"

"The hell you don't, you son of a bitch!" he stormed. "You understand every word I'm saying and you're no more Greek than I am. But the hell with you!" He strode off down the car while I quaked in terror. Luckily, he didn't cause any more trouble.

At Katowice, we left the train and walked to the border. We had no identification papers, but indicated to the Polish guards in halting German that we were Greek Jews. The guards asked many questions in Polish, but we went back to our good old stand-by in German: "I don't understand!"

They searched us thoroughly and emptied out our bags. Then one of them said to the other, "You got to search these goddamn Jews good because they all got money and jewellery hidden. If you don't get rich here, you'll never get rich anywhere. So make damn sure you give these guys a good going over!" It was hard to resist smashing him, but at that moment he held the key to our escape. We watched without protesting while the two of them confiscated everything we possessed.

On the Czechoslovakian side of the border we boarded a train en route to Bratislava. It was crowded with people speaking in an unfamiliar language. Rubin believed it might be Italian and he proved to be right. When some of them approached us, we used sign language and broken German to tell them we were Greek and couldn't understand them. But among them were several who could speak a little Greek and, to Akselrod's horror, they decided to strike up a conversation with him. What could he do? His Greek was limited to a few basic phrases, and he'd never studied Hebrew. After momentary panic, he began to recite the *Kaddish* rapidly. The man stared at him, confused and perplexed; then, at last, he interrupted him. "Excuse me," he said in German. "I speak Greek but you speak too fast for me. I can't understand a word you're saying!" And he went back to his own seat. From then on, we all used Hebrew between ourselves. Whenever outsiders approached us, Akselrod simply repeated the prayers.

A guide sent by the Bricha travelled with us during the journey. Although we never knew his identity, he passed messages among the members of our group and kept us informed. We knew, therefore, to leave the train at Bratislava and to look for reception people at the station who would escort us to a hotel where food awaited us. We rested there for two days in order to be ready for the next leg of the journey. All this was paid for by the Zionist organization.

On the second night, we began walking through dense forest toward the Czechoslovakian-Austrian border guided by a Czech and a Jew. At the border crossing, the guards, who had been paid off, looked the other way as we crossed into Austria. We had entered the part of the country that was occupied by the Russians and extreme care would now be necessary. Akselrod and I felt especially vulnerable, as we were still technically deserters.

A short distance beyond the border, we caught a train, which carried us to Vienna, and from there we were taken to the Rothschild Hospital in the American section of the city. During our week there our food was mainly dumplings made out of stale bread because the Cold War had already begun. The people of Vienna were, in fact, on starvation rations due to the Russian blockade.

Our next destination was the city of Linz about a hundred miles away in the American zone of Austria. This trip involved travelling through the Russian zone to the Danube River; once across this barrier we would be among friends. A hundred of us were loaded into coal cars under the cover of darkness. We were told to keep down until we crossed the bridge onto the American side.

Huddled together, we crouched in silence while the train chugged its way slowly westward. Then, finally, our ears told us that the train was passing over a bridge and we raised our heads into the night to see where we were going. Ahead we could see the lights of the sentry boxes and the train station, and a mass of American soldiers running toward the train pointing at us as we all stood up to see better. Instead of the warm welcome we confidently expected, once the train came to a stop, the soldiers stood with guns pointed and ordered us down from the cars.

"Who are you?" they asked in English. None of us understood English.

"We are escaped Jews!" we told them in Hebrew and Polish and Yiddish and German.

Not understanding any of those languages, they marched us off to a concentration camp for SS prisoners operated by a Jew-hating colonel responsible to the Americans. We were so stunned by what had happened to us that at first we didn't know what to do. Where was the warmth, the understanding and the sympathy of our friends the Americans? We had tried every means of communicating with them, but nothing had worked. Those who had been in concentration camps even showed them the tattooed numbers on their arms, but they seemed unable to understand the significance of them.

It was all so ironic. Here we were, imprisoned with the very criminals who had murdered six million of us, and the Americans, the saviours for whom we had crossed the whole of Europe, were patrolling outside with machine guns and dogs. To complete the dreadful irony, the Americans were often abusive, punishing those caught standing in the food line-up more than once, and calling us in for repeated interrogation. We felt that we were right back where we started.

As we did not know who our guide had been, we did not know if he had gone to get help for us, or if he was imprisoned with us. Since we had been headed for the Jewish refugee camp in Munich, we could only hope that they were aware of our plight. In the meantime, we stayed far from the German prisoners on the other side of the compound while they, in turn, ignored us and seemed preoccupied with their own predicament. When a week had passed, we began to realize that we had to find our own way out. We concocted a plan to do this that involved most of the Jews in the camp. A little after dark, we erupted out of our barracks with an enormous arranged fight in progress. Anyone not involved in it hung around the edges, egging the others on, so that there was a terrible racket that drew the guards and SS prisoners as distant spectators. The battle see-sawed back and forth, gradually moving closer to the fence near one of the guard towers. When we were sure that the guards were completely engrossed in the fight, Benjamin Akselrod, Juzek Wolynski, a former officer in the Polish army, and I rolled under the barbed wire fence and into the moat. In the compound the fight raged on.

The moat, unfortunately, contained five feet of watery mud and I could not swim. When the others realized this, they towed me across. The outer fence was made of both rolled and strung barbed wire; we wriggled under and over the strands into the meadow that was our last barrier to freedom. In a crouching run, we dashed across it and into the village nearby. What a sensation we made there. Coated with mud, our clothes and hands ripped by barbed wire, three wild men trying to figure out how to get to Linz!

Then suddenly there it was: a streetcar with the destination "Linz." No fare was needed because nothing had yet been stabilized in this part of Austria. We jumped aboard the car and it went swaying off to Linz. It didn't take us long to find the Joint Distribution Committee office and tell them our troubles.

"We are aware of the problem," the spokesman said. "But we must move through the proper channels."

"How long will the proper channels take?"

"I can't honestly tell you. Maybe a week, maybe a month. . . ."

"But what about my family?" Juzek asked. "I left them behind in the camp. How do I get them out?"

"You'll just have to wait for them, or you can take them out the way you got out yourself."

We went back to the camp, and although it was difficult, we helped to smuggle out another twenty people. Later we learned that the Committee arranged the release of the rest a week afterwards.

CHAPTER TWELVE

Salzburg: 1945–1948

Our goal now was Munich because there was a large displaced persons' camp there; thousands of Jews were making it their temporary home. It was also an embarkation point for Jews taking the last leg of the Bricha to Israel. Early one morning, we caught the train from Linz to Salzburg where we had several hours to wait for the train to Munich. Benjamin and Alter decided to use the time to go exploring and perhaps investigate a nearby camp called New Palestine which we had heard about.

Malke and I passed the time pleasantly in Salzburg while we waited for them, but when it came time to catch the Munich train they hadn't returned. We watched the cars fill up and the train depart. Still there was no sign of them. We imagined horrible things happening to them, but just when we were ready to start searching for them, they came running back in wild excitement. "You won't believe what we've found! Come on! You've got to come and see this! It's the perfect place for us!" As they dragged us along, they described the place they had found. It turned out to be everything they said: four two-storey apartment blocks with incredibly modern suites, each with its own kitchen, dining room, living room, bedrooms, and even its own bathrooms. It had been an officers' quarters for the SS unit, but the Americans had put it at the disposal of the Joint Committee for use by Jewish refugees. We were assigned an apartment of our own, and walked through it touching everything reverently. After that, we went three times a day to the adjacent barracks kitchen to collect our meals, often consisting of five courses, all supplied by the American army. It was utter paradise.

We registered with the Committee soon after we arrived, and then made ourselves known to others in the camp. Most were survivors of concentration camps, some of them determined to go to Israel and others bound for America. The Akselrods and Rubin had made up their minds to go to Israel, but I was set on America, for I was longing for the warmth of a family around me.

My father's much older half-brothers had gone to America before World War I. To me they had always represented wealth and adventure. The uncle that I had heard most about was Uncle Aaron, the eldest brother who had last visited Eisiskes in 1920. We had pictures in our living room of him standing with the town council and with the rest of my family. All this was before I was born, of course, and my only contact with him was through the big packages of clothing that would arrive periodically from New York, throwing my mother and grandmother into perfect ecstasies. I was sure that this wealthy uncle would take care of an orphan nephew if only he knew that one of them had survived. But all I knew of him was the city where he lived and his name, Aaron Don Becker. His surname was different from ours because he was the victim of an immigration officer behind a desk on Ellis Island.

"What is your name?" he was asked.

"Aaron Don Pacianko," he answered.

"Aaron Don what? Never mind, just spell it!"

But Uncle Aaron could not name the letters in English. "Well, what do you do for a living? What's your trade?"

Uncle Aaron knew the words in English for that answer.

"Baker!" he said. "I am a baker!" but he pronounced the word "becker."

"Well, why don't you say that? Name: Aaron Don Becker!"

Some of the others in New Palestine told me to go to the Committee to get help in finding him; they assured me that it was not impossible. The Committee helped me prepare an ad to be inserted in the Jewish newspapers in New York:

"Leibke Kaganowicz of Eisiskes, Lithuania, son of Shael and Miriam Kaganowicz and grandson of Benjamin Kaganowicz, is looking for relatives in New York. He is looking particularly for his uncle, Aaron Don Becker."

Then I went back to New Palestine to wait. When I had just about given up, I was called to the office of the Committee to receive a telegram. My hands trembling, I ripped it open, and found I could not understand a word of it. It was in English. Someone who knew the language was called to help and I learned that my relatives had read the advertisement.

"Saw your ad in the paper. Very happy you're alive. Letter following. Uncle Aaron Don Becker."

The incredible had become reality. I really did have a family on the other side of the ocean that cared about me and would look after me. My cousin, Bessi Colodzin, who was my father's age, had seen the advertisement and rushed to show it to her father; she had sent the telegram on his instructions. Not long afterwards, his letter arrived full of family news with inquiries about my health and what I was in need of. They were confident that I would be able to join them soon in New York, and I settled down to wait for that wonderful day. It was going to be a long time in coming, however, as the Polish immigration quota was very small, and my name was a long way down the waiting list. But I was far from unhappy in Salzburg. My life was completely secure and, for the first time since my boyhood, I was able to live without fear. I missed my family acutely, but I had long since accepted the fact that they were really dead, so at least the agony of false hope was at an end. My new family in America wrote warm and welcoming letters, and generous Americans in the occupying forces treated me with unbelievable kindness.

Despite the fact that all of us were well treated, the wounds of our past experience were always with us. We could not forget that we were in Salzburg, the home of Adolf Hitler and Adolf Eichmann, the butcher of the extermination camps. We hated all Austrians with a passion and, as a result, Salzburg was a seething cauldron of revenge seekers who, when given half a chance, took every opportunity to avenge themselves on the local populace. We had all endured immeasurable suffering at the hands of these same Austrians; the memories filled our empty hours, shrieking for retribution. I was no exception.

One day while boarding a tram, I stepped in from the front rather than the rear, which was customary for all passengers. When the conductor angrily ordered me to the rear, I refused to go.

"If you don't get on properly, I'll call you by your right name," he hissed.

"And what is that?" I asked, spoiling for a fight.

"Lousy Jew," he answered. I blew sky high.

On my return to camp, I collected a group of my friends and related the incident to them. Then we waited for the car to return and boarded it. In a frenzy of rage, we beat up the conductor and threw him through the plate glass windows, cutting his face to ribbons and blinding him for life.

Early in 1946, my old friend Aba Gefen and his brother Joseph arrived in Salzburg. Aba, who was now head of the Bricha to Israel, enlisted me to work for him, chiding me on wasting my energies on things that were not meaningful. Under his influence, my outlook on life began to change and I looked forward to my future in America with more and more excitement.

I became a guide for the Bricha, helping groups en route to Israel, taking trips back to Poland to lead others out to Austria. Several times I was approached by the Irgun and asked to join the fight in Israel, but my fighting days were over. All I wanted was a chance to build a life in peace with my American family around me.

When 1948 rolled around and I was still no closer to the top of the Polish quota list, I began to despair. I was then told that Canada was accepting immigrants and wrote my uncle asking if this would be a good alternative. He assured me that it would be simple to transfer from Canada to the United States, so I applied for entry to Canada and was soon accepted.

After a wait of five months, eighteen hundred of us boarded the American troopship *S.S. Stewart* and set sail for Canada. It was a stormy trip and we were all seasick, but I do not remember anyone complaining very much. A new life lay ahead; seasickness was a small price to pay.

In Halifax we boarded the transcontinental train. I was bound for Vancouver because my relatives had decided that it would be better for me to be closer to my relatives in San Francisco, who could be of immediate help to me. A man I had met on shipboard had also decided to go to Vancouver and was curious to find out how soon we would be there. Since I had mastered a few words in English, I decided that this was a suitable time to try them out on the porter.

"How long to Vancouver?" I asked him.

"Five nights and six days," he said matter-of-factly.

Obviously I'd used the wrong words! But I told my friend what the answer had been.

"That's ridiculous!" he said. "You could go from Paris to Moscow in that time. We've got to find somebody who speaks Polish or Russian to get the truth."

We searched the train for this person who would tell us the truth and eventually found a Ukrainian dishwasher. Would he please tell us how long it would be before we reached Vancouver? "Five nights and six days," he replied.

This was unbelievable and just a little too overwhelming. Some who had selected Vancouver as their new home left the train in Montreal instead; others got off in Winnipeg or Calgary. But I stayed on the train all the way through the Rockies to Vancouver.

This is my home now. My uncle's confident prediction that I would soon join them was misplaced. Still on the Polish quota, I was a long way down the list. But it didn't matter, for I had found an incredibly beautiful country where the people were warm and friendly, and where I had as much right to walk on the sidewalk as anyone else.

Epilogue

I am a man with two lives: in one I am called Leibke Kaganowicz of Eisiskes, and in the other I am Leon Kahn of Vancouver. Most of the time my first life is hidden so well behind my second one that few people know it is there. A good many of my friends know only the man who has achieved a joyous and meaningful life here in Canada, but the bitter experiences of that other life damaged my body and my mind for many years afterwards and the scars still remain in my soul. I still find it extremely difficult to accept the reality of my past. However, the hard facts remain. I lost my father, my mother, my sister, my brother, my grandmother, and countless close friends and relatives. Their absence is a constant reminder of what happened, and I cannot negate it.

Nor am I able to forgive those who turned a nation of peace-loving people into murderers and vengeance seekers. Doctors, lawyers and scientists, dedicated to the enrichment of humanity, were reduced to the level of animals in order to survive.

Jews have never been admired for their contributions to the worlds of art and science. These have been consistently ignored or made little of. But when Israel emerged victorious over her enemies, the nations of the world finally gave us the admiration we were never accorded before. A clenched fist and a mighty hand are not what we wish to be remembered for. But it is good to know that there were some heroes during that dark period in our history: men and women who fought the enemy in the forest and in the death camps, and even some who refused to disrobe at the edge of the grave and step into the ditches to die. As for those Jews who died without resistance, I am still torn by an intense desire to justify their actions. One explanation that comes to mind is that there had never been a precedent in the history of mankind to compare with what occurred. We had lived with the anti-Semitism of our neighbours for two thousand years, but we never realized the full extent of their hatred.

Added to this naïveté was the fact that many families went to their deaths because of the complete helplessness of their situation. No one on the outside seemed to care or show any sign of coming to their aid. They felt completely isolated and abandoned; undoubtedly this contributed to the final acceptance of their fate.

In addition, there were many Jews who went to their deaths, acquiescing to what they believed was the will of God. These were devout, deeply religious Jews who embraced the credo that whatever happened to them was an indication of a divine plan. With eyes raised heavenward they chanted the immortal words of the *Vidui,* the last prayer before death, and lay down in the ditches to die.

Not once did the thought occur to me that the murders were the will of the Almighty. This would have been a cruel and vengeful God, one I could not and would not recognize. To me, God was love, justice, truth and compassion. To think otherwise was intolerable.

Most important of all was the fact that the Nazis found an ally in the eternal tenacity of man's capacity for hope, and the refusal of any human being to believe that an entire nation could be capable of absolute evil. We knew they meant to degrade us, to make us lose faith in God and in ourselves. But that they intended our total extermination was completely unbelievable, and, to an extent, still is.

Thirty-five years have passed and I am still haunted by the question, "Why me?" Why did I survive when so many others died? I wish with all my heart I knew the answer, but perhaps I am not meant to know. I try to live from day to day and forget the trauma of the past. Yet just as I think I am succeeding, events that seem ordinary to anyone else have the power to revive all the old horrors, and I am plunged into terror again. I listen to a symphony concert and suddenly the music conjures up all the old images. In the midst of a crowded theatre, I am isolated with my fears and I struggle through those years of nightmare all over again.

At a football game when the crowd shouts, "Hold that line! Hold that line!" I am back in the forest near Yureli with my father shouting, "Hold them back! Hold them back!" I fire my gun, but the murdering Poles come closer and closer, and my bullets go right through them and they don't stop, and Freidke runs in slow motion toward me with the glint of the murderer's bayonet at her back. "RUN, Freidke, RUN!"

But Freidke is dead. And Father is dead. I stop my car at a rail crossing to wait for a freight train to pass. Suddenly it is my mother and grandmother who press against the slats of the cattle cars on their way to extermination in Treblinka. Every click of the wheels marks off the seconds until they die all over again. I am required to go to a slaughterhouse as I am involved in the sale of some cattle and have to learn how dressed weight is calculated. I should never have come. We stand in a room lined with hundreds of carcasses hanging on hooks, and I see instead the pitiful corpses of my people hanging there.

I watch a television news film on prairie cattle suffering from hoof-and-mouth disease. The farmers herd the sick animals into an open pit and shoot them from above. Instantly, the film changes. It is the *Einsatzgruppen* who are firing, and my people are falling, falling into space, their arms and legs grotesque in death and their blood seeping into the uncaring earth.

It is with the greatest difficulty that I force this other life to recede, to return to the place where it belongs: the past. I must convince myself that the struggle is over and I am no longer a fugitive. And in the end, I do succeed.

It wasn't always this simple. I remember lying in the tall rye grass near the forest in the summer of 1943, waiting for the night to come. A skylark soared up into the heavens, dived down, and soared up again, and I prayed to be transformed into a bird like that. How marvellous to have wings and fly straight into the heavens, leaving all my miseries and terrors behind. I lay there willing myself into that bird's form, just as I had tried to will myself far from Eisiskes long before. But the bird flew away and night came again.

Many years later I read a passage that helped me so much that I committed it to memory. It read: "The past is always a prelude to the present; the present, forever a preparation for the future. The past can never be forgotten, but at some point it must be forgiven if we are ever to build a world of peace upon a planet of love."

Only by striving for better understanding among people can we hope for peace. Only in peace can the horrors of the Holocaust be laid to rest at last.

Postscript: 1977

Benjamin Akselrod married in Salzburg, went to Israel, and then came to Vancouver in 1951. Abraham and Luba Asner now live in Windsor, Ontario. The last time I saw Cymbal, he had come from the Ukraine to visit me in Varena. The authorities refused him permission to stay there, and he returned to the Ukraine. Michka Dubinsky became an engineer and returned to live in Radun. Aba Gefen took his doctorate in law in Italy and joined the foreign service in Israel. He was consul general in Argentina, Peru, and in Toronto, Canada. He is now with Israel's Ministry of Culture. Bolke Maciekowski moved to Lodz and began smuggling Jews from Poland to Germany. He was caught and sentenced to twelve years in prison. After eight years, he was released and went to live in Israel. Benjamin Rogowski managed to appease the Russians after our escape from the school at Vilnius. He married there, and in the summer of 1945, escaped through Poland and Germany to Israel. He died in 1975. Lippa Skolsky escaped to Salzburg and became police chief of the Riedenburg camp nearby. He entered Israel illegally and became customs officer in the port of Haifa. He died two years ago. Abraham Widlanski escaped to the Riedenburg camp near Salzburg and eventually entered the United States. He lives in New York, where he married and became the father of three children.

Afterword

Our father, Leon Kahn, z"l,* slipped quietly but unexpectedly from this world on June 8, 2003, two weeks after he and our mother celebrated their fiftieth wedding anniversary. He was seventy-eight years old.

The legacy he left us was a testament to an indomitable spirit honed in the forests of Poland and Lithuania during the darkest years of the twentieth century. A fighter, whose Hebrew name, *Aryeh Leib*, means "lionhearted," our father depended on his instincts, courage, wits, tenacity, and an abiding faith in God to survive the Holocaust. He would apply these qualities towards transforming himself from partisan to patriarch, and building a new life and a family in Canada.

He arrived in Vancouver on September 13, 1948, a penniless refugee, with no family, no English, and no profession. In time, all that would change.

In 1952, he travelled to New York to meet relatives and while he was there attended a dance for newcomers. Our grandmother, Basia Landsman, z"l, recognized him and asked him if he remembered her daughter, Evelyn, who was standing beside her with a friend. Our father had last laid eyes on our mother in Lodz in 1945 when she had been a skinny little twelve-year-old refugee, but that hardly deterred him from answering, "Of course," and then pointing confidently at the friend. The mistake was soon rectified and a whirlwind romance followed, culminating in an engagement by the time he left town and marriage the following May when he returned. Four children quickly followed.

By the time he married, our father had already progressed from factory worker to entrepreneur. He had actually come to Canada as a tailor when the Canadian Jewish Congress (CJC) was able to sponsor a group of tailors and dressmakers for local garment factories in 1948. Having already made the decision to try and immigrate to Canada, he was certainly not prepared to let something trivial like not actually being a tailor get in the way of his plans. So he put his resourcefulness and ingenuity to work and simply paid a friend $10 to sew a pocket for him to qualify for this special quota.

His CJC assignment to a garment factory in Vancouver, however, ended quickly when the foreman noticed our father zag every time he was supposed to zig, and vice versa. He moved from tailoring to packing toys, owning and operating a grocery store, running a vending machine business, and selling Christmas trees.

In the early years of his Christmas tree business our father would leave our mother home alone with us very young children and spend three months "in the bush," cutting trees in the cold, dense forests around Cranbrook, British Columbia and managing their shipment to destinations in the United States and Mexico. This last venture may have seemed an ironic choice, but trees had sheltered our father from his enemies, and he had a special connection with them.

The year 1957 was a turning point for our father, but it was also a year that would bring emotional challenges and a new test of his faith. The joy surrounding the arrival of his first daughter was soon overshadowed by her being diagnosed with severe disabilities. Our sister, Charlene, passed away when she was eight.

The same year she was born, a chance encounter with a customer at our father's Christmas tree lot in Vancouver led him into real estate. The man he met was Henry Block, co-founder with his brother, Arthur, of a fledgling real estate concern called Block Brothers Realty.

In a single transaction, our father sold a tree and found his calling.

Block Bros. would grow into the largest and most successful real estate company in western Canada, and our father would rise to become president of its construction division. He parted amicably from Block Bros. in the 1970s to fulfil his dream of heading his own real estate development and investment companies.

Over time, through extraordinary commitment, hard work and the grace of God, the boy who was unable to fulfil his mother's dream of becoming an engineer did the next best thing and became a builder. Despite his success he remained a very humble man who never forgot his roots or his faith. He was kind, compassionate and big-hearted, and never turned away anyone who asked for help

Our father became a pillar of the Vancouver Jewish community and a respected businessman. He sat on a variety of boards, including Schara Tzedeck Synagogue, Vancouver Talmud Torah schools, and the Bank of British Columbia. He spearheaded fundraising campaigns for State of Israel Bonds and the Jewish Federation of Greater Vancouver, he was honoured with numerous awards from local and national charities, and he was recognized by the governments of Israel and Canada for his leadership role in humanitarian causes in both countries.

He was an active philanthropist who shared his wealth and counsel generously but always tried to do so quietly and, whenever possible, anonymously. He gave to a wide spectrum of charitable causes, particularly those devoted to medical research and health care, Israel, and Jewish and Holocaust education. He was a founder of the Vancouver Holocaust Centre Society and a founding contributor to the Simon Wiesenthal Center in Los Angeles. He also devoted much time to lecturing at schools and Holocaust symposiums about his wartime experiences. Recounting the traumas of his past always caused great emotional pain for days, and even weeks, afterwards. But as one of the fortunate few who managed to survive, he put his sense of obligation to educate others ahead of any personal anguish.

His vocation may have been real estate developer, his avocation philanthropy and education, but his first and true passion was his wife, his children and his grandchildren.

As a father, he simply applied the same principles to "building" his children as he did to building real estate: with a solid foundation, quality workmanship and attention to detail.

He tutored us about life, and then showed us how to live it. He taught us values, and showed us how to use them. He showed us by example how to act from the heart without the expectation of anything in return. He taught us how to be black and white thinkers when it came to right and wrong, but still recognize the greys in life. And he encouraged us to succeed at everything we tried, and then helped us understand that failure was not fatal.

Our father found a way to manage the ghosts of his past, but they forever haunted his life. He never stopped hoping that his beloved mother might yet show up on his doorstep. And he was hard pressed to hide the growing despair he felt in a world of escalating anti-Semitism and deadly prejudices that echoed those of his past.

From the time we were little our father told us about his exploits as a partisan and the horrors he witnessed during the Holocaust. To us they were spellbinding tales of a superhero who happened to be our father. To him they were cautionary life lessons to be passed on to us, our children and future generations, and we were the messengers.

The knock on the door in the middle of the night that would herald his longed-for reunion with his beloved mother never came for our father. But the strong faith we inherited from him helps us find solace in the belief that their two souls and those of the rest of his beloved family have finally been reunited for all eternity.

The Holocaust took much away from Leon Kahn, *z"l*, but also saved something very precious: our father.

He was our rock, our inspiration and our strength; our teacher, our coach, our playmate and our friend.

We were his world and he was ours.

He will live in our hearts forever.

— Hodie, Mark and Saul Kahn
April, 2004

Z"l is an acronym for the Hebrew *zichrono l'vracha*, "of blessed memory."

Index

AK (Polish Home Army) 2, 115, 117,
140–1, 146, 179
Akselrod, Benjamin 185–6, 188–98, 206
Akselrod, Malke 191–8
Alytus 173–4, 183–5
anti-Semitism 3, 5–6, 10, 14, 18, 115–6,
158, 192; among the partisans 86,
120, 123, 134
Arke (guide) 101–7
Arke the Crazy One 29–30
Asner, Abraham 135, 167, 169, 178, 206
Asner, Aaron 135
Asner, Chaim 135
Asner, Itzik 135
Asner, Luba 135, 167, 169, 206
Asner, Yankele 135
assaults on the forest 117–8, 119, 140–1
Atlas, Dr. Yeheskel 3, 135

Babisch, Dr. 132, 138, 153
Babkin (farmer) 74–5, 81, 112
Baderas (policeman) 26, 137–8, 175–7
barter/bribes 24, 27–8, 50, 51, 54, 74–5,
89, 113, 124, 144

Bartoszewicz, Pietka 67
Bastunski, Leibel 26
Becker, Aaron Don (Pacianko) 198–9,
200–1
Benjamin (harness-maker) 10
Berkowicz, Aaron 138, 140
Berkowicz, Chaim (Pietka) 169, 170,
175–7
Bialystok 190
Bielsky Otriad 135
Bielsky, Tuvia 3, 135
Bielsky, Zusia 135
Botwinick family 128
Botwinick, Isaac 128
Botwinick (teacher) 68, 128
Bratislava 194
Bricha (escape route) 192, 194, 197,
200
Buczko (farmer) 81
Bulak (brigade commander) 134

Canadian Jewish Congress (CJC) 210
Carolowa, Mrs. 27, 42–3, 45, 74–5, 168
Carolowa, Stasiuk 43, 54

Catholic Church. *See* Roman Catholic Church
Chaim, Chofetz 53
cholents 94–5
collaborators 5, 119, 169, 176, 181, 186–7
Colodzin, Bessi 199
Communists 87, 88, 114; Jewish 24, 27
Cymbal the Ukrainian (partisan) 126–8, 138, 151, 155–8, 206

Danielewicz (farmer) 109–10, 112, 166
Davidov, Captain 121, 123, 163–4, 165, 167
doctors in the forest 132–5
Dolinski family 63
Dolinski, Noah 51–2, 53–4, 58–9, 65, 68
Druskieniki 106
Dubinsky, Michka 124, 126–8, 151, 155–6, 206

Einsatzgruppen 50, 59, 63, 181
Eisiskes 9–16, 18–42, 46–50, 76–7, 90, 93, 94–5, 115, 167–9, 178–9
Eliach, Yaffa 2
Elke (leader of family group) 87–8
Epstein, Faivel 31–2

family groups in the forest 69, 82–3, 87–8, 111, 117, 120
food gathering: in the forest 83–4, 87, 120, 129–30; in the ghetto 54, 92, 94, 95

Gefen, Aba 173, 174, 184, 200, 206
Gefen, Joseph 200
gendarmerie 28, 30–1, 34–5, 55
Gershon (from Eisiskes) 36–7
Ghettos: Grodno 91–104; Marcinkonys 89–91; Radun 53–71; Szczuczin 71, 113: Vilnius 99
Gildenman, Misha 3
Goldke (from Eisiskes) 79
Grace, Elia 86
Green Hats (border guards) 176–9
Grodno 88, 89, 91–104

hangings, public 55, 98, 114

hospitals in the forest 134

Irgun 200
Itzkutzy Group 135

Jewish Joint Distribution Committee 190, 191, 196, 198, 199
Jewish partisans 83, 87, 114, 120; anti-Semitism of Soviet partisans 56, 120, 123, 134. *See also* partisans
Josephine (cook) 126
Judenrats 30, 45, 51–2, 68, 90–1, 93, 95, 100
Jurkanski, Isaac Mendel 60, 68
Jurkanski, Yudke 60
Jurzdiki 27, 31–2, 40

Kaganowicz, Benjamin (brother) 11, 14, 20, 36–45, 55–6, 69, 72–6, 79–82, 88, 89–91, 93–5, 100, 101–12
Kaganowicz, Freidke (sister) 11, 36, 38, 45, 69, 72–6, 79–82, 88, 89–91, 93–5, 100, 101–13, 117–9, 120–21, 137–41
Kaganowicz, Miriam (mother) 11–6, 24, 25, 26, 29, 32–3, 36, 38, 45, 50, 69–70, 71, 94, 100–1, 113, 121–2, 191
Kaganowicz, Shael (father) 11, 15–6, 19, 27, 33, 36, 42, 43–5, 54, 59–62, 64, 69–70, 72–6, 78–82, 84, 88–91, 93–5, 100, 101–13, 117–9, 120–1, 137–46
Kahn, Evelyn (née Landsman; wife) 191, 209–10
Kalinin (Russian lieutenant) 184–5
Kaplan, Abraham 30–1
Kaplan, Joseph 188
Katowice 193
Kielce 116
Kobrowski, Yankele 91
Konichowski, Yankele 87–8
Koppelman, Markel 51
Koppke (gendarme) 55–6, 58, 65
Korkuc (farmer) 178
Korkucian, Juzuk 51
Kovner, Aba 3

Kowner, Abbe 99
Kozlowski (partisan) 125–6, 179–80, 181, 183
Kulikowski (administrator) 51–2, 53

Landsman Basia 191, 209
Lebedniki 27, 42, 44
Lebenschein 97
Lehr, Dr. 143
Leninski Komsomol 85–6, 112, 114, 117, 120, 138
Levo family 110, 112
Levo, Isaac 110, 112, 138, 139–40, 151, 154
Levo, Sholem 110, 112
lice 76–7, 111–2, 133
Linitsa 107, 161–4
Linz 196, 197
Lipa the Shammes 13
Lipichanska forest 120, 123–4, 133–4
Lithuanian/Polish conflict 16
Lithuanian partisans 176, 179–83
Lodz 190–3, 209
Lubka (from Eisiskes) 48

Maciekowski, Bolke 185–8, 206
Marcinkonys 89–91, 119, 124
Markovicz. See Baderas
Marusiak (partisan) 87–8
mass killings 99, 116, 119; at Eisiskes 36, 37–8, 40–2, 46–50; at Radun 56, 58, 62–4
medical facilities in the forest 132–5
Meier (blacksmith) 62
Meir, Golda 71
Menkis, Sara 99
Miasnik, Dr. 134
Michalowski, Josl 146
Milikovsky (from Eisiskes) 49
Moishe (baker) 10
Mostaika 119
Munich 197
Musha (from Radun) 59, 60, 61–2

Nacha forest 81–9, 112, 113–4, 117–8, 119–20, 132, 135, 138

New Palestine (camp) 197–9
New York 198–9, 209
NKVD (Soviet secret police) 176, 180, 183; school 184–7
Nochem the Pope 21–3
Novikov, Michka 165–6
Nowicki (farmer) 139–40, 153–4

Olkeniki 46
Orzeszkowa Gymnasium 185
Ostrauskas (police chief) 19, 26, 42, 51, 171
Otriads 123–4, 135; Otriad of Special Assignments 121, 123, 164–5

Paisha (leader of family group) 88, 120
Partisans: anti-Semitism among 86, 120, 123, 134; Communist leadership 87, 169, 173, 179; conflicts with family groups 87–8; discipline 86–7, 127, 128, 139; early groups in forest 57, 85–6, 114; final operations 158, 164–5, 169–70; Lipichanska forest 120, 123–4, 133–4; Nacha forest 82, 83–8, 113–7, 119; training 84, 86–7, 113–5. See also Jewish partisans; sabotage; Soviet aid for partisans
Passover 116
Polish educational system 5–6, 14, 115–6
Persky (schoolteacher) 44, 53, 59
pit houses 111, 178
Podemby 119
Polish partisans 115, 146, 148, 178–9
Ponar Mountain 35, 99
Powielancy 54, 120, 142, 166
Pozeczy 188

Radun 42, 43–4, 45, 51–71, 78–9, 90
Remz, Leibke 49
resettlements 71, 99, 100, 101, 119, 121
Rogaczewski, Shael 146
Rogowski, Benjamin 128, 138, 142, 169, 170, 173–4, 175–7, 183–8, 206
Rogowski, Chaya 169, 175
Rogowski, Liebke 97

Roman Catholic Church 5–6, 14, 115–6
Rosenthal, Reisel 191
Rosh Hashanah 36
Rothschild Hospital 194
Rubin, Alter 191–8
Rudin (Russian general) 173–4
Rudzian, Liebe Gitl (grandmother) 12, 22, 36, 38, 45, 65, 66, 69–70, 71, 100–1, 121
Rukowicz (farmer) 110–2
Russian Jungle 119, 120

sabotage 84–5, 124–6, 128–31, 153, 154–6
Saffronov (NKVD) 176–8
Salzburg 197–200
Schwartz, Abraham 47
Sczuczinski, Israel 63, 66
Sczuczinski, Sosha (sister) 63
Sczuczinski, Sosha (wife) 63
Selo 29, 47
Shavel (cowherd) 9, 36
Shuster, Hodl 191
Simon Wiesenthal Center 211
Skolsky, Lippa 120–1, 128, 151, 162, 169, 170, 173–4, 206–7
Sonenson, Faigl 49, 64, 178–9
Sonenson, Moishe 49, 64–5, 178–9
Sonenson, Yitzhak 169, 179
Soviet aid to partisans 86–7, 113–4, 124, 133
Soviet partisans: anti-Semitism among 86, 120, 123, 134. See also Leninski Komsomol; Otriad of Special Assignments; partisans
SS 96, 97–8, 195–6
Staniecki, Joshke 113
Stankevitch (partisan leader) 86–7
Stankewicz (Stankevicius, city clerk) 26, 170
Stolnicki, Yankele 162–3
survival in the forest, factors in 2–3, 135–6
Szczuczin 68, 71, 100, 113, 121

Szewicki, Mrs. 72
Szewicki, Shmulke 72–4, 75–6, 80, 82, 89, 100–1, 168
Szewicki, Yudel 72–4, 75–6, 80, 82, 89, 97, 100
Szmulewicz, Moishe 87–8

Tarashka (farmer) 137, 147–50, 151
train derailments 84–5, 124–8, 153, 154–6. See also sabotage
Treblinka 121

Ukrainians in German uniform 157–62
United States Holocaust Memorial Museum 2

Vancouver 7–8, 201, 209–11
Vancouver Holocaust Centre Society 211
Varena (town) 35, 124, 146, 153, 154, 169–70
Varena (village) 179–80, 183
Vienna 194
Vilnius 19–20, 99, 185–8

Weapons acquisition 81, 83, 88, 112, 131
Wehrmacht 24–5
White Russians 52
Widlanski, Abraham 113, 144, 145, 146–50, 169, 207
Widlanski family 170
Winicki, Bella 100, 190–1
Winicki family 100, 190
Wittenberg, Israel 99
Wolynski, Juzek 196

Yacobovicius (partisan) 172, 179, 181
Yureli 109
Yureli forest 118–9, 120–1, 137–46

Zalusky (policeman) 59, 65–6
Zionist organizations 192, 194, 200
Zlatella (cook) 169, 175, 176
Zoludzewicz (farmer) 79–81, 89
Zorin, Shalom 3